FADING PICTURES

FADING PICTURES

Robin Bryant

The Book Guild Ltd
Sussex, England

First published in Great Britain in 2004 by
The Book Guild Ltd
25 High Street
Lewes, East Sussex
BN7 2LU

Typesetting in Times by
Keyboard Services, Luton, Bedfordshire

Printed in Great Britain by
Antony Rowe Ltd, Chippenham, Wiltshire

A catalogue record for this book is available from the
British Library

ISBN 1 85776 823 X

CONTENTS

MALAYSIA TODAY

Malaysia has changed out of all recognition from the country which so captivated me and other planters forty years ago. The slow leisurely pace of life, the relaxed attitudes and convivial company were infectious, unforgettable, and which eventually culminated in a love affair with a country and its people.

The former Malaya, built on tin, timber, commodity crops and a thriving smallholder economy, has prospered considerably over the past two decades and is now a leader in high tech and light manufacturing, possesses an efficient service sector and enjoys the fruits of a blossoming tourist industry.

The hustle and bustle of a developed country permeates throughout all strata of society. People appear content and exude a quiet confidence and their kindness remains unwavering. But beneath this surface a persistent disquiet, even apprehension exists, fuelled by an ever rising cost of living, with health, education and housing becoming especially burdensome. And this, coupled with the unappealing dourness of an imposed strict Islamic code, which has affected everybody whether Muslim or not, has influenced the dictates of social behaviour throughout the country.

Nothing remains static in life; Mao Tse-tung called it perpetual revolution. For Malaysia the physical and material advancement over the past twenty years has been stunning, but for the people, socially, fundamentalism has dampened their capacity to enjoy the fruits and pleasures of their labour.

I was lucky, for no unwanted dogma touched my life. The business and social climate continued unconstrained and hard work and diligence resulted in moderate prosperity and a contentment that an older generation probably remember with fondness, but which the young can hardly envisage.

My memories are tunnel visioned; the past was perfect, the present is not. Of course much was not perfect in the past and one cannot

1

help admiring the commercial and industrial successes of the last two decades.

Simplicity of life for the people of Malaysia has long gone, but then life is no longer simple anywhere.

My memories, however, are of a different, more relaxed period, when strains upon society were minimal and unsmiling faces were seldom seen, when colour and warmth were in and dulled people did not exist.

I was privileged to have lived during this episode of Malaysia's history; the last scene before the country emerged to take its place in the modern world.

1

A Planter I Become

Sociologists used to consider wartime babies, me and my generation, to have behavioural problems due to poor diet, the absence of a father away at war, and having to put up with frequent bombings. Thus once we reached adulthood, choosing a career such as being a planter and managing an estate somewhere in the tropics was a natural progression from those difficult times. However, although the splendid isolation of an estate was definitely preferable to the infinite restrictions of post-war Britain, even in the late 1950s, the life of an assistant manager on an estate was one of senseless harassment and bombardment from the top, usually by a despotic manager or an unsympathetic head office.

Planters were a varied species. Some were intelligent and cultivated, like my first manager. A few were slothful and devious; most were just good-natured plodders who worked hard, loved the life, the people, and, when eventually allowed to marry, occasionally their wives.

In bygone days a high standard of education was not an essential prerequisite to the recruitment process of a planter. Provided this subspecies of *Homo sapiens* could read, write and add up, any advanced scholastic achievement was regarded as superfluous. However, the recruit had to be robust, healthy – which meant active and sporty – industrious, reliable and honest.

The selection process, which could hardly be called intimidating or rigorous, came to an end when the Government insisted that all future expatriates should have reached a tertiary level of education, and that assistant managerial positions should be made open to those Malayans interested in pursuing a planting career. Fortunately for eager young recruits such as myself, few Malayans were clamouring for admittance.

The chief prequisite for a successful planter was his ability to adapt to the many changes which were forced upon him, whether it was being moved from estate to estate, the isolation he often lived in, or the gradual militancy of labour and staff who, like their trade union brethren in Britain, had begun to flex their muscles concerning pay, living conditions and working hours, which were often appalling.

The days when life was easy and labour and staff kowtowed to the assistant or manager, whether expatriate or local, were over. The new militancy necessitated managers rethinking their attitudes and man-management strategies.

For me, after leaving college, becoming a planter was not a profession that had ever crossed my mind. My father, who knew somebody who knew somebody, thought that a career as far away as possible from England would be to his and my mother's advantage.

I had an interview with Harrisons and Crosfield in Great Tower Street, London. I was an immediate success: I could play rugby and cricket. For the crusty, mean, miserable company directors this was definitely of a higher priority than knowing the physiology of a rubber tree, which I had looked up anyway prior to my interview.

I was asked whether I wanted to go to either Ceylon or Malaya. I looked at the ornate ceiling, in the dim office light, and pondered. 'Ceylon,' I replied.

Having taken 'A' level Geography at a time when students were taught the subject properly, unlike nowadays, I knew something about the two countries, which my interviewers did not, as one of them got mixed up with which country grew which crop and instead started to talk about Carthaginian pottery, which he knew about and I didn't. Ceylon, Ceylon, they said in unison, I am sure you will enjoy Malaya. Anyway, they said, as your brother is now employed as an agent in our Kuala Lumpur head office, it is better you go to Malaya. The last time I had met up with my brother was when he was about to depart with an Oxbridge trans-Saharan expedition to Timbuktu. I had no idea that he had beaten me to Malaya. Same company also. It was quite a coincidence.

My intricate knowledge obviously stunned them to such an extent that they inadvertently, in their enthusiasm for somebody who not only knew where the countries were but also the commodities,

4

forgot to reimburse my train and underground rail fares, nor did they invite me to partake of lunch or tea, even though an old crone had wheeled a snack trolley around all morning.

A few weeks later a letter arrived confirming my appointment, terms, immediate purchase necessities and travel arrangements. I borrowed my father's tin trunk, a suit was made for me at the Army and Navy Store and other items purchased included shorts, long socks, stout shoes, vests etc. A pith helmet was not obligatory, being hardly suitable attire as Britain edged into the era of the swinging sixties and the Beatles.

Except for yellow fever there were no other inoculations deemed necessary. Likewise H&C did not consider any further communication appropriate at this stage, and, except for a ticket, one way, on a Blue Funnel cargo vessel leaving from Liverpool, I did not hear from the company again until I reached Malaya. The terms of recruitment were brusque and specific. I was not to marry during my first four-year contract and if I was sacked for bad behaviour then the cost of the return homeward ticket would be deducted from my salary, if any was left, or from the Provident Fund, which the company and I contributed to on a monthly basis.

The rules were strict, with lots of don'ts in the contract and very few do's. Of the do's the most important concerned the passing of a series of examinations set for young planters by the Incorporated Society of Planters (ISP). H&C was sufficiently enthusiastic to award bonuses and salary increments to those who passed these exams during their first four-year tour of duty, particularly the language exams of Malay and Tamil. Passing these was considered a prerequisite to advancement.

I departed from Liverpool in September 1961 and arrived three weeks later in Singapore.

2

Arrival Singapore

I had read Somerset Maugham's wonderful stories of planters' lives in the Far East. All were based on characters he had met and although some descriptive embellishment had added flavour, the life he depicted certainly resembled the way of life that many of us experienced during our initial period of employment.

Singapore bustled and hustled. I was met by a young Tamil Indian who handed over, without a word, a train ticket for Kuala Lumpur and then disappeared into the crowd. As such scenes were repeated daily on the quays of Singapore, nobody seemed in the least bit interested in a white, fresh-faced young man jumping off a launch with a tin trunk and small suitcase.

Having got a ticket, I then grabbed a rickshaw to take me to the station, where I was told the train would depart in the evening but I could deposit my luggage in advance. This I did and then went off in search of Singapore.

H&C had provided a meagre subsidence allowance, which had to be accounted for, but it was sufficient to buy a couple of beers and a plate of noodles.

The rickshaw took me to a cheap part of town, the driver probably realizing that I was penniless and knowing from past experience what somebody like me could afford. I was hot, sweaty and hungry when I got off the rickshaw in a street with many bars and small eating shops frequented largely by members of Her Britannic Majesty's Forces Overseas.

Although my father had been in the army I had not opted for the cadet force at school and so knew very little about the social behaviour of the average private soldier, which in retrospect differed very little from that of a present-day soccer hooligan but without the gratuitous violence associated with modern times.

Arriving in Singapore

The most memorable recollections of that first day in the Far East were the different and exotic smells of curry and durian fruit, and a British Army private flying horizontally through a swing door of a bar and landing on the pavement in front of me. He staggered to his feet and pushed his way back into the bar.

I found this extraordinary because a minute later, as I looked back, he was on the pavement again. I wondered how long this was going to continue, for the only violence I had ever experienced had been either on the rugby pitch or in the boxing ring, but both well controlled within the rules. Violence in the 1950s was not part of our national curriculum and seldom seen in the back streets of country towns.

I eventually found a small restaurant, uninhabited, and sat down. A menu was provided and I chose noodles. While I was eating, a young pretty Chinese lady came and sat opposite me, which I considered very pleasant, but as the Chinese *towkay* (boss) could see that there was no profit in this liaison the lady soon left.

My train departed on time and slowly wended its way into Malaya, stopping at every station, where the smells of the night, the humidity and a cacophony of sound made this one of the most memorable journeys of any kind that I have ever experienced. It was a most wonderful feeling to be travelling on one's own in a country so different in every way that I felt neither homesickness nor concern at what the future held or where I was going. It just did not matter, the train would arrive, another ticket or direction would be supplied by a fleeting person, followed by another destination and eventually, hopefully, an estate.

As most intercontinental journeys undertaken in those days were by ship, one was fortunate to feel little 'jet-lag'. Each day at sea the hour was set forward, thus on arrival in Singapore one felt fit and ready for anything new. So I enjoyed the frequent stops, the somnolent hustle and bustle of the early morning, at every station the glimmering lanterns that kept me awake, and the intriguing mixture of colours.

Eventually the train arrived at Kuala Lumpur Station, an elegant Moorish building with a roof which, owing to its colonial design, could withstand a foot of snow. I was met by a cream-faced English agent, who had booked me into the hotel at the station. He was not at all communicative and suggested I washed and brushed, had breakfast, and then tottered down to the head office in Jalan Ampang. I was down to my last cent but at the time did not think of asking him for a bit of the ready to help out. My fault, but he looked the type who would not have obliged anyway.

I checked into the hotel and went down to breakfast. The steward, an elderly Chinese, asked me for my 'loom lumber', being unable to pronounce 'room number'. As I was not able to translate this immediately into English he got crosser and crosser and I more exasperated. At last I understood. He stumbled off to check that the room indeed was where I was staying. He was not very polite, but Chinese waiters and bar boys seldom were or are.

8

Harrisons and Crosfield's head office resembled the stern of a ship and housed a large number of cubicles called offices, inhabited by the agency staff who displayed a condescending superior manner. They were not polite, nor hospitable, and tried to be as brief as possible in their dealings with their estate visitors.

I met a couple of the directors, who were exceedingly unimpressive, and learnt that I was going to be sent to Sungei Wangi Estate in the State of Perak. The estate was managed by a one legged planter called Bill Harvey, who was referred to as 'Peg-leg' Harvey. He had a fierce reputation but was considered one of the company's most efficient managers. Everybody, whether in the head office or in the field, feared him. I wondered what I had done to deserve such a fierce manager for my first assignment.

The directors leaned forward, staring myopically. Bryant, they said; do you know we have a Bryant here in HO? He's my brother, I replied. Really, really, they mused. How extraordinary, they waffled; most unusual, they pondered. A long pause. He's somewhere in the office, better go and meet up. Tell him you are here. He knows, I answered. I squeezed some cash out of him. They flinched at the word money.

I left very early next morning by train for Ipoh, the largest town in the state. The train wandered its way through jungle, villages and estates, a most exotic journey, until eventually we arrived at Ipoh around midday. W.L. Harvey plus driver Kumurasamy, were waiting on the platform. I was greeted with a shout of, 'Are you Bryant? You don't look up to much, I was expecting somebody a lot tougher than you.' I replied that I was indeed his new assistant and he gruffly shook my hand and hobbled in the direction of the Ipoh Club, telling Kumurasamy to collect my baggage. We ambled across the road and went in for lunch. The dining room was full of miners and planters. Most were old, a few young, but there were no assistants of my age; a hierarchy was very much in evidence and rigorously maintained.

I was introduced as Bill Harvey's new assistant, and after lunch we left for the estate, the car being driven by WLH. During lunch he had shown considerable enthusiasm for cars and motor sports, and I had wondered how he drove with a single leg. This I soon found out, for as I sat in the front with him he give me a modified walking stick to nudge his peg-leg off the foot pedals whenever he commanded.

9

This was not simple because the roads were narrow and winding and he drove fast. He also talked incessantly. I tried to contribute to the conversation but at the same time had to concentrate intensely on road, leg, stick and on him himself. I did not find it easy. But eventually we arrived at Bilham Division of Sungei Wangi Estate where I was supposed to start my training.

3

Sungei Wangi Estate

We sped up to the assistants' house and were greeted by the cook, Ramasamy, who had been around a long time and had seen it all before. He spoke in Tamil to WLH, who was fluent in the language.

My tin trunk and small case were unloaded. I had arrived. The 'bungalow', actually two storeys, was old, wooden and needed a coat of paint but beautifully cool with fans swirling throughout.

I was shown my room. Living there at the time was another assistant, Murray Milne, who was to show me the ropes. He was not around but later bicycled up, well after WLH had driven away. WLH's parting shot to me was: Learn Tamil.

In Malaya at the time there were a whole range of plantation companies, the most prominent being Harrisons and Crosfield, Sime Darby, Dunlops, and Guthries, while companies of lesser presence included Kuala Kepong, Barlow Bousteads, Unilevers and Socfin. Each company, large or small followed a different ethos in the management of their estates. There were differences also in remuneration packages, agronomic and husbandry practices, crop production, man management and competence.

H&C estates were generally considered to have the most satisfactory agronomic and production standards but certainly not the best remuneration package for their planters. This position was held by Socfin, which delivered a most generous pension scheme on retirement.

An assistant's remuneration was not a big factor, provided it was sufficient to pay one's weekly bills and the servants, who looked after us well. They cleaned, laundered our clothes, went to market and bought the food, cooked and served it, and at month's end

11

presented the bill, meticulously detailed, for our attention and payment.

Ramasamy was quite excellent and very honest; he looked after us extremely well. He used to drink a vile alcoholic concoction, usually after serving dinner, though sometimes before. Although his English was good he spoke to us in Tamil, knowing how important WLH considered the language as the majority of our labour and staff were of Tamil origin.

For the first six months it was generally recognized that an assistant was of very little value until he could communicate with the workers. Thus one's day in those early informative weeks was spent learning the language, inspecting the tapping of the rubber trees and ogling the pretty Tamil girls in the weeding gangs. It was a blissful period of one's early planting career, even though there was always the threat of a possible visit by WLH to see how the division was being cared for.

Murray plus the divisional conductors (staff) appeared to have everything under control, and my timetable consisted of riding a bicycle and walking thoughout the estate followed by a conductor called Mahdevan, who was young, pleasant and polite and taught me the names of the plants, the essential phrases and everyday words. I wrote them down, practised and absorbed them.

I began to be able to judge good tapping from bad tapping, which weeds to pull out of the rubber rows, which plants were beneficial and allowed to remain in the field, how deep the drains had to be dug, and the many other activities that were being performed every day. For three weeks I enjoyed this carefree life and then WLH arrived on the estate. As we had no telephones nobody knew when a visit was imminent. There was no warning, no note, no shouted message from a passing lorry, he just arrived.

I was in the tapping when the doves stopped cooing, the tappers lowered their heads to concentrate more diligently on the slope and depth of their cuts. More time was taken to ensure the latex flowed into the cup and did not spill over the spout. Nervousness prevailed. Chatter stopped. A hush spread quickly throughout the estate. Staff sweated, beads of perspiration formed on Mahdevan's brow. He looked nervous; this was transmitted to me and I thought of Macbeth cursing the cream-faced loons who brought bad news, although Mahdevan's countenance was definitely not of that colour.

A Land Rover was seen in the distance. Murray was there. Relief.

12

Was WLH in a good mood or was his peg-leg itching which meant a bad morning?

I did not know whether to join Murray and go and pay homage or stay in the field and drop out of sight in a far corner. I bravely stayed. WLH got out of the Land Rover and hobbled into a distant field; he was going in the opposite direction. But no, a change of heart, suddenly a *kanakapillai*, the lowest grade of staff, was seen running at high speed through the rubber in my direction. WLH wanted me. I ran across towards him, followed by a panting, perspiring Mahdevan.

WLH's visits to the field were a continual source of anxiety. However, for the two and a half years that I was an assistant on Sungei Wangi I can only remember two occasions when he was very angry with me because of what I had done. One was justified and the other not. His behaviour then was considered eccentric. If repeated now, litigious.

On this first meeting he happened to be in a good mood and suggested, or rather told me, that as the rugby season was starting I should go up for the State trials. I pointed out that I had no vehicle to go to Ipoh. This was not a problem as a driver plus the Willy jeep would be made available. But his bonhomie did not last long as he started to question me on my Tamil. He was disappointed that my progress was slow. As Murray was going to take his Tamil exam why did I not go up as well and try, he suggested. I reminded him that I would have been in the country for just three months and that to pass an exam in such a short time would not be easy. Pass he never expected, but as I had taken Latin at school there seemed no reason whatsoever that I should not be entered for the exam.

Now, being hot, weary and with an itching leg, his good humour began to desert him. For the rest of the morning I kept quiet, leaving Murray to keep him calm.

Realizing the seriousness of the situation, I became more diligent in learning the language.

Then Murray and I separated. I was sent as Assistant i/c of Division I. Ramasamy followed me there, as Murray had recruited an old Chinese lady to look after him. Ramasamy soon learnt through the grapevine that I was to sit the Tamil exam in Kuala

Lumpur the next time round. He also knew that if I passed I received a salary increment and a small bonus, part of which he hoped would come his way.

Enter Ramasamy's youngest son Kathirivellu, whose command of English was excellent. Although only twelve years old he was patience personified. Probably he was the best language teacher I ever had. Every afternoon for two hours we spoke, read and digested Tamil. Ramasamy thereafter never spoke English to me, only Tamil. I talked to the tappers, the staff, the pretty weeders, the drainers, the drivers; anybody who could speak the language became an integral part of my learning process.

When I met WLH in the field, fortunately infrequently, he spoke to me in Tamil, until he dismissed me as a hopeless case, there being not the remotest chance of my passing the exam. This spurred me on.

Murray and I went off to KL to sit the exam. He found it easy and got distinction. I found it easy but scraped through. To this day I have never been quite sure if the oral teacher really thought my spoken Tamil deserved a pass mark, or, because I was one of WLH's boys, he did not dare fail me.

I received a congratulatory letter from Mr Gunton, who was Chairman of H&C. He also thought my pass should be entered in the *Guinness Book of Records*, for nobody had passed elementary Tamil in three and a half months.

WLH was astounded, but pleased. Ramasamy was happy receiving a portion of my bonus and so was my young tutor. I earned a raise, although having passed I realized that it changed nothing. The language remained difficult to speak and the pretty girls in the weeding gang still did not always know what I meant. But by now I was enjoying the language and I started to learn and write Tamil script. When assistant in charge of the factory, I spent the long evening hours learning the complicated alphabet, much to the amusement of the staff, whose only desire was to learn English.

My father put my success down to the monetary incentive on offer. He was only partially right.

My first muster as assistant in-charge. A chilly, misty morning, I am cycling hurriedly along the estate paths, taking short cuts through the rubber to get to muster before roll call.

My arrival is unheralded; I slip from my bicycle, hundreds of pairs of eyes watch me, following each movement. A cacophony of coughs greets me as I stroll towards the waiting conductors, who are eager to commence their daily ritual of muster.

Good morning, sir, the conductors whisper. Roll call starts. Workers acknowledge their names, betel nut juice is spat vigorously onto the ground, brown discoloured teeth and red-tinged mouths masticate the sludge, slurping it from side to side. Some smile, some grimace; shy giggles are heard from the young girls in the weeding gang as they daringly stare at me while I walk along the rows of shuffling, sleepy workers.

Everybody is accounted for except a small group standing close by the office. Who are they? I ask. Those persons you see before your eyes are sick, sir, says the attendant hospital dresser grade III who presides over the Division's clinic. They will report to the doctor when he comes early morning, but these men, standing here, sir, these dirty rascals, are very much infected with VD. Would you like to see the Sick Register and then you will see some surprising things?

I read yesterday's and last week's reports. Tuberculosis appears frequently; dysentery, sores, boils, septic wounds are mentioned daily. So is VD.

Surely VD can easily be treated nowadays, I ask, as I dredge from my memory hurried glimpses of well-thumbed books, filched from the school library, relating to the pleasures of sexual indulgence.

Indeed, sir, indeed VD is easily treated, replies the dresser. Then why are these six workers continuously off work? Ah, sir, ah, these are very dirty rascals and are always going with unclean women. Look, sir, look – and he orders the men to drop their shorts or dhotis, and, picking up a ruler off my desk, points to the offending portions of their anatomy.

I peer and look away at this unappealing sight. Surely the doctor issues the appropriate medicine, I ask. Indeed, sir, he does, sir, but sometimes he just signs the register and then goes to the club for a drink without even inspecting these dirty rascals.

The men by now have bent down and lifted up their attire. They are not in the least embarrassed at our intrusiveness. The dresser shifts his position and leans slightly forward. If you would write

15

in the Sick Register that these dirty rascals must be treated promptly and properly, sir, no doubt he will fulfil his duty forthwith. I turn back the pages of the register. The previous assistant has also commented upon the desultory treatment that some of the patients, VD sufferers and others, have received. Perhaps the good doctor drinks too much, I speculate. I choose my words carefully and sign. The dresser looks down appreciatively. Thank you, he says, very good, the doctor I am sure will take much notice.

I doubt it, I mutter quietly to myself.

My new life has just begun. My first contribution to managing an estate, inspecting the anatomies of six dirty rascals.

The months turned to a year. A social life developed and a new assistant joined the estate and stayed in my bungalow, which was large and roomy.

Geoff Brown came from a long line of planters and had been born and brought up in Malaya. After schooling he joined the Merchant Navy as a midshipman but longed to return to Malaya. He spoke fluent Malay.

Up to his arrival I had concentrated on Tamil, but it was very much the language of the estates rather than of the villages and the towns where the Malays and Chinese lived. Thus it became obvious that to enjoy a social life to its fullness speaking Malay was essential. Geoff could communicate with everybody, also with those Tamils who spoke some Malay, whereas I could only converse with the Tamils, which was of little advantage if one was in a bar in Ipoh or chatting up a dancing girl at the Great World Dance Hall on a Saturday evening.

Fortunately English remained widely spoken in those days, especially in the towns. On the estates all the conductors could speak excellent English and all reports, directives and messages were written in English.

WLH, who was considered a Tamil scholar, also wrote fluently in English and had the habit of communicating with his assistants by means of written instructions as we had no office telephones, faxes or emails in those days. The messages when received were read, acted upon and signed, and commented upon, if necessary.

Many of the messages were pithy, pertinent and often amusing. One on drainage, directed at me, pointed out that the drainage system in question had been adequate for over seventy years and that he really could not understand why I, who have been here only twenty-four months, should now feel it necessary for the configuration to be changed. Please clarify, it concluded.

Another, 'The standard of weeding work being performed in field 17 shows every indication of being jaggered [*jagga*, Malay, for being looked after] by an ignorant clown. Please comment.'

Rugby was played extensively throughout Malaya. Standards depended on the catchment area of players. Perak drew from planters, miners, schools e.g. Malay College, and the Commonwealth and Malayan Armed Forces, school teachers, banking personnel and others.

Perak State team was very much a multinational team and played some exciting rugger. We played against visiting teams, the most notable being the Oxford/Cambridge touring side, New Zealanders on tour, the Thai army and the redoubtable Fijians. Perak had two especially talented wings, both from the Malay College. They were fast, side-stepped at great speed and, being small, were difficult to catch. The forwards were generally slothful, cumbersome miners and planters, except for one enormous Sikh and a broad, rotund Tamil excavator driver who worked for the Public Works Department, both of whom were extremely mobile.

While working on Sungei Wangi I played two seasons for the State; Saturday afternoons, and evenings, were pleasant interludes in the humdrum life of the plantations. We reached the Malaya Cup final each year, won once and lost the other.

My driver, Vadivellu, thoroughly enjoyed watching the games as much as I enjoyed playing in them, and would always sit in front of the stands on the grass and opposite the halfway line. But it became very obvious that while he enjoyed the game and knew a surprising amount about its intricacies, one of his duties was to report back to WLH on how well I played. Next morning I was often woken up by a telephone call from WLH asking why I had missed the penalty in front of the posts, or kicked to touch when the wing was begging for the ball.

After a game at Seremban during which I dropped the ball at a scoring opportunity which decided the fate of the game, I was harangued over the telephone a few days after my return, and

Playing rugby with Vadivellu in attendance

accused of being totally responsible for the team's loss and that it must never happen again, or else. I sought out Vadivellu and told him to stop feeding WLH with match reports which were not fair and were causing me a lot of strife. If he persisted I would use another driver.

Rather than lose the privilege of an afternoon off, he made his reports more glowing and acceptable.

In the evenings we always had a good time, even when spending money was in short supply. I often had to lease my watch or my car's spare tyre – I had purchased a Mini by then – as security for the beers I drank and the food I ate. The tyre and watch were later retrieved, after I had been paid at the end of the month.

The Chinese hotel and restaurant owners realized our penniless predicament and were generally helpful and considerate, never minding if payments were delayed. Unfortunately this happy state of affairs did not last and towards the end of the sixties, when I returned to North Perak for a short management input, the scene had changed as cheques bounced and debts were not settled.

The culprits were fortunately seldom planters, who were generally honest in all their dealings while in town. The *towkays* also knew the estates where we came from and if a debt was not paid, the assistant would be reported. Certainly none of my close acquaintances were involved in unpaid bills. But it saddened the local people, probably more than us, when this breakdown in honesty and trust occurred, and I remember one hotel owner showing me a cheque which had bounced and then asking me if I knew the signatory; which I didn't. I later understood it to be that of an officer of the Irish Hussars based in Ipoh. Army officers were considered in those days less reliable than the other ranks; NCOs being the most honest.

4

Troubled Times

The first strike ever by the National Union of Plantation Workers on Sungei Wangi estate occurred when I was on Division I. It was not sudden, but a release of energy, resulting from a build up of resentment which slowly gained momentum and for little reason. Agitators in those days abounded.

WLH, initially, was not a great help to us as he had never experienced any trouble before, and, because of his personality, knowledge of Tamils and their language, it was totally beyond his comprehension that his beloved workforce would ever be anything but compliant. And it must be our fault, the assistants, anyway. Thus we were on the receiving end of some ugly scenes, as were also the staff. We never dared to go to WLH for his help nor to his deputy, a fine old Indian gentleman called T.A.P. Menon. Both extended an aura of dignified silence but they observed and were well aware of what was going on.

The Indian assistants had the hardest time of all for as they spoke the language, so the Tamils, all natural lawyers, could argue and press their claims more comprehensively. While on the divisions managed by the expatriate assistants, the shortcoming in fluency could be a help, as meetings became restricted, governed by our ability to converse.

This resulted in meetings breaking up early with handshakes all round and happy smiles; signifying little had been achieved but at least the workers had had a hearing and their grievances aired. In the early stages of labour militancy this was sufficient. Only when more educated trade union leaders became involved did relationships turn sour between workers and ourselves, which on a few occasions led to damaged rubber trees and other acts of sabotage.

* * *

20

On some estates there was violence and intimidation. Many of the union leaders had left-wing socialist backgrounds and some were affiliated to communist cells. Although these had effectively been stamped out during the communist insurgency of post- and pre-war Malaya, a following amongst some of the Indian and Chinese workers had continued.

At this time British trade unions were also beginning to make themselves felt, with successive governments appearing feeble and weak in constraining the excesses of the TUC movement. Poor company management did not help either.

TUC influence was felt in Malaya, and as foreign firms were most affected, the Government adopted a hands-off policy, which gave the unions the wrong signal. Continual threats to strike unless their demands were met became a feature of life on some estates; an aspect of man-management which we had little experience of, but soon became familiar with and adept in handling.

However, we managed to keep our presence and 'cool', and, except for a few hotheads, most workers really only wanted a quiet life.

On Sungei Wangi as time went by, WLH's personality, influence and experience came to our aid as no unionist wanted to tangle with him. Owing to his linguistic fluency and knowledge of the Tamil labourer, and, as many of the most influential union leaders were well known to him, sometimes through a previous relationship on an estate that he had managed, a brief telephone call to union headquarters would result in the estate union backing off after being told by their leaders not to damage their personal relationship with Peg-leg.

Other estates were not so lucky and some estate managers endured continual union problems, especially on those where there was little respect for the manager or his assistants, resulting in working relationships becoming wafer thin.

On Division I the NUPW was not strongly represented, but a small band of hotheads led by a handsome, erudite young Tamil called Arumugum did their best to cause trouble for me.

There were walkouts from the field and on occasions the liquid rubber (latex) was left uncollected; everybody seemed to complain of the unfair tasks they had to complete before being paid and the severe discipline imposed upon them by the *kanganies* (foremen). Much was fabricated and just bluster, exaggerated by Arumugum and his cronies.

The conductors and I knew that we had to rid ourselves of Arumugum before peace could be restored, but without violence or threat. Then our luck changed and a misguided adventure turned to our advantage.

Arumugum, being young and virile, enjoyed the company of many of the pretty young Tamil girls who adorned the various divisional work gangs. One in particular, Veemala, was particularly attractive and, it was said, she and Arumugum were betrothed.

However, Veemala was an exceedingly jealous young lady and if Arumugum should so much as glance at another girl she would vent her anger most hotly.

One day she decided to teach him the ultimate lesson, by half committing suicide, not an unusual practice amongst lovesick Tamil girls. In effect, she believed by playing with her life, it would show how much she loved him, and he in turn would respond in sorrow and anguish, with equal portions of love and devotion thrown in.

Thus the scene was set and as I returned one midday to the office I noticed a crowd gathered by the dispensary. I rode my bicycle over, dismounted and made my way through the throng. What is going on, I asked the hospital dresser and nurse who were standing by a bed upon which reclined a dying Veemala. Oh sir, they cried, Veemala has poisoned herself. Whatever for, I asked; Oh sir, because that rascal Arumugum no longer loves her, wept the nurse, indeed, sir, that is very true. You will notice she is much sick, she has drunk poison and will die unless we pump the poison out of her belly.

I looked her over. What did she drink? I asked. Oh sir, sodium chlorate, the dresser answered. Oh well, not as bad as sodium arsenate, I muttered. Quick, get her upright I ordered the dresser and nurse. She was raised, flopped ungainly and then was steadied, head lolling. I looked at my hands and went to the sink to wash.

Open her mouth, I commanded and then I slowly pushed my fingers down her throat. She retched, gurgled, and pulled away. I withdrew my fingers. I washed again and tried once more. There was a sudden rush and her food and drink spilled out, tinged in blue, not pleasant to view. Again I tried, until she flopped back exhausted, but now purged.

It is over, the curtain comes down, a small smile figures delicately on Veemala's pretty face. Has she accomplished what she hoped to achieve, I wonder.

But where is Arumugum? He has disappeared, probably the consequence of being the cause of Veemala's near demise has frightened him, for her brothers will surely seek revenge.

At next day's roll call Arumugum is nowhere to be seen, nor the following days. The rascally band of mischief-makers soon breaks up and peace on the division is quickly restored.

It was many years later that I met up again with Arumugum, this time on Sungei Sabling Estate, where he was a senior *kangany* and much changed; a good example of poacher turned gamekeeper.

5

Sitiawan and Lumut

Although I tried to go to Ipoh most weekends the district of Sitiawan and Lumut was a very pleasant place to live in. The local club was the focal point of entertainment for expatriates and locals alike. Tennis was keenly played, also football, and a school of poker players placed frighteningly large bets while gambling.

I played tennis. There were only four regular players, all of whom had played Davis Cup tennis. Moses Tay was the best, followed by our own estate doctor, U. Menon, Ah Kow, a contractor, and Mr Cheah, the Chartered Bank manager.

Playing every week with them raised my own standard, and when I played my brother in KL I was able to beat him easily, something previously I had never managed before.

I sailed off Pangkor Laut, close to Lumut. There was a small club and I purchased a sailing boat from a departing planter.

We sailed most Sundays and races were held to and from Pangkor Island, now a very posh seaside resort, but then a picturesque island with pretty fishing villages secluded amidst the jungle that bordered the shore.

It was not far from Sungei Wangi and I borrowed the Willy jeep to go down late in the afternoon when breezes blew from north to south, sufficient for a brisk sail until dusk.

Nightlife consisted of a cinema in Sitiawan town and the frequent visitation of funfairs, dancing groups, Indian and Malay, the occasional circus, and, of course numerous Chinese eating shops which were not the most salubrious of dining establishments but served a

24

delicious range of Chinese dishes, each shop producing one or two specialities.

At the funfairs we all participated in whatever action was being promoted, especially the *jogets* (Malay dances), during which the audience was invited on stage to dance with the young ladies. We all rushed forward when the opportunity arose, hoping that they would come out with us later in the evening.

Other activities included boxing; one planter, Chris Ing, an ex-amateur schoolboy boxing champion of some repute, would take on the funfairs' exhibition boxers and usually win.

The circuses were equally fun and would provide all sorts of entertainment. Elephants did their tricks, tigers too. On one afternoon the camels escaped and found their way into Peg-leg Harvey's garden. Murray and I were having tea with him on the veranda when a camel poked its head through the rattan sunblinds. Harvey blinked and, turning to Murray, asked what was this animal doing in his garden, please remove it immediately. Murray knew little about camels, but got up to do as he was bid. Fortunately at that instant the camels' trainer arrived and took the animal away.

One boastful strongman demonstrated his toughness by having a Land Rover driven over his body. He then called for somebody from the audience to do the same, thereby showing the watching crowds that the stunt was not a fake. A young planter got up to much acclaim and offered his services. The stuntman lay down on the ground, two wide planks were then placed against his body to facilitate easy access on and off his stationary torso.

The young planter gleefully watched the preparations. He got into the Land Rover and started it up and at a signal slowly drove towards the reclining strongman. Up the plank he went, the front wheels riding over the body and down the other side. Then suddenly the Land Rover stopped with the rear wheels heavy on the strongman's throat and lower anatomy. Our friend cried out that the engine had stalled. The crowd screamed with delight, the stuntman hollered in anguish. We rushed to the Land Rover. It's all right, the driver whispered, I just wanted to see how much this fellow could stand. He started the engine again and drove off.

Immediately the stuntman was surrounded by his followers and helpers – being Indian, there were many – and carried him away to his tent. The crowd were delighted, particularly the Chinese, who squawked and shouted with glee.

25

Testing the strength of the circus strongman

The older planters in the district seldom invited the assistants to their homes. There was a creed of amicable separation, neither side particularly desiring the company of the other, especially as young assistants 'nowadays' showed little deference or respect towards their elders and superiors.

There were, of course, exceptions. Bill Harvey was one who often invited us round, Charles Cooke, who had taken part in the last charge of the Mysore Lancers, another. WLH was, unlike his contemporaries, knowledgeable and intelligent. He read avidly and once when his stump was giving him a lot of pain and he was

26

confined to bed, I had to take some letters round for him to sign. He was lying propped up in bed reading a book on Greek pottery. He then discoursed for an hour on the great civilizations of the world and their impact upon modern society.

There was also a great cross-section of personalities and abilities. The younger planters were generally more able than their elders and many had acquired over the years a variety of talents by which they augmented their meagre salaries, and later depended upon when they left planting.

Murray, now unfortunately dead, was an extremely talented trombone player, ex-Aberdeen University, where many planters were educated. He supplemented his meagre salary by playing poker amongst the rich members of the Chinese and Indian communities. He was very successful.

Another, who lasted only a few years as a planter established an escort service in Japan, where his good looks excited a great deal of attention amongst older Japanese ladies seeking a good time after years of hardship.

An ex-Harlequin rugger player who was so poor he could only afford an old battered BSA motorcycle left the profession and become a vicar. Probably in atonement for the debauchery we all enjoyed after games of rugby on Saturdays.

A good friend left to take up law and another became a professional pilot, while Ian Barnwell, a well-known motor-racing fanatic and a manager, joined the French Research Institute, IRHO.

Brian Vaughan, an assistant on Sitiawan Estate, was an especially versatile artist and after a brief interlude as a planter gave up and went to Hong Kong to work as an artist and cartoonist.

His successor, a placid young man, had a clever wife, the daughter of a missionary who had spent a large chunk of her life in China and was fluent in Cantonese, which most of the Sitiawan Chinese spoke. Because they lived fairly frugally, unlike other planters, she did her own shopping and marketing. This necessitated visiting the local markets in town to buy her vegetables, fruit and meat.

As most of the stall owners were Chinese, she received excellent service, once the Chinese realized she could speak their language. However, when she first arrived in the district and went off to the market, her arrival was greeted with many ribald and obscene comments, which only the Chinese are capable of inventing. Not to be swayed by their coarseness, she went from stall to stall to look and inspect their wares amidst a cacophony of raucousness, finally stopping at one stall owned by a little old Chinese lady. She then asked for what she wanted, discussed the relative merits of the various items on offer, chattered about the weather, seasons and her grandchildren.

The market quietened instantly with her calm fluency of the language. Then picking up her full baskets she departed the way she came in, stopping only once to castigate a particularly vociferous stall owner, whom she described loudly as being as worthless as a pimple on a face and that she hoped his wife gave him syphilis and that he would die in excruciating pain.

Having vented her quiet rage she departed the now silent market, and thereafter never had any trouble.

On occasions we went to Lumut, to the rest house, where there were get-togethers: a dance, a party, a meeting or a gathering of expatriates and locals.

It was while at a dance that I first heard of the Beatles and their quick rise to fame. The person who confided this piece of information was the District Commissioner's daughter, who had been in the UK visiting her brother at university. She was very attractive, but as my dancing did not impress her she soon found somebody more attuned to modern music.

Later that night we walked to the eating stalls haphazardly erected on the narrow promenade that bordered the sea, and there enjoyed a late-night snack and a beer. It was a star-bright night; the light breezes from the sea suppressed the humidity and everybody was in good spirits.

After eating, we slowly dispersed to our cars as it was now getting quite late. Just as I was about to start my Mini I heard the unmistakeable wail of a person in grief. I looked around; cars were reversing and then revving off.

I could see nobody but the sound was easily distinguishable and coming from a table at the far end of the small eating square. I walked hurriedly over. There were two girls sobbing. Are you all right? I asked. It was unusual to meet up with young people on their own in Malaya; back-packing had not yet really got started in the early 1960s.

Have you not heard? they asked. They were Americans. Heard

28

what? I asked. President Kennedy has just been shot, they sobbed. I left them to their sorrow. A brief era of such promise, all gone.

My days on Sungei Wangi were drawing to a close. Like all assistants, I had learnt a lot and the confidence gained from being on a premier estate helped me cope with future assignments.

Unlike other assistants I had been very happy there. Perhaps Peg-leg was mellowing but he wasn't the martinet I had expected. My wife, who met him in 1977, when we had just married, liked him immensely, finding him easy to talk to, gracious and charming.

He was always a good host and, as I have said, was one of the few managers who would usually invite his assistants along to his house when he was having a party. On one of these social occasions he had his cook concoct a drink with the aim of knocking out a group of garrulous wives, married to managers who resided in the locality, and whose company he had little regard for and in some cases actually detested.

The concoction was a liqueur mixed with fresh orange to disguise the taste. It was shaken, stirred, tasted for alcohol content and remixed to achieve the most potent strength. It was an immediate success. Eyes of the memsahibs became glazed; some sank low in their chairs. One backed through a panelled screen. Everybody waited, nobody moved, mesmerized; would she topple over the veranda into the flowerbeds below, or not? WLH watched, as did her husband, in limbo, praying for an early release from her wounding and barbed expletives. Instead she toppled back into the room crashing to the floor unconscious. We raised our glasses.

A drink was born, the Harvey Wallbanger.

The birth of the Harvey Wallbanger

6

I am Transferred

My sojourn at Sungei Wangi came to an end and I was transferred to Carey Island, a plantation off the coast of the State of Selangor. If Sungei Wangi could be likened to a state penitentiary, Carey Island was not dissimilar to the castle fortress Colditz of World War II fame.

Separated from the mainland by three hundred yards of tidal water, crossing was only possible by a manually operated ferry, later to be replaced by a motor-powered vessel. Owing to the speed of the tidal flow the ferry could only operate when there was calm water. Once on the island it was not easy to get off and the frequent tropical rainfall resulted in slippery rutted roads, making driving a fraught experience.

Most managers and assistants just did not bother to go away. On the other side of the island was a golf course and a very pleasant club while a ferry service, an ancient powered boat, operated between the island and Port Swettenham, the principal port of Malaya and only an hour away.

The island was divided into three estates: South, West and East. These three very unimaginative names were indicative of the mentality of those who had managed the plantation in the past when the island was one large plantation. Dividing it into three separate integral estates ensured better management control. Also, H&C did not like large single-management units with an all-powerful manager who would be difficult to keep to heel. H&C preferred compliant managers who were not going to treat H&C agency staff like office peons, as WLH enjoyed doing.

On West Estate the manager was Jack Moorcraft, who had been

the previous General Manager of the whole island estate. He had a certain charisma and charm. He seldom wore a shirt, believing that as the Indian labour did not wear shirts then neither would he nor his assistants. So we all on West went about our duties shirtless, except in the mature rubber, where mosquitoes abounded and protection was needed.

I did not mind not wearing a shirt as I soon became tanned, but for others, especially the pink-skinned Scots, not wearing a shirt was a recipe for peeling skin and probably later cancer. One assistant who suffered more than others reverted to wearing an enormous pith helmet, which kept his body well shaded.

Jack had been an army officer in the war and was tough and handsome. He could speak Tamil well, but not with the fluency and scholarship of WLH. He could, like all managers, be extremely kind and generous but was more often than not arrogant and intolerant.

West Estate for me was not a happy experience. There were four divisions on West and during the year I was on Carey Island I was moved from one to another. The principal reason for my movement was probably due to my own fault as I just did not get on with the senior assistant, a Tamil and a promoted conductor. Nor did I try.

He had been around a long time, as had all the senior conductors, who regarded any assistant as a usurper to their authority, which over the years had become considerable. Especially when management had allowed their conductors more and more influence on the divisions.

Assistants on Carey Island often became sidelined by the managers and, coupled with the promotion of some conductors to senior assistant status, a powerful hierarchy of favoured local senior staff emerged. This often resulted in confrontation between the assistants and promoted senior assistants, many of who could be extremely devious. All this made our lives difficult and the situation was further exacerbated when on occasions orders were countermanded by the conductors with the connivance of the managers.

For me Carey Island was not a pleasant place and this was not helped by having a manager who relied upon spies, selected from the staff and labour, to keep him informed of what was going on. I wrote a letter to the manager complaining of this powerful coterie of junior and newly promoted senior assistants. This was not a

32

wise move, but at least my dissatisfaction was out in the open, and because I had a disagreeable confrontation with one junior staff member, I was moved to another division.

As I was considered a troublemaker I was moved four times. I was perpetually in transit until I was eventually posted to Division 4, where my house was just two hundred yards from Jack's home. I had arrived, for the worst possible reasons, to what was called Rotten Row, an exclusive avenue of beautiful homes where all the senior personnel resided, and now me. Jack had decided to keep an eye upon his assistant at close quarters.

My divisional office was the other side of two fields of coconut palms and the quickest way through was by bicycle along the many harvester paths. By using shortcuts I could be at muster in ten minutes, by road half an hour. Jack had to drive by road; I bicycled. Should he decide to go to muster he passed by my house at 5.15 a.m., I left at 5.20 a.m. to arrive one minute before him at 5.30 a.m. He was usually in a bad mood and tried to direct muster rather than leave it to the junior staff. This would lead to conflicting orders, a melee of workers wondering where to go, and a sneering uncooperative me. Which was not helpful and did not improve his mood.

There were few good aspects of life on Carey Island. I did not play golf, but I did manage to play rugby and cricket for Klang Club, close to Port Swettenham, where there were lots of Saturday parties to go to, hosted by the shipping agents who resided near to the port.

In those days, pre-Muslim fundamentalism, Malaya exuded a happy-go-lucky atmosphere with complete integration of all races, particularly of our age group, having never been tainted by racialism.

On the estate the club was the centre of our social life on the island. There was a golf course, two tennis courts and inside the clubhouse, billiard tables, a table tennis table and a library which inhabited the corner of an upstairs alcove.

It was a splendid building, built of brick and wood similar to all the houses on the island. Upstairs a huge sitting room encompassed the whole floor plus a large bar. Here we gathered once or twice a week with the specific aim, for some of us, to drown our sorrows for having been incarcerated on this remote, dreary island.

Not everybody disliked the place: some of the managers, and most of the local Indian assistants were quite content, especially those who had lived and worked throughout their planting careers on the island and knew no other estate.

It was obligatory that we were present at film nights every Wednesday and also at the weekly curry tiffin on Sundays. Wednesday evenings were especially fun and nighttime revelries continued well into the early hours of the morning. Like most assistants, I stayed on after the film, as did also a few of the managers. Jack, having learnt that I played the piano, although I was now out of practice, insisted once the jollities were over that I return to his house and play duets with him, sometimes until early morning, when I would depart on my bicycle to attend muster.

However, club life was a pleasant interlude in our highly regulated existence of checking tapping standards, maintaining the interminable drainage system which bisected and trisected the island, and supervising the weeders and the railway maintenance gangs. All the oil palm fruit, copra (coconut albumen) and latex in those days was transported by locomotives (made in Hull) pulling long streams of clanking wagons.

Unfortunately, one blight upon club life was the senior bar boy who, having fled from Mao Tse-tung's advancing communist armies, eventually arrived in Malaya and soon found employment. Now middle-aged and grumpy, he, unlike most Chinese, could not add up without making mistakes. And as he never kept notes of who drank what and how many, invariably made mistakes when entering into each individual's bar account book the amount of liquor that had been consumed. Each time we had to check, each time he protested that we had consumed what he had written. Balls, we cried, I drank four beers only, not five. Why have you written whisky when I only drink gin, another would argue.

Finally it come to a head when, one evening, an assistant who hardly frequented the club, living at the furthest corner of the estate, found in his bar book entries made when he had not even been present. He erupted, enraged, and demanded an explanation from the bar boy. The bar boy jabbered with fear, for the assistant, Latimer Beatty, cut a fine figure of manhood, being an ex-rower from a well-known Thames rowing club. Latimer, incensed, picked up the bar boy and hoisted him out of the window. We watched this breathtaking drama with cries of support for our hero. The bar boy dropped from the balcony onto the ground below. Fetch a coffin, shouted one assistant distastefully. Fortunately the bar boy's fall was broken by landing on the soft tarpaulin roof of Jack M's Land Rover. He stumbled up, shouting obscenities at us as we craned our necks outwards and downwards to voice our opinion of his parentage and his cheating habits.

The few managers remaining, sitting in a far alcove reserved for 'top people' only, shambled over to us to break up the conflict. At last some semblance of order was restored and we explained to the managers the reason for our anger. Needless to say, they were surprised as the bar boy was considered honest and trust-worthy.

We pointed out that of course he would never dare to manipulate a manager's bar account, but there was more than sufficient evidence that he was certainly altering our bar accounts whenever a loss occurred, especially when stocktaking after an evening's drinking session. At the same time we agreed that he was probably not manipulating our bar accounts for his own monetary gain, but just to cover any loss which may have been incurred owing to his inability to perform simple arithmetic.

The managers realized we were not going to be fobbed off and so an assistant was appointed to check the accounts monthly. The assistant, Joe Clifton-Brown, was a scholarly individual who, after leaving university, was undecided what career to pursue. Instead of the army, first choice, or the Church, last choice, suitable only for misfits and the unemployable, he considered a planting career might be to his liking.

Our troubles were over, our bar book accounts would now be in safe hands.

It was after one Wednesday evening thrash that I lost my cricket cap, much to my dismay. It was very special as only members of the Madhatters Cricket Club, a wandering team of players who roamed the Kent and Sussex countryside looking for opposition to play, were entitled to wear their colours. The cap, of red, green and white circles, was comfortable and cosy to wear, and, being of good quality, warm when riding a motorcycle to muster in the mornings, or returning from a late-night binge, or after piano duets with Jack M.

On that night as I was speeding back to my bungalow, on a borrowed motorcycle, I slipped violently off the road at a sharp bend and was thrown into the drain alongside. My motorcycle disappeared beneath the brown peaty water, and I with it. Sodden, cold and dripping, I emerged, my head rising slowly above the water level, but without my cap. I looked around and scrambled onto the bank. My hat was nowhere to be seen.

I was bedraggled and very wet, so I set off at a jog to return home. There my cook, on being awoken, made me a hot lemon toddy, fearing I would catch pneumonia.

In the morning I gathered some workers and we went to retrieve the motorcycle and, hopefully, my cap. The former was manhandled easily out of the drain; of the cap, there was no sign.

Oh sir, oh sir, the Tamils exclaimed, it is not here. Of course it must be, I replied in Tamil, it cannot just walk away. They laughed, ha ha, how can a hat walk away sir, oh no sir, hats cannot walk. Well, where is it? I retorted.

We searched high and low. The water in the drain was stationary so it should be close by. Unfortunately it wasn't; my cap was lost.

A few months later when I arrived to supervise a railway maintenance gang, I espied in the distance a dhoti-clad worker with a splash of colour on his head. I walked over. Good heavens, I exclaimed, there is my cap. You scoundrel, you rascal, I shouted, you are wearing my cricket cap. Oh no, sir, said the guilty party, I bought this cap with my own good money at the Sunday morning market. Impossible, I replied, let me show you, my name is inside. He handed me the cap. My name was no longer visible, nor the maker's crest. See, sir, see, your honoured name is not in the hat.

It is mine, I cried. No, it is mine, the labourer replied in anguish. I paid good money for this very nice hat. It is mine. Please, sir, look see, it is mine; on the back of the cap he had written, A. Krishnasamy. That is my name, sir, he said.

There was silence, I handed the cap back. You must always keep this hat clean, I told him. Oh yes, sir, of course, sir, this I know is a very special hat.

I left them to their task, he the proud owner of a Madhatters Cricket Club cap, the only one in Malaya.

Life off the estate was always fun, on the estate it was long hours, meaningless slog, which management, mistakenly thought, desirable. Planting on Carey Island was a state of attrition, seldom was a simpler method investigated or employed to carry out a job. Just as soldiers in the First World War were often led by unthinking officers who knew of only one plan of attack, over the top, so similarly on the estate there was only one way of doing a job and that was the one prescribed twenty years before. Innovation was not management's strong point. And should an assistant suggest something new, it was dismissed as inappropriate or too difficult to implement, or just ignored.

My end soon came. Although socially Jack was thoughtful and kind, I was not the type of officer he wanted on his estate. I played piano duets into the early morning with him when ordered to his bungalow at midnight, and he did not mind me taking time off to play sport. However, he did not like his junior assistant telling him what was going on and contradicting him if he had got it wrong. Which invariably happened.

He decided we should part company. He had been angling for an excuse for a long time and, as the assistant of an adjacent estate on the mainland was moving up-country, my transfer was simply executed.

His parting words to me probably summed up his attitude: 'What I have seen of you I dislike intensely.' Management in those days paid little heed to the feelings of their subordinates or to any form of political correctness. Termination was brief and brusque. As I was twenty-three years old his bad temper was of little concern, I was departing this cursed mosquito-infested island, thank God.

I packed my tin trunk and suitcase, put my cook and dog in the car – I had now changed my Mini for an MG TD – and drove to the ferry. It was waiting. As I glanced behind I noticed Jack's Land

Rover the other side. He was leaning against the bonnet. I blew him a kiss. He didn't reciprocate, though surprisingly he waved a tired salute. I never ever saw him again, although I returned to Carey Island on two further occasions.

7

Dusun Durian Estate

How different was the manager of Dusun Durian. Hans Veldhuis was a Dutch refugee from Indonesia; he was competent and innovative but couldn't handle labour, being either too strict or too lenient. Typically Dutch.

The estate was mostly oil palm with a little rubber. It was by the coast, located amongst an array of Malay kampongs (villages). A convivial environment far removed from the peat swamps of Carey Island and its geriatric and oppressed managers. I was to stay on Durian for the rest of my first tour of duty.

In 1962, 'confrontation' between Malaysia and Indonesia suddenly erupted. Indonesia, poverty-stricken, badly ruled and corrupt, fabricated a confrontation with Malaysia concerning, principally, the ownership of Borneo Island, part of which was deemed Malaysian and part Indonesian. The Indonesians wanted it all. Malaysia was well governed and content, the Indonesians were governed by a popular, charismatic despot presiding over an ever-increasing population, eighty per cent of whom were living in squalor. It was a tinderbox of discontent about to ignite. Confrontation was to last until 1965.

Fighting broke out on the borders of Sarawak and Sabah (Malaysian Borneo), and Indonesian Borneo. Sukarno, the President of Indonesia, also threatened an invasion of the Malaysian mainland and sent his soldiers by sea and air. Dusun Durian was on the front line, being by the coast. I was armed with a revolver, and a Sikh watchman was posted as guard, but as he slept throughout the night he would have been of little use in an emergency. As there was a curfew at night I was not supposed to go out, although I did. The only difficulty for me to overcome was stepping over the

Waiting for the Indonesians to invade

watchman, who lay propped up fast asleep against the front door, spread eagled.

There were roadblocks, and some British Army personnel had taken up positions along the beach as it was rumoured a large Indonesian landing force was heading our way.

Further along the beach in a small fishing village there resided an old retired planter who had been made a *dato* (a lord) for services rendered. What services I never found out but he was kind and hospitable and enjoyed company. As I left my sampan (boat) in his garden, which stretched out to the beach, I got to know him well and his ready supply of gin and tonics were very welcome after a hard sail.

40

His peace was disturbed firstly by the arrival of the army to defend his beach and secondly the threat from an invading force of Indonesians. It was suggested he leave, which of course he didn't, but instead increased his stock of gin and whisky just in case the war should cut his supply line to Banting, the nearest town.

I visited him most evenings, using village paths. We waited, in vain, for the arrival of the Indonesian fleet, gin in hand. They never arrived. The army retired to barracks and peace returned.

Nobody seemed to want my revolver back so I kept it, and the Sikh guard stayed on, for whatever reason.

However, on one fine night, down the road at Sungei Sedu Estate, a parachute drop of airborne Indonesian troops did take place. At the time a field of rubber was being replanted with oil palms. The charred, smoking remains of the clearing had caught the eye of the airborne commander, who thought that the burning wood was a town on fire caused, supposedly, by an advancing force of his compatriots.

He jumped, and so did his troops, into the burning replant. Their fluttering parachutes were noticed by watchmen overseeing the fires, who rushed to the manager's house for assistance.

The manager lived with his mother, a redoubtable old lady called Mrs Lawrence, who it is said spent more time on the estate than her son. Both rushed to the replant to find the Indonesians up to their knees in burning rubber wood, crying out for help.

Lorries arrived from the estate factory and the enemy soldiers were herded in, thankful to be away from the fire, particularly as the soil was peat, which burnt to the depth of its decomposing layers.

The soldiers were taken to the factory and stood against a wall and hosed down with water under the belligerent eye of Ma Lawrence. Then the police arrived.

That was the end of the war for this particular parachute regiment. Soon after, Indonesia's most senior generals ousted Mr Sukarno and then purged the country of all communists and anybody they did not like. Peace between the two countries was quickly restored.

At the same time a new era unfolded with the cementing of ties between Sarawak and Sabah and the Federated States of Malaya and, for a short period, with Singapore. At last Malaysia became an established country.

41

To achieve maximum production from oil palms it was necessary to pollinate the female flowers until such time as there were sufficient male flowers on the palm to ensure natural pollination. Nowadays a weevil, *Elodobius kamerunicus*, introduced from the Cameroons, West Africa, provides a satisfactory pollen coverage, but thirty-plus years ago during the early stages of palm growth pollination had to be performed manually.

My predecessor organized a gang of the prettiest girls to perform this not very arduous but vital work. He selected well, and as most of the workers on Dusun Durian estate were Malays there was an abundance of attractive girls to choose from.

How lucky we were. Ayatollah Khomeini was not yet on the scene in Iran. His arrival in 1979 altered the moderate Islamic landscape of countries such as Malaysia to one of vigorous, dogmatic, unforgiving fundamentalism. Such an alien religion for an undemanding and contented people.

The Muslim communities in the 1960s remained effortlessly hospitable, kind and tolerant. Like most rural communities throughout the world, they lived a slow, easy and refined life uninterrupted by the unattractive drive for wealth. A Malay man was always a gentleman and a Malay woman a graceful lady with an equal measure of charm and guile.

Surrounded by such people, no young assistant could remain unmoved for long and I soon was on good terms with the surrounding villagers. My fluency in the Malay language began to improve under close tutorial guidance.

Supervising the pollination gang, although an experience we all enjoyed, including Veldhuis the manager, had a serious side to it. The work necessitated the girls going round the estate daily, pollinating the flowers and, when required, climbing the taller, older palms. During one outing a girl got her sarong and leg entangled in a frond petiole, which although pruned close to the stem snagged her foot, which snapped. She was rushed to hospital in agony.

It was time to try and introduce a method by which the pollen could be blown onto the flower while the girl stood on the ground, thereby eliminating the possibility of another climbing accident.

Veldhuis realized the necessity of fabricating an instrument suitable for this purpose. We racked our brains for inspiration and came up with the novel idea of blowing up a tube fixed to a pole with a container full of pollen tied to the upper end. The tube was blown through and the pollen puffed onto the flowers.

The girls were equipped, they could now blow the mix of talcum powder and pollen easily onto the flowers. It worked well initially but the muslin covering the bottle soon became damp from the girls' breath which clogged the powder, so we needed to modify the apparatus and try a different approach. Fortunately Veldhuis, while in the barber's one day – he was always getting his hair cut, as do all Dutch – realised that the powder puffs barbers used to apply talcum powder could be fitted on to the pollinator. He rushed back to the estate and tied a puffer to the end of the tube. Instead of blowing, the girls had only to manually puff it.

The design was sent to H&C, who forwarded it to all oil palm estates. The pollinator became known irreverently as the 'Veldhuis tool'. They are still being used throughout the oil palm growing regions of the world whenever artificial pollination is required.

Days and weeks hurried by. The estate was well managed, and in my MG TD I went to Klang most weekends to play rugger or cricket. I was captain of the cricket team.

It was during a game that I learnt, to my indignation, that I was supposed to be having an affair with the English wife of one of the research officers. This was not pleasing news as no self-respecting assistant would have ever looked at a white wife, who were, with the odd exception, usually bedraggled and limp. With so many beautiful Asian girls around, there was no need. It was incomprehensible. As this particular piece of tittle-tattle arose during a cricket game at Klang, I was eager to know who was responsible for this gossip.

As her husband was fielding at second slip while I was at first, the subject was quickly broached. The wicket keeper, who was the principal mischief-maker, listened intently and dropped a catch while concentrating more on the gossip than the game.

Yes, indeed the second slip had heard that his wife was having an affair with an assistant but he didn't know with whom. He presumed because I lived close by and knew both parties that it was me.

It was outrageous that he should have thought that I, or any other assistant, would have found his wife desirable. I told him I had no designs upon his wife and nobody else's either and there the matter rested. Not until the mid 1970s did I learn that they were divorced and that she had returned to England and he had married again.

By chance during a cricket game against the Singapore Cricket Club in 1975 the subject of who had been involved with his wife arose. As some of the players on that Saturday afternoon were the same as those who had been playing for Klang ten years before, we chattered about old times in between overs.

It was while batting that I started reminiscing with the opposition fast bowler, ex-Klang club, about times past. The affair was mentioned and I reiterated my innocence and that I had never been involved. His reply, against a backdrop of club, law courts, a well-known cricket field and a busy harbour in the distance, was like a scene from a Somerset Maugham novel. No, he replied, he knew that it was not me. I asked him, if he knew, why had he not responded to the gossip in my favour, particularly as I had later been sent to Sungai Samak Estate after my return from leave; an estate as far away as possible from Dusun Durian, and for that very reason. It had been completely unfair.

His response was unexpected. How could I support you over this, he answered, when it was me who was having the affair. The game continued. We lost.

I was due for leave and a replacement was being sought. My tour of duty of four years was over, but I continued until the assistant due to take over returned from leave.

He was Duncan Blincoe, a cricketer and pianist with a degree in geography. He loved Dusun Durian as much as I did and settled quickly into life. My Malay by now was fluent, owing to continual exposure, and, because we enjoyed the same things, he soon slotted into the comfortable life of the estate and its surroundings.

Except for the *dato* and the odd VSO or Peace Corps recruit who stayed in the district, our social lives tended towards the villagers rather than the other planters, most of whom were married.

At weekends we travelled to Klang or Kuala Lumpur, where planters used to gravitate. In a street of bars, the Rex, Tivoli and

Paramount were well-known meeting places where the drink and food were cheap and the company convivial. British Army personnel also used to inhabit these drinking holes and fights would occasionally break out. Fortunately, though, usually between drunk squaddies.

Fights never seemed to perturb the bar staff. In fact, once a year fights were positively encouraged in order that a huge inflated bill for broken glasses and furniture could be presented to the army authorities of the offending battalion for immediate reimbursement. The bills were paid up and new sets of glasses and furniture purchased. This method of equipping such hostelries was adopted by most bar owners as an acceptable standard procedure and considered a small price to pay for the damage caused.

In 1964 in Malaysia, and up to the Vietnam War, all solders were Tommies, British or Commonwealth. Only when Kuala Lumpur became a rest and recuperation centre for the USA forces engaged in Vietnam did Americans become more prominent in the town.

One evening, with a Peace Corps friend, we went to a cabaret in town and were soon joined by girls wanting us to buy them drinks. My friend was asked where he came from. Sticking out his chest he said loudly and proudly, from the United States of America, to which a girl, turning to me, asked which part of England is this United States of America.

How times have changed and that was less than forty years ago.

8

I Go on Leave

I returned to the UK by air in a VC10 and caught a train from Charing Cross railway station to Tonbridge, where I hoped my parents would meet me.

At the station I purchased a Tamil newspaper to see how far my Tamil linguistic skills had deteriorated after speaking Malay continuously on Dusun Durian. I was surprised that I could still read the phonetic script, but found it difficult to understand the meaning. I was about to put the paper away when a businessman in pinstripes, sitting opposite, leant over and asked if he could borrow my newspaper. He read it thoroughly and got out at Sevenoaks, returning the newspaper as he left the compartment. He mentioned that he had often sought a Tamil newspaper in London but never at Charing Cross railway station.

My parents were at the station. The weather was glorious, an Indian summer, and we drove to the village of Speldhurst, where we lived by an old water mill. The mill still worked, the house's lawns were a vivid green and my father had left the tennis net up as the weather was so dry. They still played tennis, though unenergetically.

It was a perfect day and setting, calm, peaceful and undisturbed. I almost felt that I had never been away; the gentle, tranquil sameness of the English countryside seemingly unaltered over the past four-plus years that I had spent in Malaya, now Malaysia.

I was entitled to six months' paid leave. After the first few weeks, during which I did very little except help in the garden, cut logs for the fires and play rugby for Tonbridge town, my enforced idleness began to pall and I decided to take flying lessons.

46

The nearest club was at Rochester. As I had already hired a car from a friend for my leave period at the princely sum of £45 per month, I set out to find the club and enrol.

The club had two planes and the instructor, an ex-wartime pilot, took perverse delight in scaring his pupils. But he considered that until a trainee had experienced all aspects of flying and conquered all his fears, then and only then would he become a good pilot.

I felt very confident with him and I enjoyed our half-hour lessons. However, one of the planes crashed and the club was overrun by officialdom scrutinizing the books, planes and returns. Sadly the club was closed temporarily. I left and decided to wait until I returned to Malaysia before flying again.

Next, I put an advert in a newspaper stating that I would be willing to do anything and go anywhere. There were a few replies. One was selling perfume, not quite what I had in mind. A group located at Victoria, London, wanted me to investigate slave trading in Bermondsey, East London, in which the residing Pakistan community was supposed to be involved. I was told it would be a dangerous assignment and that the previous recruit had been tortured unmercifully when he was sent into the area to spy. I decided against this as I wanted to return to Malaysia in one piece, and also the job was very poorly paid.

I was given an air ticket by a consortium of businessmen to inspect some apartments being built in Tripoli. As my visa and passport were not in order I was bundled back in the first plane out and arrived in Rome, where I had to purchase another ticket to London.

After this I stayed in England and helped my father prepare the vegetable garden and cut more logs for the fires as winter was upon us. Life meandered along. It was enjoyable but I missed the tropics and Malaysia.

My six months drew to a close and I was sent a ticket to Malaysia via Calcutta. It was the month of May; I remember it well.

The plane broke down at Calcutta airport and I was put up at the rest house in the suburb of Dum Dum. As flights to Malaysia were not frequent I had to wait. Rather than continue in the slum of Dum Dum, I went into Calcutta and stayed at the splendid Grand

Hotel. A considerable contrast to the poverty-stricken surroundings of the city.

Two days later I returned to the airport and caught a plane to Bangkok. There I waited for my connection to Kuala Lumpur that didn't arrive. The airline staff were apologetic and helpful and I was booked into a smart hotel. I had little money, but I was told all expenses would be to the airline, which was MSA, Malaysia Singapore Airlines.

Again, after a wait for a day and a night, a bus came to pick me up to return me to the airport. I checked out. Who was to pay? There were no MSA representatives around. I had no money and even if I had I would have refused to pay. It was hardly my fault the plane broke down.

The reception staff politely told me that all non-alcoholic drinks and food were to the airline's account, but not the other bits and pieces I had purchased, eaten or drunk. However, they obviously did not want me around any longer and I certainly had had enough of the travel industry. I was already three days late. So I was loaded on the bus and we set off for the airport.

After an uneventful flight it was a relief when we touched down at midnight at Subang, Kuala Lumpur's international airport. I hurried out to find a taxi to take me back to Dusun Durian Estate, where all my worldly possessions were stored.

There were few taxis waiting and all looked obsolete, but I found one driver willing to take me to the estate and we set off. The vehicle was not in good repair and the engine overheated continually. Stops became ever more frequent, but at last we rattled and burped our way up to the bungalow.

The Sikh watchman, the same one as before, was asleep, but once woken up told me Blincoe had been transferred and that no new assistant had yet arrived. The house was empty and locked.

The driver meanwhile was becoming restless for his money and wanted to return to KL. I had no money left. Fortunately, the senior conductor, Mr P. Thomas, was at home so I woke him up and he kindly paid my taxi fare. He also kept a duplicate key for the bungalow, which I thankfully borrowed, I went straight to sleep on a hard uncovered mattress.

The next step was for me to go to H&C's office in Kuala Lumpur to report my arrival, which owing to the many delays was long overdue. My car, which I had left at the estate factory, seemed to be in a reasonable but dusty condition, so I left immediately for KL with my tin trunk and suitcase.

Halfway there the MG came to a shuddering halt. I had forgotten to check the oil and the main bearing had seized. The very worst that could happen. I waved down a lorry, loaded on my trunk and case and asked the driver to take me to Jalan Ampang straight away. He was going in a different direction but seemed happy to detour. Fortunately my brother was in the office and after asking why I was three days late took me back to his house in Petaling Jaya, a suburb of Kuala Lumpur. There I phoned up Dusun Durian Estate factory and asked the engineer if he could retrieve my vehicle. My brother suggested I hired a car to take me to my new posting at Sungei Samak Estate. He lent me some money, so I phoned a taxi firm, negotiated a price and we set off.

The journey through Lower Selangor then on to Ulu Perak took five hours. To reach the estate one had to go by river transport, ferry or speedboat, a two-hour journey along the Sungei Bernam River. I found the small quay and the speedboat that had been ordered to pick me up three days before and was just about to leave without me. We set off. Luxuriant jungle bordered the river and small kampongs dotted its banks. It was fun and for the first time in over a week I felt more relaxed. However, this was not the end of my travelling horrors. Suddenly the boat stopped, with the engine over-revving. The pin which attached the propeller to the drive shaft had snapped, the dismembered propeller dropping out of sight into the murky water below.

No propeller, no pin, but all was not lost: the driver had an old, warped, spare propeller with a pin. Owing to its poor state of repair, the remainder of the journey would be slow. Fortunately, the tide was in our favour and we meandered unhurriedly along, the sun percolating through the forest and sparkling on the water. It was tranquil but the propeller, which made funny rattling noises as it bit into the water, kept us alert. I felt sure the pin would break again at any moment.

Some hours later Sungei Samak came into view. Our passage had been noted by passing boats and the manager, Ewart Bracewell, had been informed that we were on our way.

May had not been a good month for me and once on shore I

vowed I would not leave the estate for at least three months. I therefore stayed put and the next three years, my second tour of duty, was to be a very happy time indeed.

9

Sungei Samak Estate

H&C estate managers, compared with managers of other companies, enjoyed far more freedom to manage their estates without the constraining interference of head office staff turning up and interfering. Visiting agents inspected the estates twice annually and, except for the occasional visit from research staff advising on fertilizer recommendations and visits from the company's engineering department, managers were very much left to their own devices. This suited most of us very well. Visitors were not encouraged. On Sungei Samak we seemed to have less contact with the outside world because of our isolation, especially when compared to those estates close to KL or in more accessible locations.

Next door to Sungei Samak was a property owned by the East Asiatic company, founded by a bunch of Danish army officers wanting to escape the deprivation of Europe after the First World War. They moved into Asia and travelled extensively, opening up trading posts and then establishing estates, mostly in the Ulu Bernam and Teluk Anson districts of Lower Perak.

Both estates had planted oil palms, the flat, riverine and peat soils being ideal for these two crops. For H&C, growing oil palms was a comparatively new venture but for East Asiatic, oil crops were dominant on all their plantations. As the price of crude palm oil began to rise so H&C and other companies started to replant their rubber and coconuts with oil palms.

Management on Ulu Bernam Estate was a mix of Scots, Danes and Malaysians. Their engineering department was sophisticated and advanced and was managed by two Danes, both of whom flew their own planes, purchased with their excellent bonuses, which dwarfed the miserly handouts that the scrooges of H&C afforded their planters and engineers.

Life, however, was fun and work was hard. Both communities got on well, although personality hiccups amongst senior staff members became more visible when Ewart got married to a bossy woman who tried to establish a hierarchy amongst us planters and engineers. She failed because the numbers involved were too small and most assistants couldn't care less who invited them to dinner. They only went along for the food and the booze anyway, certainly not the company, which was generally tedious in the extreme.

As it was, our social life revolved around a number of activities. An extremely competitive football league was enjoyed by everyone. Often fisticuffs broke out between the two rival camps of supporters when a referee's decision was disputed. Volleyball and badminton were also keenly played. Water-skiing on the river was popular, and traipsing along the jungle fringes looking for rhinoceros, whose spoors were frequently seen, captured our spirit of adventure.

There was in those days plenty of wildlife and I saw my first tiger, unfortunately shot for sale by the aboriginals, the indigenous people of the country who resided principally in the jungle and lived off its flora and fauna. It was a most beautiful animal and I felt immensely saddened to see such a beast killed in order to carpet somebody's floor. I have never understood, except for fox hunting, shooting vermin or for the pot, the pleasure people get from killing wild and beautiful animals in the name of sport. Now too many species have become almost extinct.

We regularly went hunting with dogs at the weekends for wild boar. The meat of young pig is delicious and when one was shot we all shared the carcass, hunters, workers and ourselves alike.

The riverside was a gallery of wildlife with many varied species of hornbills and monkeys. Outside my bungalow at Sepong Division, a tributary of the Bernam separated the estate from the jungle as it wound its way past the edge of my lawn. A small landing stage jutted out into the river, from which my gardener fished, but usually only to catch catfish, which teemed in the waters. While tortoise, during periods of high water, often got washed up and stranded on the lawn.

Small fish-eating crocodiles inhabited the banks. One lacerated Ewart B's finger when he was about to water-ski from my jetty. Needless to say, this incident was exaggerated out of all proportion,

Waterskiing at Sungei Samak

to such a degree that it was common knowledge in most clubs up and down the country that Ewart had been savaged by a giant crocodile up the Bernam River and just managed to escape with his life.

Crocodiles, the bigger version, were frequently seen upriver and occasionally in our waters. Their presence did not put us off taking part in one of the most enjoyable of all sports, water skiing.

Conditions were not exactly ideal. The water was murky and silty, especially after rains in the hinterland. Water lilies, weed, logs, tree trunks the occasional crocodile, and small Malay fishing boats were all major obstacles that one had to contend with while skiing. But it was great fun. A small speedboat was fitted with a

60hp engine, which provided the power but was easily damaged, especially when hitting submerged logs.

The scene is hard to imagine: a murky river, a group of planters and engineers jump starting off a jetty on a pair of wooden skis into a swift-flowing river contaminated with a mix of partly submerged vegetation. We had a course, were timed as we raced, while the Chinese and Indian workshop staff bet on our times.

On these days the Malay fishermen would paddle to the riverbank to watch in anticipation, hoping for a spill so that they could rush out in their sampans to help the bobbing skier, and later be compensated for their efforts. Everybody had a good time. The bravest and riskiest of the participants was the estate's engineer, Hugh Fraser, whose burning ambition in all sports was to beat the planters, whether it be at snooker or volleyball, football or water skiing. He was a fierce competitor, but affable, kind and good company. He had a gorgeous wife whom we all admired (and probably secretly propositioned) and whom all the other wives envied. This was so often the case when a beauty was found living amongst the beasts.

The small speedboat used for water-skiing was also my only means of getting off the estate, which I managed every month. Having enjoyed my first flying lessons, I decided to try for my licence. KL was the only place one could get proper flying tuition. The Royal Selangor Flying Club located at Sempang Air Force Base was active and most of the instructors were RAF personnel seconded to the Royal Malaysian Air Force. They enjoyed club life, and by giving flying lessons earned themselves free drinks and free membership. For me to reach the club entailed piloting my little speedboat at high tide up a tributary of the Bernam which led to the back of a huge irrigated rice development scheme. There I left my boat, caught a bus or grabbed a lift in a lorry to the town of Kuala Selangor. I still had no car. Fortunately a friend living close to Kuala Selangor usually gave me a lift to Kuala Lumpur. By leaving at daybreak I would be in KL by mid-afternoon.

Later I purchased a car, a Ford, hot and cumbersome but reliable, and sold my MG TD for 500 Malaysian ringgit (about £100). Ten years later an MG TD or TC would sell in Penang for 12,000 ringgit. The ringgit had now superceded the Malayan dollar.

My flying instructor, Lenny, a Canadian, was patient and good humoured. Once I had completed seven hours he acknowledged that there was little point him sitting next to me, for each time I flew I continuously made every mistake in the book. Better he got out and let me try on my own, as I showed little improvement while he was alongside. A very different attitude to nowadays!

At the edge of the runway he left me to go solo, echoing the kind words, You have yet to make a good landing, so try one now, but please the right way up. He then stalked off back to the clubhouse.

One's first solo is exhilarating rather than frightening and once airborne all those instructions which are compartmentalized in the brain quickly emerge.

I call the tower, which gives permission for me to line up. I follow the usual checks more assiduously than before. There is clearance from the tower and off I trundle. Take-off speed 90 m.p.h., up and away. Turn left at 500 feet, continue climbing; turn left again, now you are parallel with the runway and downwind.

At this stage I dare to look around: the airport to the left, the city, the rugged jungle-clad hills making up the spine of Malaysia in the distance, the Bentong pass over to the right and Batu caves, where the Indians worship their gods, to the far distant left. I contact the tower and turn left to commence descent and then left again to final approach. I line the plane up and call the tower. My air speed is too high, I have forgotten the flaps. I pull the flap lever up; the plane rears, nose up. I apply more power and push the nose down; we flop; the speed increases. All wrong as usual, but I have control, just.

The tower gives me clearance to land, no more flaps are required. Speed too slow, I push in the throttle and lower the nose. We hover sluggishly and then sink. Three wheels hit the tarmac. I breathe a sigh of relief and slow down. I request permission to taxi to the club. I am exhilarated. The club engineer, Kurasingham, congratulates me and passes a cursory glance over the undercarriage. I enter in the flight book exercise details and times and write FIRST SOLO in capital letters. I walk up to the clubhouse proudly.

My instructor glances up and remarks, You are back, and returns to his beer and chat. Nobody says anything, except, stalls and spins next week, don't be late. I realize a first solo really is just a minor part in the process of learning to fly.

I only really begin to enjoy flying when I am allowed to go cross-country, firstly with my instructor and then on my own.

We fly into rough grass strips on plantations, onto strips laid in the jungle used previously by the army during the communist insurgency days. We land at small jungle army bases, on short narrow airstrips by the sea and at the international airports of Singapore, Subang KL and Penang.

My skills improve and I am ready to take my pilot's flying licence, but the sad death of my instructor while flying over the mountains of North Perak on a military exercise puts my test on hold.

After the accident the Air Force immediately implemented a complete investigation into the airworthiness of its planes, particularly the airframe, the wings of my instructor's plane having fallen off in severe atmospheric turbulence, which occurs frequently over the mountains during the afternoon.

As the club is located on the same base as the Air Force, the effect is quickly felt; planes are inspected for metal fatigue. The engineering staff work overtime to ensure that the planes remain in their usual excellent state of airworthiness.

I was fortunate that my next instructor was equally as patient and long-suffering as Lenny had been before. Pat Lewis, a Wing Commander, thought like Lenny that the quicker I passed my flying exam the less time he would have to spend sitting alongside me trying to instil the intricacies of good flying skills which, according to him, were lacking.

I took my test after seventeen hours and passed. I felt at last that I had arrived. There is flying, and there is flying. I realized how fortunate I was having been taught by such professional instructors, for however bad a student I happened to be, their advice and knowledge always came back to me when situations became sticky; especially when trying to land on short jungle strips. Then their instructions and directions would quickly surface, enabling me to retrieve a difficult and mildly dangerous situation because I had been so well taught.

I flew everywhere, sometimes on my own, sometimes with friends. I also carried out a survey for H&C on the extent of damage caused by flooding in the Temerloh region of Pahang, and another time assessing the extent of damage caused on Sungei Sabaling Estate by a herd of rampaging elephants.

Once, I took up a photographer who was part of a team involved in a Guinness advertisement. He was Chinese and prior to take-off insisted on removing the passenger seat door. Once in the air, he pulled out some rope and while I fought for control of the plane in the afternoon turbulence, because the light had to be right, he tied his waist with rope to his seat and then lowered himself onto the wing strut. He appeared to have little fear or concern for his safety and, to achieve the correct picture angle, he clambered under the belly of the plane, startling me, as he looked into my window mouthing directions. The advert was a success, so was he, and I got paid for my flying, which was most satisfying.

I did not just fly; I worked as well under Ewart's tender loving care. Labour relations were generally harmonious. Annual replanting programmes resulted in large areas of young palms having to be maintained, necessitating the employment of huge gangs of workers. Some were Malays from nearby kampongs but most were resident Indians.

The work was long and arduous, particularly on the peat soils, where one could sink up to one's thighs in the black deep-littered earth. As time went on, it became obvious that manual weeding was becoming less popular amongst the workers. Certainly the Malays did not find it to their liking and fewer and fewer sought this kind of employment. Fortunately, chemical control of weeds was becoming increasingly widespread and labour input was halved by using herbicides to reduce the weed population. Ewart was enthusiastic about anything new and a series of trials confirmed the suitability of a range of chemicals being manufactured by companies such as ICI, Monsanto, Dow Chemicals and others.

Small gangs of sprayers superceded large gangs of weeders in controlling weed spread. But of course this meant workers being laid off, and those returning to the kampongs lost their sole means of income. Some could be used during the clearing and planting work, but many activities were becoming mechanized. Agronomic practices were beginning to change with mechanization being swiftly adopted. Instead of 500 workers being employed only 300 were now necessary. The old Tamil population of Sungei Samak Estate soon became depleted as the young left for the towns and other jobs; the vacancies, if any, were filled by the Malays.

My household now included a dog, a cat and a mouse deer. I no longer had the inestimable Ramasamy, but a Malay family looked after me, and would do so for almost ten years, accompanying me around the countryside, except for a brief interlude when a most unusual Filipina lady became my cook.

The Malay family consisted of two sisters and the elder sister's husband, who acted as my driver when and if required, which was seldom. Mariam, my age, cooked the most delicious Malay food, while Esah did the washing and cleaning. After Mariam returned to the kampong to bear yet another child, Esah carried on by herself and then was helped by another sister sent from the village.

Looking after a bachelor planter was not an onerous position. However, it did not always meet with approval by the village elders, although they realized it was modern to do so. Nowadays it just would not be allowed, more's the pity, as they were good company. Esah was attractive and indulgent, Mariam robust and pleasant; both enjoyed the convivial atmosphere of an estate and the hum and buzz of plantation life. The eccentricities of planters amused them, and one young Malay planter friend continually came to the bungalow to court Esah, who fortunately resisted his charm and advances.

As further recruitment of overseas planters was no longer permitted by the Government, some companies adopted an active policy of employing ex-Malayan Army officers as assistants. Meanwhile, my Malay contemporaries were now being promoted as senior assistants and managers. This policy generally worked well and it was recognized that an ex-Malayan Army officer was not only adept at controlling Malay labour but also Tamils, who soon realized that Malays were becoming increasingly the dominant force not only in politics but within the civil service, police and army.

In most district and regional government offices, senior positions were reserved for the Malays. Sharp-tongued Tamil lawyers had always considered themselves to be a match in their dealings with foreign managers, principally because the latter, due to their foreignness, had to step warily to avoid offending. But now dealing with Malays, the dominant political caste, necessitated labour leaders having in turn to be equally careful and not cause offence, so easily done.

The winds of change were blowing. The emancipation of the Malays from a rural setting to a major dominant force was gradual and inexorable. The passage of time for Malays, which had stopped for so long, was now being unlocked. Malaysia would never be the same again. The riots of 1969 saw to that.

10

Redundancy

The selling price of both crude palm oil (CPO) and rubber dipped dramatically. Rubber was especially affected and some small rubber estates became no longer profitable.

Cost cutting measures and mechanization were introduced, including oil palm fruit and rubber transportation, clearing for new plantings, drain digging, road building and field maintenance. These no longer necessitated the large labour input of years past. Excavators dug and cleared the drains, graders maintained the roads and fleets of lorries collected the crop.

Labour numbers declined, but this did not halt trade union leaders seeking higher salaries for their members. Not all estates were able to take on the extra burden of spiralling wage increases and their effect upon the cost of materials which all added to the estates' revenue expenditure.

H&C had only one answer to this and that was by cutting management costs on the estates. A planter with a wife and two children managing a small estate was a luxury the company could no longer afford.

Throughout Malaysia, H&C and other companies followed a policy of retrenchment. Not all the managers had expensive families, some were made redundant due to incompetence or waywardness in some form or other. Compensation in the mid 1960s was unheard of, and except for their provident fund and a ticket back to wherever they came from, these unfortunates received little else to assist their rehabilitation. Assistants, some of them friends, were also retrenched, both expatriate and Malaysian, but usually expatriate.

On Sungei Samak, one assistant, a Canadian, was retrenched. He was my chess partner. We played daily. A chessboard was laid on the veranda of my house and whenever one of us passed by we

Playing chess at Sungei Samak with Fletcher

made a move. It could take a week to finish a game. I never understood why he had to leave, he was conscientious and clever. After returning to Canada he studied law and became an extremely successful lawyer, and his wife a high-profile fashion model.

Some assistants looked to other companies for jobs, but there were few around. Most returned to the UK, one or two went to Papua New Guinea and Indonesia. One planter became a pilot and joined Air Narua in the Pacific. Another opened an escort agency in Japan. For an assistant on his own to seek employment was not difficult. Unemployment worldwide was not a factor which one considered, unlike today. However, for the family man it was not easy to return to the UK to find a job, especially when unqualified, except for managing Tamils – a qualification which western-based companies hardly regarded as an essential requirement for engagement.

A few families opted for Australia and the Outback. Fortunately some planters had married wives with a qualification or skill e.g. nursing or teaching, which could easily gain them entry anywhere. Wives in these initial stages of upheaval often become the principal wage earners. A few planters moved out to West Africa and joined the huge estates of Socfin and Firestones, later to be caught up in the blood letting which periodically flared up in that part of the world.

I was not made redundant. My brother thought it was probably due to the fact that I had passed all my exams and that nobody had surpassed my three-month record in passing the Tamil exam.

None of WLH's ex-assistants was made redundant, which was an interesting inference. Possibly my brother's presence at HO may have helped, but I doubt it; he was much too straightforward to allow our family ties to influence the company's directors cost-cutting decisions.

For us lucky ones, the future appeared reasonably bright. H&C adopted a policy of replanting as much oil palm as possible. With demand for CPO beginning to escalate, it was predicted by the World Bank that CPO would become the cheapest vegetable oil on the market, as it has since turned out to be. Small rubber estates were sold or amalgamated with adjacent estates and relegated to divisional status. In Perak, some unprofitable estates were fragmented amongst the workers. This policy was generally unsuccessful and the Government became concerned that a smallholder culture for growing commodity crops would not produce the volume required to keep the country's coffers full.

The economy of Malaysia has always depended upon tin, rubber and other commodities. Oil palm was now superceding rubber, but agriculture still remained the dominant industry of the country. It was to continue thus for another eighteen years.

11

The Bund Breaks

There are no seasons in Malaysia, although peak rains, the monsoons, arrive annually and influence the estate's activities. Planting takes place just prior to these rains. Drains are deepened and the assistants anxiously wait on their divisions for the first deluge and then the proliferation of weeds in the fields which the wet conditions quickly encourage.

Managers become annoyed to see yet again the rapid annual emergence of unwanted vegetative growth. There is a little one can do to control the weeds. Daily rain prohibits spraying, weeders sloshing through the field pull out what weeds they can but by their movement press into the wet soil more than they actually remove. Roads became rutted and slippery. Tractors and lorries slide off into the drains either side of the road. Tempers become frayed as the rain increasingly pelts down.

On Sungei Samak, surrounded by river and jungle, more rain than usual means rapid-flowing rivers and rising tributaries, the force of which can result in breakages of the bund walls (embankments) which separate the jungle from the estate, and which are built to keep the floodwater out.

I am awoken at two in the morning by frantic shouts that a bund has broken due to the force of water in the streams and rivers. I had been holding my breath for weeks, hoping and praying that the monsoon would move away, enabling the rising water to recede. Workers patrol the bunds to report of cracks and breakages, but none have occurred. However, the river at the end of my garden is now gradually easing its way onto the lawn. Such rain has not been experienced for ten years. With the labourers' excited calls, I get out of bed and speed to the farthest end of the estate, where the cracks have begun to appear in the bund.

I ride an old Ariel motorcycle, which weighs a ton and slips and slides its way down the road. It is pitch black and raining. Eventually I arrive and notice the fingers of floodwater seeping through the palm rows. I leave my motorcycle and join a team of labourers waiting close by for instructions.

To get to the bund we have to wade through the rising water. A python glides by unperturbed; I fall into a small drain but get pulled out. We crash on and eventually come to the bund and climb up. A gushing sound can be heard further along, and there an enormous gash of forty feet has opened up, allowing a turbulent cascade of frothing floodwater into the field below.

There is nothing that we can do until daybreak, but I stay; the return journey now is much too difficult to undertake. I write down a series of requests and orders for the labour needed, sacks to block the hole, poles to brace the sacks in place, rope, planks – everything we would need.

A worker is given my note. He drops into the field and half swims, half scrambles to the distant road, pushed by the rushing water, and then vanishes into the early morning gloom, running. We wait. Fortunately, the rain begins to abate and we survey the scene. A torrent of water is vomiting through the gash into the field. The hole is beginning to widen and the sides of the bund at the mouth of the hole have started to crumble, resulting in an ever-widening gap.

As a glimmer of light emerges in the east, the sounds of tractors and people can be heard. There is a lot of shouting, calling, swearing, tractor revving, backing, followed by unloading of sacks, poles and planks. A tractor digger has arrived to help fill the sacks, and a clanking locomotive bringing up supplies hoots as it approaches shrouded by the early morning mist.

A hundred workers start to wade through the rising water, carrying poles and planks on their heads. A strong ladder is constructed and placed against the wall of the bund so that the workers can carry the equipment along the top to us.

First comes the heavy manually operated rammer to ram the poles into the ground in order to provide the structure for the repairs. It is heavy; we all heave and drag it along, while the frame is rolled on logs. It is erected and work is immediately started.

The hammer lifts and then slides smoothly down the shaft; a pole is rammed in. One sunk, ninety-nine to go. The hammer lifts and falls again. A rhythm is set and a chant follows, timed to the rise and fall of the ram.

The relaxed, timed motion of labour is infectious and soon all the work is performed to a beat, a chant and sigh. In the field one hundred and fifty female workers are carrying filled sacks on their heads. Although the water continues to rise and is up to their waists, they wade and sway through on an invisible stamped-out track. There is an occasional slip and a sack splashes into the water. A snake causes screams and once a bear is seen swimming agitatedly with the flooding flow. In the jungle monkeys chatter non-stop, watching us as we labour.

We are beginning to enjoy ourselves. The sun is up, the hard work is exhilarating, the hundreds of workers are talking, singing, shouting, sweating, plodding through the water, calling to their friends. It is fun to be doing something different instead of the monotonous day-to-day chores.

I am stripped to the waist, helping on the rammer, placing the poles and aligning the planks. The senior conductor, Munusamy, is organizing the laying of the sacks. Three rows are now in place, the gap is reduced, but the rush of water remains a torrent.

Break time approaches. A field kitchen has been set up and the workers down their loads and scramble over to eat their fill. Ewart is also there, and the senior assistant. They wave then splash across the field and join me on the bund. They bring a thermos of coffee and some chapattis. They are delicious.

Ewart remarks how suddenly the breakage must have occurred. He had motorcycled along the top of the bund the day before and had noticed no cracks. He commends the work performed and, unlike some managers would have done, blames nobody for negligence.

By evening the worst is over and the hole size is shrinking but not the velocity of the water. The engineer, Hugh, and his lovely wife Doris also arrive and wade across. The labourers enjoy the sight of a white lady getting soaked and the effect of the water upon her clothes, making them cling to her figure. They cheer the spectacle.

They bring fresh supplies for me and the staff. The workers have been changed for a new shift and oil lanterns on poles are strung across the field to provide guiding lights for the bearers carrying the filled sacks.

The manner of work does not alter even with the new teams, who immediately slip into the same rhythm as their departing friends. I am really no longer required, but stay and chatter to Hugh and Doris. The gap is sealed. There are great cries of exaltation and grinning black faces, white teeth glinting in the lamplight.

Those who were filling sacks and working out of sight of the bund splash through the water to glimpse the repaired structure, which through their hard work and effort has halted the flow of water.

It is midnight. The stars are out in their masses – it is a clear night, the first for a month. A straggling line of workers moves through the water to the waiting locomotive, lorries and tractors. The staff count numbers, take inventories and return to find their motorcycles. I wade back to Hugh's Land Rover. I have no idea where my old Ariel is but it does not matter, tomorrow is another day.

Hugh drives me back to my bungalow. We sit outside on the veranda and Esah brings some curry puffs and we drink beer. The end of a long day, a job well done, but should I not have seen the impending tell-tale signs of a possible bund collapse? I just hope the water level falls before the visiting agent's arrival next week. At least all the weeds will have died through drowning.

12

Social Disturbances

Ewart, for some unknown reason, decided to get married. He had always seemed to enjoy his state of bachelorhood and most of us thought that for him to marry would be a disaster. Who would put up with his carefree ways?

He married in Scotland and brought his severe, over-educated wife back to Sungei Samak. Opposites usually attract but such diversity in personality and attitude was just not sustainable in a marriage, as time would show.

Our social lives altered dramatically as partitions between the managers, engineers and various other members of the hierarchy separated themselves from the junior rabble – us, the assistants. This enforced social engineering did not include Hugh and his lovely wife as both ladies showed a considerable degree of animosity towards each other, culminating in Hugh and Doris becoming excluded from the hierarchy after a vitriolic exchange of words.

We assistants stood on the sidelines, but gravitated to our engineer rather than the lady manager. But at the same time we remained loyal to Ewart, who continued to be avuncular in his attitude to us, especially when out of range of his wife. It all sounds worse that it was, for life continued its merry way and we could always avoid any persons we found caustic and petulant, and there were many.

However, the final straw came about on Ewart's birthday when, after an exceedingly delicious dinner, we returned to our bungalows. On the way we decided to come back and provide a twenty-one gun salute with our shotguns and our old Malay cannon, which, when filled and rammed with gunpowder taken from detonators used for quarrying stone, could produce a mighty bang. We had also fashioned in the workshop steel balls which when exploded

Firing the cannon on Ewart's birthday at Sungei Samak

from the cannon's mouth could pierce a plank or bungalow wall a few yards away, as we had already found out.

In Hugh's Land Rover we went down to the main office and lifted the cannon from its plinth overlooking the landing stage. It had been installed because we lightheartedly thought that it would act as a deterrent to union officials. I rushed to my store to get some gunpowder plus shotguns and returned to find Hugh and the others unloading the cannon by Ewart's fishpond. As all good or bad events happen at midnight, we waited for the witching hour to strike. All lights in Ewart's house were out, all was quiet. We loaded our shotguns and the cannon. I rammed a ball home. Hugh, being the only one who smoked, reached for his cigarette lighter.

68

At 12 o'clock the fuse was lit, the detonator ignited the gunpowder, the cannon exploded and the shotguns fired. The noise could be heard miles away. The cannon belched flames, the iron ball shot downward onto the grass and ran at high speed toward the small fishpond, where it disappeared below in a spout of water, throwing fish to the surface.

We thought Ewart would be pleased with this outburst of loyalty. He was, but his new wife wasn't. A window was flung open and a head appeared, from which a volume of expletives were flung at us, many of which were unfamiliar. Ewart was cross, because he had to support his wife. The explosion had frightened the dogs and the cannonball had disrupted the life cycle of the fish. The noise had woken the servants, the police, the watchmen and the Scottish manager on Ulu Bernam Estate, who arrived bristling with belligerence, and a primed antiquated revolver to hand. It was pantomime. Our salute had misfired, its purpose misplaced.

We all returned, chastened, to my bungalow, where Esah brought out curried prawns, chapattis and beer. We ate and drank and at 5.30 a.m. I went to muster, not pleased that our efforts had been wasted. Ewart was cheerful in the morning and tried to make conversation. I apologized for disturbing the fish and dogs but not his wife, and reminded him of occasions past when he would have been at the forefront of any high spirits. I left him in the field looking sombre and went about my duties.

Their marriage fortunately did not last long.

It was an interesting social and personality observation that managers who exuded a happy, jolly disposition usually married less convivial types, while the more evil-tempered and irascible managers married the most sweet, mild and charming ladies. Such managers were often Scottish and their wives were generally from Highland farms where patience and steadfastness were definite virtues.

It was like chalk and cheese on Sungei Samak, for Ewart, the most pleasant and good humoured of persons, had married somebody definitely not possessing a pleasing temperament. On the other side of the fence, the manager, a Scot with a legacy of bad temper whose idea of man-management was to try and reduce everybody to a state of total submission, had a most charming and good-natured wife, completely unperturbed by her husband's bluster and bad temper.

Owing to the small size of the community, we assistants on Sungei Samak offered up thanks to the good god Shiva that we were on this side of the fence and not the other, and that our mixing was social rather than through employment. How I would have survived on Ulu Bernam under such a manager I dread to think.

13

Christmas

Other marriages did last. On either side of the fence, managers, engineers and assistants lived in a generally harmonious state of married bliss.

Those of us who were unmarried had girlfriends or mistresses hidden away discreetly, some not always so discreetly. One of the Danish engineers seemed to have a never-ending supply of sisters and cousins who visited the estate; while during the Christmas holidays an assembly of young ladies and men, a cross-section of nationalities, joined their relations, expatriate and Malaysian senior staff, for their holidays.

At Christmas there were numerous parties. Using an old projector I showed old black and white films: *Casablanca* with Humphrey Bogart was a favourite. Esah and Norah prepared Malay food, the satay being especially excellent; whisky, gin and beer were drunk, seldom did anybody serve wine as it was regarded inappropriate for the humid tropics. As the river outside my house was clean we went swimming, all the silt from the rains having settled on the bottom or washed downstream to form ever-moving sand banks. The exercise and cool waters clearing our coagulated minds.

As Christmas was approaching, most of the younger planters stayed on to dance and be merry. Some of the older planters too, but most husband and wife teams left soon after midnight, especially if they had babies or young children out for their holidays from school. Some of the Malay assistants had very attractive wives and a few who had been educated in the UK had returned with English wives. Most had adapted well to estate life and the carefree existence that we all enjoyed.

Most Malays were careful over their drinking habits, but some enjoyed spirits, brandy especially and not always in moderation.

Their wives generally did not drink anything alcoholic but as an evening wore on, their spirit and jollity were seldom inhibited.

Those days are now but fading memories, pictures that will never be seen again, wiped out by the arrival of Islamic fundamentalism, which shook the world and interrupted, probably permanently, the way of life and freedom which all of us, expatriate and Malaysian, had so much enjoyed. How often a religion spoils the fun, to the detriment of society, and results in disagreeable enforced obedience.

Christmas Day seemed to be one long day of drinking schnapps and eating smorgasbord in the Danish homes, turkey and Christmas pudding with the British. We all drank too much and when well over the limit, whatever that was, indulged in frantic motorcycle or go-cart races, water-skiing, and football matches which usually ended in bloodshed.

On one Christmas we all went down to the furthest division of Ulu Bernam Estate for a swimming race. The river was wide, with crocodiles still residing there. The aim was to swim across the river and return without being eaten by a crocodile. To safeguard the swim two watchmen with rifles were installed on a high point by the bank.

We raced down to the riverside and waded in, keeping a wary eye out for crocs. None was seen and we started to swim across against a falling tide, which swept us downstream. We reached the far side some distance from the starting point and noticed the Samak senior assistant, Tom, struggling. We watched. We liked him and didn't want him to drown, but the alcohol and the speed of the river had sapped our strength. So we waited and watched, hoping he could struggle towards us, which he managed, but he was definitely not in good shape, having drunk much too much. His wife, an Indian lady, on the far bank looked concerned as he struggled white-faced towards us, schnapps and river water deposited in equal quantities in the falling tide.

We had to return before the ebb became too strong, which would make it difficult for us to swim back. Tom would have to wait for a boat. The rest of us dived in and swam as powerfully as we could. The flow of water pushed us downstream but we used the ebb to our advantage and eventually arrived well out of sight of the bungalow.

Swimming the Sungei Bernam

We struggled up the bank and through the narrow belt of jungle which bordered the river, to a road which ran around the periphery of the estate. We walked back to the bungalow, to be greeted by those who had remained behind. Beer was offered but most of us declined; enough was enough. It was after about an hour, during which we had laid ourselves out in the sun to dry and get our breath back, that we realized that our party was one short, Tom. His wife, who had been more involved with her babies than her husband, a normal scenario, thought that he was lounging around with us. We had forgotten all about him.

It would take a long time to bring a boat up from the factory landing stage, which was three miles downstream. So instead we found a long rope and set off in the opposite direction to our arrival point, in order to use the tide.

Tom was the other side, sitting on the bank, looking forlorn. There were no crocodiles so he was in no immediate danger. The best swimmer, a young Dane, volunteered to bring him back. We tied the rope around his waist and he splashed into the river and started his swim across. After a struggle he reached the other side and tied the rope around Tom's waist, who then splashed, swam and struggled, with us pulling him slowly in, rather like a fish at the end of the line. He was a sorry mess. When he eventually was pulled ashore, he vowed never to do anything so stupid again, especially after admitting that he could hardly swim.

The young Dane was said to have won the race, quite rightly. To thank the watchmen for being so patient on this day of rest and festivities, I took them some food, but when I arrived at the vantage point where they had been posted neither was in sight. Instead a small boy of about seven, armed with a wooden spoon, had been ordered to stay there and shout and bang his spoon on a metal bar should he see a crocodile. They had then gone off with the rifles to join a group of hunters upstream pursuing wild boar. We had been left in the capable hands of a little boy armed with a wooden spoon. Fortunately the crocodiles were also having a day off.

It was indeed fortunate, for medical facilities were very rudimentary on both estates. On one occasion I got a large thorn stuck deep in my thumb, and as the dresser did not want to pull it out he sent me to the hospital downriver at Jendarata Estate, the East Asiatic HQ, where the doctor, a Scot, resided. I drove myself there in my speedboat.

Surveying the thumb he gave me a local anaesthetic, and then proceeded with a shaky hand to pull out the thorn. A nurse afterwards bandaged the thumb and he invited me back to his house for a beer. The combination of alcohol and an anaesthetic clouded my brain and the journey back in my little speedboat was extremely erratic, but at least I did not hit anything.

It was to that same doctor Doris Fraser sent her young son to be treated for tonsillitis, accompanied by the amah. They went in

74

the company speedboat and arrived safe and sound. Three days later the boy still had not returned. They radio-telephoned. All is well, said the doctor, they will be sent back tomorrow.

Sure enough the boy and amah arrived back. Why so long? Not only had the doctor removed the tonsils, but he had circumcised the boy as well.

14

I Go on Leave Again

My contract of thirty months drew to a close. The long four-year contracts were a thing of the past as most companies had decided that the advantages of shorter contracts outweighed those of the longer sojourns we had all experienced before.

We needed the leave because we seldom took time off during the year except for weekends and public holidays. Most of us could not afford a holiday, but over the years as we were transferred from estate to estate we saw a lot of Malaysia during the course of our work.

H&C and other companies considered it necessary that we took our leave in a cold climate (thickens the blood and all that). As most of the overseas planters came from the UK or Denmark, and the occasional one from France, it was natural to gravitate to where our families lived.

I was to go back to the UK but organized my return trip via Thailand, having never been there before. I stayed for a few nights with a Thai friend of my brother's who had been at Cambridge University with him. He had a beautiful sister, an ex-beauty queen, and the three of us toured the Bangkok high and low dives together.

I then went down to Pattaya. In those days it was a picturesque sleepy fishing village, but now it is a disreputable tourist resort. I stayed at a very posh hotel with about ten per cent occupancy, which included a drunk English arms dealer, a trumpet player who had played with Frank Sinatra before deciding that Thailand was more enjoyable than the hassles of Vegas, and Henry Cabot Lodge plus wife, the American Ambassador to Vietnam, who was surrounded by a coterie of bodyguards and a very shady officer from the CIA with whom I struck up a long-standing friendship.

The war in Vietnam was starting. Which war, one may ask, as

there had been so many over the past one hundred years in that part of Asia. This, however, was the real one. The Americans were propping up an ailing, corrupt regime in the South, while on my left in the red corner were the communists who inhabited the North.

The North, led by Ho Chi Minh and marshalled by General Giap, had already duffed up the French at Dien Bien Phu in a most controversial fashion, from a French point of view. The French, who since the time of Napoleon had been generally emasculated by all and sundry, particularly during the two world wars, decided that they would show the world a glimpse of their fighting prowess. Their strategy was based on luring the communists into a heavily fortified valley and then exterminating them as they charged down from the hills.

The plan was flawed; they had forgotten the communists had access to some big weaponry, which was manhandled in the surrounding forest by thousands of peasants who positioned the guns within shelling range of the French positions. They then blasted away happily day in day out.

Thus, on a fateful day in May 1954, with 13,000 dead, the French surrendered and were hustled out of Vietnam.

I remember the day well for we were playing cricket and our umpire was the French master, probably the only ethnic Frenchman who not only enjoyed the game but also umpiring. At teatime the scale of the tragedy became apparent. We boys noticed his misty, glistening eyes as he realized the enormity of the defeat and its repercussion worldwide.

The empire game was over and with it decades of French colonial rule.

The Americans have never taken history seriously, having such a short one themselves. Although they tried to get Britain involved, the then Prime Minister, Harold Wilson, refused to be drawn into a conflict whose end was predetermined by the march for freedom and self-government all around the globe.

In 1967 the Americans thought propping up a corrupt dictatorship was better than allowing a bunch of communists to take over the country. They also firmly believed that without their intervention the whole of Asia would fall to the communists, especially with Mao Tse-tung behaving belligerently in China. The domino theory was born.

Of course nothing of the sort happened. The South fell after a bloody, miserable conflict, without any further communist uprisings (in SE Asia) eventuating. Quite the reverse. Mao began to have problems with his students and everybody from Singapore to Laos wanted a good time, no restrictions, no black pyjama uniforms, but all the good things in life: drugs, women, plastic bags and Japanese motorcycles. Culture was out, consumerism in.

Mrs Lodge taught me to water-ski on one ski and also how to take off from a beach wearing a suit without getting wet. My CIA friend asked if I would like to join him to fight for their cause. The shady arms dealer asked if I knew anybody who would like a truckload of weaponry which he had hidden somewhere in Bangkok.

Pattaya is not like that now, rent-a-boys and girls have replaced Mr Lodge, the arms dealer and the CIA, and everybody has a good time when they holiday there.

Malaysia and Singapore remained havens of peace and prosperity during those troubled times. Malaysia after the Second World War had suffered from a communist insurgency and knew all about the hardship incurred during this kind of warfare.

However, the insurgency, referred to as the emergency, was cleverly stamped out by Commonwealth and Malayan forces. Coupled with a real desire to succeed and a political will not to fail, Malaya's success was ensured.

The lessons learnt from twelve years of war were lost on the Americans, who needed to keep their huge arms industry ticking over. And, by dropping a greater tonnage of bombs on Vietnam than were dropped during the entire Second World War, made certain their defence industry prospered.

They bombed the jungle, the beaches, the sea, cities, towns, villages, wherever they perceived some threat. Neither their soldiers nor the South Vietnamese trudged the jungle to weed out the enemy to the same extent as the British, Commonwealth and Malayan forces had done during the emergency.

The Southern Vietnamese possessed neither the will to fight, nor respect for their leaders, who behaved in a similar fashion to Nero at the fall of the Roman Empire: they just fiddled.

* * *

I returned to Bangkok and stayed with my CIA friend. I overstayed my welcome, according to the immigration authorities, but when I did leave, his influence ensured a swift passage out.

After having me around he had a slightly more illustrious person to look after, Henry Kissinger, who later shared a Nobel peace prize for helping to end the conflict.

Money played a considerable part in achieving this diplomatic settlement. In centuries past diplomacy could hinge around a gunboat's presence or a flag raised above an outpost in the desert, whereupon all the world leaders would put their heads together to find a solution to the problem. Money was not bandied around; compromises were sought, boundaries re-drawn, a treaty sealed. All very refined and civilized, although not always appreciated by those being colonized. However, in the late 1960s and 1970s money was the key and the USA had loads of it, also bombs, and both were used. Particularly the former, as the Americans decided to attack Cambodia as an accessory to the war.

Henry Kissinger, learning that Cambodia was harbouring men, supplies and armaments for the communists in Vietnam, instigated the bombing of the country along the border initially, then inland, with devastating results.

Meanwhile waiting in the wings was a dissident movement of illiterate peasants called the Khmer Rouge, whose ideological aim was to rid their country of the present regime and implant a bottom-up peasants' development scheme upon which a utopian society could be built.

It is reckoned that two to three million Cambodians died at the hands of the Khmer Rouge during the bloodletting of 1975. For to achieve this peasant ideal, they decided to liquidate all the elite, anybody who could think and later anybody who could read. As this resulted in the demise of the country's intelligentsia, Cambodia became quickly and completely ruined and all that remained were the Khmer Rouge, their few supporters and a multitude of illiterate farmers. It was the kind of social engineering often discussed but never performed: the creation of a completely new infrastructure and social strata. A modern day NGO's delight, but executed with horrific violence.

The means by which this utopia was being achieved were over-looked, or, not understood, or, the ghastliness of it all, not believed.

Cambodia as a nation ceased to exist, and still appears to be in a state of limbo. It is surprising that no real action was taken against the perpetrators of these horrors either by the Americans or Western powers. Fortunately, over the border the newly victorious Vietnamese decided enough was enough and having booted out the Americans, invaded Cambodia. The Khmer Rouge had by now experienced enough bloodletting and their armies folded as the Vietnamese advanced.

Most stories have happy endings. The Americans' armament factories had prospered during the war, the communists had taken over Vietnam. Mr Kissinger's persuasive monetary and military diplomacy earned him a Nobel Prize, and a new peasant state had been born. Everybody was happy. The extreme suffering endured by millions was hardly mentioned.

And this conflict was not about oil, just doctrines, and dominoes which did not fall. Millions of soldiers and peasants died for nothing, but that is the usual way as it has been for centuries.

Mr Kissinger was and still is lauded for the part he played. It beggars belief when you think about it.

Meanwhile I was enjoying a good cricket season in the village, untouched by the tragedies of the Far East. If one mentioned them, one was gently rebuked for being too serious on such a lovely afternoon, or told what a spoilsport one was.

The beautiful weather continued but England's fervent green never dulled. Beatlemania had taken over from shipbuilding as the country's major industry; fashion and records, four young men setting a trend that never looked back.

Miners, ship and car workers, anybody engaged in the heavy industries seemed to be able to hold the Government to ransom. More money, without a please. Having been to H&C's offices in London on my return, I was not surprised that the workers were up in arms when observing the managerial somnolence exhibited by many company directors. Fair play was out, greed and envy were surfacing, and 'them and us' was frequently heard, referring to the workers and the managers.

But there still remained a quiet contentment. Village life had not changed. The pubs were always full, while the churches emptied. Village cricket dominated our rural community and the Test matches were eagerly watched or listened to.

At home my parents hadn't invested in a TV and any empty hour was spent gardening or kindly watching me play cricket, or going for walks in the beautiful countryside which still existed.

15

Prang Besar Estate

I returned to Malaysia and was posted to Prang Besar Estate, the premier rubber estate and research centre of H&C. I was senior assistant, which meant very little, except that I became more aware of the duties of a manager rather than just looking after a division.

The manager was a genial Scot, John Mackintosh, known as JBM, who never raised his voice and thoroughly enjoyed introducing new ways and means of improving productivity. He was referred to as a modern planter. He was also a pilot and had at some stage flown Tiger Moths (bi-planes) so did not mind me running off to fly from KL, which was only three-quarters of an hour away. In fact he paid for me to take photographs of Prang Besar for the Board of Directors.

Then one day he decided that he would like to go and bomb his brother, who managed an estate in the north of the country, with flour bags. Although I never ascertained why he wanted to bomb his brother, I was more than pleased, for he was paying and I would gain more flying hours.

I reserved a Club Cessna 150, which was small and cheap. I thought it adequate for the venture. I checked out the plane in advance of JBM's arrival and fuelled it up to the maximum, four to five hours of flying time. Just enough, but if necessary we could put down at Ipoh on the return trip.

Then JBM arrived. I had not realized what bombing his brother entailed and registered disbelief when JBM unloaded from his Land Rover bags of flour plus his son, who although only twelve years old was very large. JBM also was thickset, which meant the plane would be seriously overweight. However as he was paying he insisted that all sacks and son were loaded on board. He had a habit of whistling through his teeth when happy and he was feeling exceedingly content with life; particularly the proposed afternoon's bombing of his elder brother's home.

I got permission to proceed to line up for take-off. However, the control tower, noticing the plane when taxiing down the runaway appeared tail-heavy, enquired how many persons were on board; I replied there were three. This did not satisfy the tower, who then asked what else. Rather than tell them I suggested to JBM that we return to the hangar and offload some flour, as the tower would not give us permission to take off in our present loaded state.

We returned to the club hangar, but instead of off-loading some of the flour, his son was told to leave us and return home. The flour remained on board, the bombing raid was not going to be curtailed on any account.

After rearranging the load, I sought permission to taxi and off we went. We took off very sluggishly. The tower, I am sure, was watching with interest but made no further comment. We were happily on our way.

We climbed to 6,000 feet and settled our course to Kuala Ketil Estate in the State of Kedah. The weather was perfect for flying and JBM took the controls. He hummed and whistled through his teeth happily.

After about three hours of flying we approached the estate. I had not yet asked JBM how we were going to perform this bombing exercise, so I thought it was time a plan of action was agreed. It was quite simple: the window on his side of the plane would be removed and he would push out the bags. From 6,000 feet accuracy could not be assured, so I had to descend, then swoop just above the roof, whereupon he would release two bags at a time.

We descended and made a pass overhead. Two figures hurried out of the house and waved energetically. JBM returned the waves and I banked around to come in lower. Aim for the water tower, he commanded. I did. The house was on a hill and I came up from the rubber below and climbed as the house came into view. JBM concentrated, two large bags in his fists, waiting for the right time. The waving figures were still there. Just above, he released the bags, which dropped and splattered on the lawn. JBM cursed. I flew round; he armed himself again with two, and two more on his lap. The roof, he said. I flew for the roof. Two bags gone and another two on the garage. Direct hits. He was jubilant and so was

83

I. The figures were no longer waving; one had gone inside and returned pointing a stick at us, a shotgun. We banked steeply and came up above the pointing figure. He fired, and we bombed. A hit, he was covered with flour.

The bags were finished and we headed away from Kuala Ketil. We decided, as nightfall was approaching, to drop down at Jonny McGovern's estate to spend the night. The estate was difficult to find in the gathering dusk but eventually we came across a small strip on the lower portion of a hill close to the estate.

After passing over Jonny's house to attract attention, we landed on the strip and waited for him to come. He eventually drove up. An extremely angry brother had already been on the telephone to him, suggesting no sustenance should be offered should we seek his hospitality.

Our bombing escapade had used more fuel than I had estimated. Setting off early after a delicious breakfast of *laksa*, a mix of vermicelli and fishpaste, and other delights, I decided to land at Alor Setar to take on more fuel.

Weather reports for the remainder of the journey were not good and the aircraft controllers suggested we bypass Ipoh and go out to sea to miss the haze and low cloud base.

We refuelled to capacity and set off. JBM had not forgotten his own flying skills and was soon relishing the opportunity of flying the plane himself. Although I thought it prudent to miss Ipoh, he thought otherwise. He wanted to practise flying by instruments. We charged into the murk, which came streaming towards us. Ipoh control didn't think this a wise move but there was no cumulus, just very poor visibility and drizzle.

We climbed; the visibility was only a few feet. The conditions were bliss for JBM, who whistled and hummed as he piloted the plane, his instrument reading immaculate. I navigated, trying to keep to a course, but I didn't know if there was wind blowing us off line or where we actually were. I decided to turn right and head for the coast. Gradually the cloud thinned and we were able to make out the coastline.

I reckoned we were in the vicinity of Kuala Selangor and after a few minutes the town came in sight. Inland to the east the weather still continued to look bad. But we had to get to KL somehow, so we pushed south towards Klang and then took an easterly path around the back of Petaling Jaya.

Visibility was down to nil. JBM had control, thankfully. I called KL (Subang tower), who had us on radar and handed us on to the military base and home. We descended. A patch of cloud opened to reveal our position over the Hotel Merlin's swimming pool. At 1,500 feet the cloud lifted slightly and we found ourselves over the railway station. Only a short hop to Sempang.

We received permission to land but as we approached, the murk returned and I went round again. Another patch opened, so I went down vertically, got through and landed.

JBM had had a lovely time. I reserved my thoughts and feelings. As we left together in his car, he turned to me and said flying was only really fun when one ran into foul weather and therefore had to use instruments.

When I got out off his car at my bungalow, he leaned over and said, 'You really should use your instruments more often, you know. It is such fun.'

JBM became listless. He was not well. He lost weight and had no energy. The doctor came and pronounced him to be anaemic, which was very surprising because he always ate well, and anything which was served.

One occasion at breakfast he threw a bowlful of flowers to his Great Dane, named Gnasher, and then demonstrated how to eat a glass vase. Having just arrived on the estate, I suppose I should not have been surprised that my new manager ate glass and his dog flowers. Glass-eaters in the UK are confined to the circus or country fairs; in Malaysia they were two a penny.

While dancing at the Singapore Cricket Club after a game, the drink I was holding was grabbed and downed, drink and glass, by a particularly obnoxious evil-smelling gent who was showing off to his Chinese girlfriend. I had not seen it done before until I came to Prang Besar.

So JBM was sent to hospital, the Lady Templer in Kuala Lumpur, to recuperate. Gnasher howled and thereafter joined me for breakfast each morning. He had an enormous appetite: bacon rinds and sausage ends were snapped up while I dug into my breakfast. I offered him flowers and made a mental note of which ones he enjoyed most.

Roses were top of the list, followed by lantana, which is generally considered poisonous. Not for Gnasher, though, who crunched up the leaves with no ill effect.

During JBM's stay in hospital I looked after the estate. Before he left he handed over the safe keys, and a specimen signature was sent to the bank to enable me to sign cheques.

I wasn't quite sure whether to use JBM's office or continue in my own, so I compromised and continued in my office but signed all paperwork in his. I tried to look managerial and grave and rode about the estate in his Land Rover, getting the feel for the future. Gnasher came too.

After a week I went to visit JBM to find out how he was. He looked much better: obviously the medication was working. I presumed iron injections and plenty of steaks, but no: under his bed was a case of red wine, which he was drinking at the rate of a bottle per day. Could I get more?

I drove into KL and purchased a case from the Weld supermarket and took it back to the hospital. As wine by the caseload is not normally prescribed by doctors, I wondered how to bring a dozen bottles in without being stopped. I hadn't a suitcase or a bag but noticed wheelchairs unattended by the door and loaded the bottles on the seat and covered them with a folded white sheet. I wheeled JBM's instant cure into the hospital. He was very pleased and I stashed them in his suitcase under the bed.

16

The Acting Circuit

I stayed four months on Prang Besar and then was posted to the place I hated most, back to Carey Island.

The island had undergone a mild transformation and most of the old managers and senior assistants had retired and a more equable crowd were now on site.

I went to South Estate, where the manager, Rod Mackenzie, was trying to put right all the problems which had occurred due to the previous managers' negligence.

Rod was a gentle fellow whose main claim to fame was being able to complete two hundred press-ups with his nine-year-old daughter sitting on his back, and boxing Billy Walker, the British heavyweight champion, while at university in Scotland.

He is still around, a very amiable friend, who almost died while deep sea diving. Now pensioned, he can be found in the remotest Highlands of Scotland, tramping the hills.

We got on well and the estate gradually reverted to normal.

I was then transferred to East Estate, where the manager counted pencils and screws and could not acclimatize to the larger picture of management. He, poor man, became a scapegoat for our frustrations, and East Estate was packed with disgruntled, ambitious assistants longing for their own estate. Murray Milne was there, also Geoff Brown, newly married, having forsaken a beautiful lady of royal lineage for a pretty English girl who had lived next door in Esher.

We were all fed up and it was bad luck for the manager that we were all together under one roof. Our fun was juvenile and absurd but at the time amusing, relieving the boredom of being an assistant, which by now we had grown out of. Once, I found Murray grading only one side of a road because his divisional boundary was the middle of the road. I retaliated by digging only one half of a drain and leaving the other clogged full of weed. Another time, I intercepted a dozen lorries full of hardcore meant for Murray's division to repair roads and used them instead on my roads, for which the estimate had been spent.

The manager could not cope. However, Murray suddenly was requested to go immediately to an estate as acting manager. I drifted on; the new assistant wasn't much fun. Then out of the blue I was told to go to Sungei Sabaling Estate to take over from the manager, who was going on leave. I had joined the acting circuit at last!

17

Sungei Sabaling

Sungei Sabaling Estate was managed by a knowledgeable planter of mixed Russian and English parentage. The union produced a severe individual, until drunk, whose humourless demeanour extracted the most out of his labour force, but without doubt of all the managers I had ever come across, he was the most lacking in jollity and good temper.

However, the estate was well organized and efficient, costs were the lowest in the company and he was scrupulously honest. His loyalty was never rewarded by H&C and after resigning when the company was taken over, he died in suspicious circumstances in Indonesia. He had already divorced his Chinese wife and had taken up with an Indonesian girl who was supplying him liberal doses of an aphrodisiac concoction to keep him young and virile. Probably he took too much.

Sungei Sabaling was all rubber, planted on gently undulating terrain in the centre of the State of Negri Sembilan. This was the first time I had left the coastal plain and been assigned to an inland estate.

It was a pleasant location. Jungle bordered half the estate, and the bungalow was situated on a hill overlooking the office, workshops, and labour lines. A small swimming pool was conveniently placed at the rear of the house close to a veranda, the roof serving as a diving board.

H&C in their wisdom had now introduced another cost-cutting measure. Since retrenching large numbers of managers and their families, their mean, myopic eyes alighted on management travel, the Land Rovers and Jeeps managers used to go about their duties. It was decided that only managers on large estates should be issued with a Land Rover, while on small estates an increased travel allowance would be paid, allowing managers the choice of purchasing a vehicle, motorcycle or bicycle to carry out their supervisory role in the field.

On Sungei Sabaling the manager had purchased a vehicle, which on my arrival he locked away for safekeeping. I therefore had to procure my own means of transport to carry out my duties. Fortunately in the town of Bahau I managed to find an old, battered, topless Morris Minor belonging to a local petrol station owner. It cost 250 Malayan ringgit and turned out to be one of my better buys as I sold it on to a Eurasian assistant on a neighbouring Dunlops estate for 350 ringgit when I left the district.

When the manager and his family went on leave for four months I was left in charge. It wasn't much different from being an assistant of a division except that one was ultimately responsible for everything and everybody.

The estate was well maintained by excellent staff, while the workers were well trained and competent. However, there was little to cheer about. Football was seldom played and when a game was arranged there was not much enthusiasm exhibited by the workers or staff.

Murray Milne, now married to Maude, an Anglo-Indian lady, was residing on a nearby estate and occasionally visited.

The community of planters was generally good fun and my supply of beer and gin had to be replenished weekly to keep up with the drinking habits of those who invariably dropped in morning and evening.

One planter, now abstemious, would on these social occasions finish off a bottle of brandy without any external or physical sign of inebriation. He would then drive home without mishap. The only time I noticed that drink had affected him was when he arrived on Sungei Sabaling one early morning with a thick slab of plaster across his nose, which he had almost sliced off while shaving. He used a cut-throat razor, which needed a steady hand. His wasn't that morning.

18

Elephants

The only excitement that occurred during my stay on Sungei Sabaling was a visit by a small herd of elephants which trampled down a young three-year-old planting while enjoying a romp and thereby destroying a three-acre patch of H&C's latest high-yielding prime clonal planting material. They must have had a very jolly time as much of the rubber had been pulled out, rolled upon, or used to scratch their itching backs and bottoms. We managed to chase them away from the rubber by firing guns and beating drums.

Elephants are animals of predetermined habits, particularly concerning their travel itinerary around the country, which never appeared to change from generation to generation. Thus should a new planting be established in their path, or their route blocked, they paid little heed to the obstacle but ploughed through regardless. Plantings could be decimated, any newly erected habitation destroyed, and crops eaten or trampled upon.

As plantations expanded and land schemes were established or villagers extended their cropping area, so elephant routes became more and more restricted and thereby disturbed. This resulted in numerous instances of confrontation between man and beast.

I informed H&C and they asked me to carry out a survey of the damaged areas and plot them on a survey map. Dunlops requested that I do the same for them as they had also suffered from extensive elephant damage.

I booked a plane and called up my Chinese photographer friend, Tan, and we discussed and planned how to carry out an aerial survey. I managed to procure some detailed survey maps of the district and Tan purchased a huge quantity of film and a new camera, the latest Canon version.

We flew from KL in a Cessna 172 and landed on the Dunlop

Elephants damaging the rubber on Sungei Sabaling Estate

golf course close to Sungei Sabaling, which had served as an airstrip during the communist emergency. We took off the door and Tan tied himself to the seat and off we went.

It was late afternoon and we had approximately enough light for two hours of filming. This was sufficient to survey the closest damaged fields. There was a little turbulence, except over areas which had been recently felled, resulting in bare conditions. This caused hot air to rise, creating downward and upward currents. Once over the rubber and jungle, there was less turbulence as the warm, moist air rising from the trees below blended with the cooler air above, producing calmer conditions.

When turbulent conditions exist, a small plane can lose or gain 500 feet in a few seconds, due to the build-up of thermal currents during the day.

We soon found the areas damaged by the elephants and a clear pattern of movement began to emerge. Their tracks from jungle to estate, although not seen, could soon be guessed, and Tan drew a configuration of the elephant's routes on the maps.

As we had no real knowledge of mapping elephant incursion nor knowledge concerning an elephant's lifestyle, our survey was very rudimentary and involved showing where the damage had occurred and where the companies had infringed upon the elephants' routes. All this was entered on the survey maps and Tan took a series of photos of each area.

Two years later, the arrival of a young zoologist, Robert Olivier, heralded the beginning of a more serious and professional input to elephant conservation, especially elephant movement. I became very much involved in his plotting and mapping activities over Taman Negara, the National Park of Malaysia, and in other areas of the country.

Next day Tan and I flew northeast to central Pahang to access the damage caused on the H&C estates in the Temerloh district of the state.

Damage to the estates' new rubber plantings was slight but on all the new government oil palm development projects, considerable damage had been caused. Young oil palm seedlings are very much enjoyed by elephants, who can rip out an acre of newly planted seedlings within half an hour of arrival. Wild boar were also a problem and could cause as much damage by devouring the succulent palm bole, which they regard as a delicacy.

How to contain animal damage in these wild-forested areas was a managerial nightmare, but little thought was ever given to finding acceptable measures of control. Expansion meant cutting down the forest without ever taking into account the existing wildlife, and never were natural barriers such as rivers, streams, animal tracks, swamps and steep hills considered useful as boundaries to development. It was a mess with little thought applied as to what appropriate action should be implemented. Not only to safeguard an estate or land development project but also the wildlife, which abounded in the jungle close by.

Animal damage can be minimized or at least controlled without bloodshed. Unfortunately, during the 1960s and 1970s environmental issues were never considered important, especially in Southeast Asia. The concept of preserving rain forest was submerged under the desire for newly developing nations to follow policies of aggrandizement. And of course the easiest way was to plunder the natural resources that were so readily available, particularly the existing hardwoods of the forests.

During colonial times logging was a major industry, but as the equipment was mainly manually operated and unsophisticated, the area of forest felled was relatively small. Forestry officers also restricted the companies to mature trees only, which allowed the immature stands to develop. A cycle of logging once 50–70 years soon became 20 years and by the mid 1970s, 10 years. Government agencies after Independence did not change these policies, but greed, easy and quick returns soon influenced attitudes, resulting gradually in large tracts of land becoming deforested, with mature and immature trees regularly extracted. Honest officialdom could not stop the outflow of timber, and illegal logging became a major issue in Malaysia.

Unfortunately, as areas become deforested, so the weather pattern changes. Land temperatures soar, rain clouds disperse, and droughts became entangled with floods, while convectional rain, the farmers' rain, soon disappears for ever.

Few plantation companies were permitted to expand into prime forest areas, but the government allocated large tracts of deforested land for huge settlement schemes to which the rural and suburban poor were encouraged to migrate. Some schemes were specifically reserved for personnel who had completed their stint in the army.

Some of these schemes have been very successful. Planting trees, rubber or oil palm, on denuded ex-forestland being considered a better option to pursue than leaving an abandoned devastated landscape of bush, grasses and deep eroded ravines.

Awareness to the fragility of the environment is a comparatively new issue. Certainly none of us living and working in Southeast Asia during the 1960s and 1970s gave much thought to the environment. Sometimes, when and if we wandered into the jungle, we became aware that trees were being cut and removed by villagers for either their own use, or for sale. Valuable timber abounded and there was no reason why a village dweller should not occasionally cut down old trees to benefit from their sale or to use to build their houses.

However, it was the logging companies which did the most damage with their giant heavy machinery, logging roads and the pervading squeal of chainsaws, a few minutes to fell a tree that had taken two hundred years to grow.

From the air Tan and I could see all this. On the ground it was not easily visible. The periphery of the forest remained in situ, but beyond the frame of the picture the jungle was being felled not only by the loggers but also for the new agricultural schemes which were beginning to become established.

It was all very depressing, as degradation of the forests became the principal means of progress for the future.

Meanwhile Tan had taken a wealth of photos, the details of which were then positioned on the maps. Whether or not the company's directors took much interest I never knew, but the damage caused by the elephants and their locations were now easily identifiable.

While I was waiting for Tan to disembark from the plane with all his equipment, Murray arrived and wanted to view his estate from the air. I obliged and lifted off once again. It was now getting dark but we swooped low over his house and new plantings.

On landing I suggested he came up to the house for a drink. Tan meanwhile had sloped off to stay with an old friend of his on a neighbouring estate.

That evening we both drank much too much and I put on the record of the day, Neil Diamond's *Jonathan Seagull*. After a lot of gins, and whisky for Murray, we both attempted to soar into the sky above the swimming pool.

Our leaps from the roof of the veranda bordering the swimming pool were effortless, the splash huge as we belly-flopped into the water clothed and drunk. Jonathan Seagull soared much more gracefully than we were ever able to.

19

Kuala Reman Estate

Four months is not very long and time passed quickly. As my stay on Sungei Sabaling neared its end, H&C directed me to go to Kuala Reman Estate, near Kuantan on the east coast. The manager of Kuala Reman, Bill Martin, was an elderly bachelor who was due to retire and I had been asked to take over until a new manager was appointed.

Once the Sungei Sabaling manager had returned, I loaded my tin trunk, suitcase, Esah, Norah and dog into my Ford and off we went. It was now September. The monsoon season was building up, and the main rains were due to start in late November.

The drive along narrow winding roads through jungle and villages was very pleasant and picturesque. The topography was gently undulating while the mountainous spine of Malaysia could be seen stretching into the distance, a hazy mist of jungle and mountains, but always with a darkening mass of cumulus enfolding the tops and peaks in a forbidding embrace. I never liked flying towards massive, accumulating cumulus; it was always so threatening.

Eventually we arrived at the town of Kuantan and found the road to the estate, where I was greeted with pleasant bonhomie by Bill. Staying at the time was an old planter called Berkeley, who told of his life behind enemy lines during the war, having been asked to stay back as the Japanese overran the Malay Peninsula.

He recounted amusingly how he intercepted enemy lorries carrying stores and how he rifled amongst the stores once the lorries had been captured in search of whisky. Food was certainly of little consequence to him and he considered that whisky, rice and dried fish were all that was needed to keep body alive and fit. For the three years he endured staying behind enemy lines he scorned army rations, which were periodically dropped for him.

During the morning and afternoon I went around the two estates that Bill managed. He wanted to be away as quickly as possible so he was pleased that I was quite happy with a quick handover. He departed with his cook, who went back to her village. I was to remain on Kuala Reman Estate for six enjoyable months.

The estate was close to the sea, so at the first opportunity I went around the town and neighbouring villages looking for a sailing boat in order that after work I could sail along the beautiful coastline, leaving the boat in a nearby fishing village during the evening.

I managed to purchase a boat from the manager of the Mercantile Bank, but the winds were very erratic and as the monsoons approached the sea became turbulent, with deep swells. Going out was difficult while returning, one often surfed back to the beach with mast and sail trailing in the water and the boat upside down. The fishermen regarded my seamanship as a joke but were helpful and always assisted in pulling up the boat and looking after it when not in use.

One afternoon as I was drifting aimlessly out from the coast, the wind having dropped as usual at 3 p.m., a great bank of thunderclouds appeared on the horizon, from which came warning shafts of fierce winds. There was very little I could do, being so far out to sea, other than use the winds as they advanced towards the coast with thickening cloud behind.

My sails soon came to life and I started to streak back to the coast, with the wind gradually taking control of boat, sail and rudder. It was exciting but alarming as the swell pushed me on and into the ragged troughs, drenching me and the little boat with spray and spume.

It was a very rapid return to the beach. I had now lost complete control and decided it would be better that I cut my losses and jump overboard as the boat was being swept onto the beach, to become a tangled mass of ropes, planking and sails. Half-drowned, I struggled to shore, where some of the fishermen, seeing my plight, ran out to help. The boat was hauled up to the village. It was not badly damaged and the fishermen obliged by caulking together any open seam of planking, while wooden plugs were used to repair the damage to the hull.

However, this prelude to the South China Sea monsoons sapped my enthusiasm for the time being, and not until there were calmer seas, after the storms, did I venture out again.

I joined the Kuantan Club, which was a very pleasant place to visit in the evening. There were few planters, most members being either in banking, the public works department or tin mining; plus officials from various government departments. The local Circuit Judge, a tall Malay, was a prominent figure who devoured James Hadley Chase novels as a means of relaxation. He deplored the fact that Malaysians never read books in their spare time, in contrast to Europeans, who were always reading.

A senior PWD engineer, who although very competent was also extremely vague and had just married a charming American lady while studying in the USA, asked if I would be interested in bringing back a newly purchased launch for the PWD which had been built in Singapore. All my expenses would be paid and he would supply a helmsman and crew for the journey.

He wanted the boat urgently, prior to the monsoon, which was due shortly. He himself could not go and knew of nobody else he could ask. I agreed and we set a time for the following weekend.

A car picked me up on the Friday and drove me down to Singapore to the boatyard where the launch had been built. The helmsman and crew were already there and they suggested we depart immediately. They were very nervous of the weather and the reports were not pleasant reading. The monsoon was arriving early.

The builder, the crew and I boarded and we set off. The launch was powerful, driven by two Perkins diesel engines. We had charts and for two hours we powered our way through the straits which separated Singapore from the State of Johore.

The boat builder, satisfied that the launch was behaving as designed, called a tugboat trailing behind to come alongside and jumped off to return to his boatyard. We continued our journey to the open sea, to be met by a racing swell. We proceeded north, hitting heavy seas bow on. Our weather information report had not quite described these conditions, but as we had a radio on board we contacted the Singapore meteorological station to find out whether or not the weather was going to deteriorate further. It was, they said, but we had approximately twelve to fifteen hours of moderately rough conditions to negotiate before the full force of a severe weather front became a reality.

I calculated that we would not be too far from Kuantan by then. We increased speed and hammered north.

After another three hours our progress was not as calculated. We had had to reduce speed because of the heavy seas. The boat performed admirably and ploughed on, but being in open sea, we wondered what action we should take with a monsoonal weather pattern approaching rapidly.

The helmsman was skilled, as were the boat crew. I could read a chart but my knowledge and seamanship were limited to sailing boats. From the charts and positional aids we knew exactly where we were, but there was a lot of sea before we would reach Kuantan. So instead I drew a course for Mersing, which had a natural harbour, protected by adjacent islands, and which could provide shelter and anchorage.

By late afternoon Mersing came into sight and we navigated our way slowly towards the town, now broadside to the sea, which made our passage very uncomfortable.

At last we reached the lee of the nearest island, which broke the rough seas, but the deep swell remained. I told the helmsman to continue to the small group of islands protecting the town; there we could anchor and shelter.

The sky was now darkening as we approached the islands and we took repeated compass bearings of the lighthouse to ensure that we were not going to be washed up on any coral reef or rocky outcrop. Fortunately, the launch had searchlights and with these we managed to find a sheltered position where the swell was slight. We dropped anchor with relief and I then tried to call the PWD in Kuantan to let them know that we had anchored and all was well.

There was no answer from the PWD, of course, because it was Sunday, so I went ashore by dingy to telephone the engineer at his house. Luckily, he was in and listened intently as I described our journey, which I embellished elaborately. He seemed not in the least perturbed, except when I told him we hadn't eaten for thirty-six hours. This he found distressing and he promised to send a vehicle down with food and give me a lift back as I had to return to the estate by early morning.

Late at night a vehicle arrived with food and mattresses for the bunks. I then boarded the Land Rover and we sped north to Kuantan, arriving at daybreak on the estate.

Later that day the engineer came around to my office, where I again embellished my account of the journey. He was certainly very pleased that the boat was safe and sound and anchored securely at Mersing.

The launch remained there for a further two months as the monsoons struck early and the boat was not able to venture away from the security of its Mersing anchorage. They did manage to change crews and I met up with the helmsman in town, who then recounted the various incidents that had taken place, such as the anchor coming adrift, the dingy being stolen one night, attempted piracy and many other happenings.

The monsoons arrived with a vengeance and it rained from 20th November to 23rd December non-stop. On the estate 1,450 millimetres of rain were recorded during this period. Rivers flooded, banks burst, half the estate was underwater, and no work could be carried out until late afternoon when the rain abated for a few hours. The rubber could not be tapped and only a few tons of oil palm bunches could be harvested by the dripping-wet harvesters, who had to raft the fruit out to the roadsides.

Then just before Christmas the sun suddenly emerged. I wanted to go to Kuala Lumpur for Christmas so I packed my car and off I sped. Many of the roads were under water, but by following tracks and lanes in the higher terrain I avoided the worst parts.

After many hours of driving I eventually arrived in Kuala Lumpur, where I stayed with my brother, his wife Clem and their two children.

20

The Riots

I was in Kuala Lumpur staying with my brother when an eruption of violence between the Malays and the Chinese broke out. It was a turning point in Malaysia's history and became known as the riots of 13th May 1969.

Up to that point the Malay, Chinese and the Indian populations had lived in reasonable harmony. The Malays were prominent in politics, the civil service and the military. The Chinese generally scorned the public services and were interested only in business, while the Indians were generally either lawyers, shopkeepers, public servants and clerks, or employed as workers or staff on the estates.

The population was roughly 50 per cent Malay, 42 per cent Chinese, 6 per cent Indian, plus 2 per cent European, Middle Eastern, etc. The fact that all appeared content in their individual but integrated pursuits should have meant that, provided the Malays could govern and the Chinese make money, everybody ought to have been happy. However, this was not the case, for the results of a recent general election, which were part reason for the riots, showed that in the urban areas there were many discontented people. These were mainly Chinese and Indians, who had voted for socialist candidates rather than the governing Malay-dominated conservative party.

Socialism was anathema to the Malays, who had been the principal fighting force against the communist terrorists, predominantly a Chinese-manned guerilla organization. The Malays regarded themselves as the *Bumiputera*, sons of the soil, and the rightful owners of Malaysia.

The Malays were therefore fearful that socialism would spoil their tranquil lifestyle, unhurried and simple, with a king at the helm. The Chinese and Indians, on the other hand, felt that they

101

were long overdue some political influence in the country in which they had now been settled for almost seventy years, and had adopted as their own; a land which they had helped to make prosperous.

The election results showed a big political swing to socialism. Jubilant supporters of the newly elected socialist members of parliament rushed around Kuala Lumpur in motorcycle cavalcades. Some of the jubilation was just high spirits but insults were also traded between the Malay supporters of the incumbent government party and the Chinese and Indian supporters of the socialist parties.

To run amok describes a person who loses complete control of his temper. All he sees is a curtain of red mist that blurs his thought process and results in extreme intemperate behaviour.

Anybody can run amok, but the Malay people are particularly prone to this form of frenzied outburst. Many Malays ran amok during the riots when they felt threatened and goaded beyond endurance. Amed with swords, they hurled themselves at the Chinese and slaughtered many. The Chinese retaliated but certainly did not kill or rampage to the same degree as the Malays.

The riots soon got out of hand and soldiers were brought in to halt the bloodshed. Being mostly Malays, some were accused, mistakenly or otherwise, of joining in the fight against the Chinese and Indians. A curfew was called and the Prime Minister, Tengku Abdul Rahman, broadcasted to the nation, pleading for calm.

On the estates all was under control, although some Malays had gone by bus to Kuala Lumpur to indulge themselves in this blood-letting frenzy. Fortunately roadblocks had been erected and nobody was allowed to enter the city. I phoned my brother to ask if he and his family would like to come down to the estate and stay until the violence was over. As they were not in the firing line he thought it better to stay, especially as their servants were Chinese and needed all the protection and assistance that he could provide.

Amok behaviour soon runs its course and the frenzy passes. The Malays quickly returned to their usual good-natured selves. Although the violence ceased within five days, the legacy of bitterness remained and the riots brought to a close an era of racial harmony.

It was realized by the rulers that the Malays had to enter the twentieth century, they couldn't remain outside; they had to learn to compete in business and industry and could no longer hover on the periphery of the country's economic life. They had to change and join the modern world.

A Malay assistant of mine said of his own people, 'The only thing we have is our religion, Islam. We have nothing else to hang on to.'

It was sad that they should have felt so inadequate, and perhaps this is why so many embraced the fervour and dogma of Islamic fundamentalism which took root amongst the Islamic people of Southeast Asia when Ayatollah Khomeini came to power in Iran. The Malays felt they had nothing except their religion to hold them together.

And yet, some of the cleverest people in Malaysia were Malays, certainly the best judges, lecturers and civil servants. The Chinese were good businessmen but not necessarily especially intellectual, they were just good at making money through their commercial endeavours, while the Malays were not. And thirty years later they still remain backward in the ways of commerce.

21

No End in Sight

Throughout 1967–70 I travelled the acting circuit, going from one estate to another occasionally for a six-month stint but usually for three or four months' duration only.

After the initial three or four actings, the pleasure and relief of joining the circuit palled; journeying from one estate to another, north to south, east to west, became a tedious chore. Estates were never the same: a different manager, good or bad; staff and labour, some good, some lazy; signing the cheques, signing for crop received, end products going out, the stock checks fortnightly and monthly, always the same system. H&C's method of management was considered by far the most superior and effective compared to that of its rivals.

There were, however, casualties amongst the managers and engineers on the acting circuit, especially those who were married, as this unsettled way of life was not appreciated by the young wives. While a bachelor could load all his goods in his car and speed off, the nature of marriage is such that a couple seek to be settled and stable, happily surrounded by their chattels, not speeding around the countryside living in one house and then moving to another as though they were nomads.

However, some planters, both married and single, looked upon the continual change as an aphrodisiac, like jet age travellers who are always urging the present to slide away, willing a new journey to commence, anticipating the pleasure in store, the next experience. But to most it was just a disagreeable routine.

Manageable for us single planters, but not the kind of lifestyle a successful marriage is built upon. One engineer admitted that going from one factory to another had affected his marriage, and although he and his wife continued to live together, the continual movement influenced their relationship and eventually they divorced. So sad for the children, whose lives needed to revolve around two parents, not one. Divorce in those days was not in vogue and most marriages were a ready mixture of somnolent awareness, vacuous contentment, weekend sex and affable companionship.

As air travel became increasingly accessible some wives took the opportunity of returning 'home' more frequently than before. Contentment for them was to be back under the dripping skies of the UK or wherever. They longed for the streets, the suburbs, the corner shops, mum and dad down the road, brothers and sisters not far away.

It was extraordinary how a bleak street in Aberdeen or Orpington held so much appeal and fascination for these wives who scorned the bright colours of the East, the delicious smells, the gentle people and warm climate. For what? The teeming hordes of unwashed, sleep-eyed commuters hurrying to work; dismal shops, poor service, foul coffee in unclean cups, speckled grey sugar lumps.

These picturesque scenes of urban England or Scotland were treasured and recounted when they returned to their not always waiting husbands, who during their spouses' absence had often re-opened links with their previous mistresses, sadly put aside once a wife appeared on the scene. For marriage was what the community expected, being happy or otherwise was immaterial.

Young brides, however much they enjoyed the novelty of their new life, became quietly contaminated by their older and more experienced contemporaries who, having returned from their short stay back home, recounted the excellence of life, the friends they met and the invigorating climate which had replaced their dull, wan complexions with a tinge of pink to their cheeks. How fit and well they felt.

Just to be with their husbands, they had forfeited this wonderful life back home. And now look at our husbands, they would say, red and blotchy, perspiring, some heavy with drink, hairy legs. They would reminisce about how handsome their husbands had been when they first met, tanned, slim and desirable. How different everything was now under these hot blue skies.

What a gloomy picture I have painted. Of course some wives thrived and had no desire to return to wherever home supposedly was. They enjoyed the freedom, the casualness of life and its comparative luxury. Many busied themselves in the house, with their children, if any, and good works. Some taught; my wife became very much involved in the music scene of KL. Many gardened and became extremely knowledgeable about tropical plants.

Children were generally brought up by house staff and particularly by the amahs, with whom a special bond developed over the years and was never relinquished. Even later, when they grew up, the amah would continue to discipline them as though they were still children.

When Geoff Brown married he called up his parents' old cook to come and work for him and his new wife, Lyn. The old man happily obliged, but forgot that he was now working for a married couple and not looking after children. When I was visiting them one evening, he came onto the veranda to remind Geoff plus wife that it was bedtime at 10 p.m. Geoff dutifully thanked him and said goodnight. I got up to return to my bungalow and Geoff and Lyn went off to bed.

22

Sungei Sedu Estate

Sungei Sedu was not far from Dusun Durian in the Banting District. The Lawrences had lived there happily for years but had now retired. I was asked to relieve the manager, who was being posted to another estate. I hoped I would be asked to stay on and become the substantive manager, but I was still too junior.

Esah was now about to get married to a soldier and it was decided she should return to her kampong. She also wanted to open up a small eating shop. Now a good cook, there was no reason why she should not be a success. After eight years on the road she and her sister departed. It was very sad but inevitable.

At the Flying Club I was told that as the Station Group Captain, plus family, were returning to the UK to resume duty there, his Filipina cook was seeking another position, and would I like to take her on. Her name, abbreviated, was Epi. As I urgently needed somebody and the Group Captain was departing soon, I decided to meet her and went round to her employer's house.

Epi had had a chequered career. She had worked as a singer on a troop ship, and swallowed swords and fire in circuses. She had been married to an English stores clerk and then separated from him; she had managed strippers in cabarets and had various nefarious connections with royalty and the higher echelon of the country's political circles. I couldn't imagine her settling down to the mundane life of a planter's cook/housekeeper. However, she seemed quite willing. Her employers mentioned that although she was not your typical type of servant she was an excellent cook and organizer.

Epi returned to Sungei Sedu with me.

It wasn't long before her many talents, desirable and undesirable, were revealed. My first experience with Epi's eccentricities occurred while busy in the estate office, my car suddenly entered the office

107

compound with Epi at the wheel and an embarrassed driver alongside. He had been cleaning the car, when Epi decided to go for a spin. She had a very persuasive manner, and was able to wheedle most things out of a person, whether he be a king or a countryman.

I was not exactly pleased to see her and asked her what the hell she was doing. I did not expect her reply, for she had decided to inspect the estate. She then recounted that some workers had been sitting by the roadside idling their time away. She had told them to get on with their work immediately, or she would report them to the boss, me, which she had now done.

Her behaviour during the following two years under my employ can only be described as bizarre and possibly unique. She was indeed a very good cook and organizer and loved parties, although the guests were never quite sure if Epi was one of them, or the hostess, as she would greet them at the door and usher them in and then introduce them to those already enjoying themselves inside.

She prepared the food and, helped by the driver and gardener, laid the tables and served the guests. I really had nothing to do except chat and drink. Epi was everywhere, totally immersed in her duties, which she thoroughly enjoyed, and, flirting with the odd stray elderly bachelor whenever time allowed. Epi then must have been forty-five years old.

She was not elegant, a little dumpy, and certainly not attractive but had a ready smile and an exuberant presence, which conveyed to the average staff member or worker 'play around with me at your peril'.

At the same time she was aware of her position and always knew when to stop and draw back from the lead role she often adopted, to return to becoming a retainer again. She had a special liking for young bachelors and would try to flirt with them. But being much older, she very soon realized that however much they found her entertaining, her undoubted charms of yesteryear were no longer sought after by the young and single.

She took an instant liking to Robert Olivier, who had recently arrived on the scene and was good-looking and young. Living in KL, he soon had a circle of friends, female and male, which he brought down to the estate on any pretext. Especially if a party was arranged.

*   *   *

108

Sungei Sedu being close to KL, one hour by car, we saw many visitors, some more welcome than others. Engineers seemed to be always prominent, arriving to inspect the mill. Also research officers to conduct fertilizer trials, and agency staff to interfere and irritate. As the bungalow also had a swimming pool and a tennis court, many friends and acquaintances drove out of the city to visit and enjoy the estate's special ambience at the weekend. Epi was in her element: people, fun, gossip, news, and lots and lots to drink.

One evening, she asked if I would put up two friends of hers in the house later during the week. I asked why could they not stay in her house at the back but she replied it was unsuitable. She was persuasive and I agreed, but for one night only.

Returning from the office later that week, I espied a red MG near the garage with my driver lovingly cleaning it. I got out of my Land Rover under the porch as Epi hastened towards me. Her friends had arrived and were by the swimming pool drinking tea. I wandered over to behold two bikini-clad young ladies sunning themselves. One was English, the other Australian, and both were on their way to Singapore to perform in the latest cabaret. They knew Epi because she had been the 'madam' of a group of girls who plied their trade around the Far East. Their pale skins and voluptuousness were very much in demand by male Asian audiences.

They were extremely nice and good company and stayed until the end of the week, when they departed for Singapore. I never saw them again but Epi, who kept in touch with all her girls, told me that one had married a wealthy Chinese *towkay* (businessman). She was apparently quite happy with her status as number one wife, provided he remained rich.

23

Borneo

From Sungei Sedu I was directed to go to Borneo, to Giram Estate, which was located at the far northerly tip of Sabah. The nearest town was Tawau, where H&C kept an office and trading post.

Rod Mackenzie, ex-Carey Island, was manager and about to go on leave. He was then to be transferred, back to the island, which he adored, although his wife Wendy certainly did not.

I caught a plane for Sabah with Epi in tow, and arrived eventually at Tawau late afternoon. Rod was waiting. The drive through logged-out jungle was slow and tiring as the roads were graded tracks used by the logging trucks and heavy machinery. The jungle had been savagely depleted, much of the immature wood having been extracted as well as the mature trees. There appeared to be no control in either the species of timber harvested or the trunk circumference of the trees felled. Immature and mature stands alike were removed; the jungle looked as if it had been recently bombed, with broken trees and holes where stumps had been uprooted; wood and debris littered the ground. Giram had been planted on such a landscape. At least uniform plantings of oil palm were more productive and pleasing to the eye than partially destroyed, abandoned forest.

Rod decided to show me the estate in detail. We marched from field to field and along the boundaries; we waded the rivers, inspected the new plantings and the factory and workshops. He was fit and so were all the staff, who followed his active supervising inspection techniques without question.

The labour force was a mix of Malays from Sarawak and Malaysia, Bugis from Sulawesi, Indonesia; Ibans and Kadezans who inhabited the jungle regions of Borneo, Cocos Islanders from their Indian Ocean homelands and Filipinos, many of whom had been expelled from the Philippines by President Marcos for being political agitators.

Epi was in her element. She was able to chat with the Filipinos and enjoy their culture, particularly the music. She relished the racial mix on Giram and all the amusing and enjoyable aspects of life that were afforded by such a diverse community.

Rod departed for Scotland and I took over the estate. It was all oil palm, 6,000 acres, with further plantings programmed. Oil palm is not the most exciting crop to manage but on Giram there were so many problems which had to be overcome, or at least needed one's undivided attention.

Insect and animal pest damage was prevalent. Wild pig invaded all four quarters of the estate and although the hunters killed many, there were always the same number entering the next day. They swam the rivers, avoided the guns posted to control their entry, outmanoeuvred the dogs and, when in a herd, would simply charge straight at you without deviation. The boars possessed sharp-pointed tusks which could kill a dog, slice a leg and, as I found out, without ill effect, puncture the radiator of a moving Land Rover. Some boars were very big and once on the move would charge dogs and hunters, cleaving a swathe through. They were also fast.

All the workers, excluding the Muslims, enjoyed eating pig and at the weekends the meat was readily available at the Saturday market, which opened after work.

Epi, unlike most Filipinos, did not enjoy the meat, finding it tough and too lean. It was therefore surprising when she suggested that as a special visitor from KL was coming to stay on the estate for a couple of nights, she would cook a joint of pork. The visitor, a director of the company, was accompanied by the Tawau agent. I never ever had any concerns regarding the suitability of a dish that Epi might concoct; however, as pork was on the menu I did mention to her that I hoped it would not be too tough. She put my fears to rest, mentioning she had procured a small baby pig. I queried her no further. The food that evening was delicious, both guests remarking on the pale-textured flesh. It was a pig, I knew, but not one recently hunted, for wild boar meat is dark in colour.

I thought no more of it. The director was in good humour and

Epi playing snooker

all was well. But some days later, as I was sitting on the veranda one evening, there were some angry shouts and cries, which abated as quickly as they had begun. Epi ventured in, exhibiting a contrite exterior, a familiar demeanour that meant trouble. A Chinese smallholder had lost his prized piglet and, learning that it had been stolen by Epi, demanded full retribution: the value of the pig at maturity, had it been allowed to live.

This was annoying but after prolonged negotiations, I paid, although more than I should have. I called for Epi and told her I was going to deduct half from her salary for having stolen the pig. She stiffened. Why? We had enjoyed the meat – it was not fair. But indeed it was. Chinese smallholders don't like seeing their succulent little piglets being lured through their fences as this one had been. I fined her; she was cross and immediately sought out the person who had betrayed her to the Chinaman. He was, needless to say, terrified as Epi threatened him with two hundred and fifty Filipino labourers who would flay him alive. He took off in great haste and was never seen again in the district.

The Giram Estate community was very active and, being isolated, a whole range of pursuits and activities were followed by staff and workers alike.

Gambling was forbidden but rife, especially amongst the Filipinos. Snooker was played by all and, of course, the best player was Epi, followed closely by the engineer whose sombre demeanour had changed visibly since Epi's arrival and was now quite jovial. There was talk of nightly visits. Probably true, and nice for the old boy for he had little fun in his life. Nor was Giram much fun for me.

It was an unwritten rule that one never struck up a liaison with a female from the workforce. Many problems could result, especially from the girls' brothers, who often had a proprietary hold over their young sisters' behaviour, even if the girl wished for the liaison to go ahead. Epi occasionally offered to find a nice young lady to help her in the house. I was never quite sure if this was to be for my advantage or hers. As it turned out, principally hers, as she found a pretty young Cocos Island girl who lived in a village nearby and was willing to do all the chores which Epi now found demeaning.

Not far from Giram was Mostyn Estate, owned by the Commonwealth Development Corporation, where there was a club, a swimming pool and a squash court.

The senior assistant, John Walton, was an exceedingly good squash player who beat me repeatedly, as did the manager, Bill Tully. However it was good to get off Giram and enjoy the sparse but convivial atmosphere of the club.

John's wife Rosemary loved the life. They had three young sons; one was at boarding school in the UK, while the other two, taught by Rosemary using a correspondence course, lived carefree, blissful lives. They were such a happy, well-balanced family, completely opposite to the uncomplimentary picture I depicted before. Sadly, Rosemary died of cancer early in middle age.

Other than Mostyn, there was no other entertainment until one reached Tawau, which also was hardly exciting. Cricket was played during the season, and the small number of planters, many of whom had their own estates, were generally extremely hospitable. But it was a long way to go to find sociable company.

On the estate the many different ethnic groups were always seemingly celebrating a festival of some sort. The Cocos Islanders, who had arrived on Giram Estate after a harrowing journey across the Indian Ocean, brought their simple culture with them, namely, Scottish dancing and the homely jigs of the Highlands. These they had been taught by the owners of the islands, the Clunies-Ross family, who had settled there many decades before.

The Cocos Islanders were very gentle, shy people and, when scolded even mildly, would run away and hide. They were, however, excellent carpenters and could make anything from a boat to furniture without any plans. Some were homesick for the islands, having left to seek work and prosperity abroad, and would play and dance the Scottish reels, reminding themselves of happier times and families left behind. It was an incongruous sight watching them perform the intricate dancing steps, the men often wearing wellingtons or army boots, shorts, long-sleeved shirts and ties; the women in skirts, with tartan shawls tossed casually around their shoulders. The violins and violas played; they danced, sang and crooned. As the sun set below the mountains, leaving an amber glow behind, the emotion it aroused was palpable.

The Filipinos were very hard to please. They were good mechanics and artisans but did not enjoy working in the weeding gangs and only a few would harvest.

Most of the clerical positions were taken up by Filipinos, who were also the drivers. They lived together in longhouses, separated from the other races, with whom they always seemed to be squabbling. On one occasion I found the Filipinos carrying their camp longhouses from one plot to another, having fallen out with their Bugis neighbours. I was taken aback to see a couple of hundred men, women and children lifting up complete blocks of houses with long poles and carrying them to a distant portion of the workers' camp-site.

My senior assistant, Ismail, was not at all surprised, as he described how easily they became slighted for no real reason, and, rather than stay any longer close to those they disliked, moved their houses instead.

While I was on Giram on two separate occasions they moved their longhouses to different sites. Better that they move than have a bloodbath, which had occurred a few months before. Then the Bugis and the Filipinos drew daggers and tried to slaughter each other. It was a very messy affair indeed.

I went shooting for the pot most weekends with the Iban hunters. I am not a good shot and once, having failed at close quarters to shoot a charging boar, the hunters preferred that I stayed to the rear of the expedition. My driver was not pleased with my performance.

Deer abounded in the forests and were good eating. Except for meat shot on the estate or in the jungle beyond, the labour had no fresh food. Vegetables were hardly grown and did not seem suited to the basalt soil upon which the oil palms thrived. Even the Chinese smallholders found growing vegetables difficult, and the labour force had to make do with produce imported from Tawau.

Likewise there was little variety in fruit. Pineapples were grown and so were passion fruit and papaya. The latter was in plentiful supply around the workers' camps, and my bungalow had a number of trees growing in the garden. Rice, the staple food, was brought down by lorry every fortnight, as was tinned food, which was greatly enjoyed but exorbitantly expensive. Needless to say, fresh meat was greatly prized.

24

I Return to the Mainland

My six months were up and a new manager arrived, Bill Greasley, who had been a manager on Carey Island for a long time. He was a Scot, affable and good-humoured and easy company.

There was little point in staying long to hand over as he was well experienced with all the intricacies of management, and therefore there was no need to delay my departure. He signed on the dotted line and I was off.

Epi sadly packed her bags; the engineer had propositioned her no further and Giram was hardly her scene long-term, however enjoyable it had been.

We drove to Tawau. The plane had arrived, and after saying our farewells we awaited our departure. I was flying first-class and Epi at the back. John Walton also turned up and asked me if I would put his eldest son, Mark, on the plane back to London. He went and sat by Epi.

The plane was late departing and an attractive Australian girl in the aisle opposite kept anxiously looking out of the window as though searching for somebody. I asked one of the stewardesses why we were late taking off as everybody seemed to be on board. She was apologetic but the plane had been told to wait.

After about half an hour a limousine sped up and a Government Minister entered the plane and sat next to the girl. She seemed relieved that he had at last arrived. I had met the Minister before and we chattered about Sabah and Malaysia. He was concerned that many people in the State would have preferred to be independent of the Federated Malayan States; similarly Sarawak, which had been coerced into becoming part of Malaysia once the confrontation with Indonesia had ended.

After taking off, the plane set course for Singapore. It was a short, comfortable journey and before landing I went to the back of the plane to make sure Epi disembarked with the boy.

I found her surrounded by passengers and crew. She was singing and had a very good voice, as do most Filipinos. The audience, who were either sitting or standing in the aisle, were listening appreciatively. The boy looked embarrassingly content and pleased to be associated with somebody of such star quality. I told her I would wait for her outside the plane by the disembarkation corridor. I knew she wanted to go on to KL and not stop in Singapore, for I was being asked to go to an estate close to Johore Bahru; Epi was not happy about this.

Once I left the plane, I awaited the boy and Epi. The boy arrived but not Epi. He gave me a note saying that she would come to the estate on Monday but must go and visit her children first. This surprised me, for her children, as far as I was aware, were staying with their father in Rochester, Kent, England. It was a little far for her to go for the weekend.

Epi could never quite make her excuses plausible.

25

South Johore

Changi Airport, Singapore, at the time of our arrival from Borneo was in the process of being constructed, although part of Terminal I was in use. I took the young boy to the departure hall, which was in a state of chaos. Signs were pointing in every direction, Chinese, Malay and Indian ground staff were twittering and shouting to each other and appeared just as confused as the passengers. It wasn't an edifying experience, unlike nowadays.

Holding the boy firmly by the hand, I took him to the BA check-in counter. He had only hand luggage, fortunately, and after receiving his boarding card we went to the departures entrance. I was told politely but firmly that I couldn't go through, as it was not allowed. I pointed out the boy was ten years old and I certainly had no intention of leaving him on his own. The officer wasn't impressed and spat out a spate of obscene verbiage in Hokkien, which I could understand, about the ghastliness of white people in general and me in particular. I answered what a bunch of mean fornicators they were and that they must have been born without mothers. This impressed them considerably as they had never heard a white man talk back at them in their own language.

However, they were still adamant that I had no permission to go through, so I went back to the check-in counter and asked for assistance. Needless to say, as they were Chinese, there was none forthcoming. Fortunately, I espied a large Indian lady who seemed to be wielding considerable power. I went over and, using my best Tamil, asked for help. Her face lit up, impressed, and asked me how I had learnt the language. We then chattered about all her relations, who either seemed to work on every plantation up and down Malaysia or were employed by Malaysian Railways as train drivers.

Realizing that this was not getting me anywhere, I asked if I could get permission to see the boy into the departure lounge and thereafter through the departure gate and onto the plane. He was very young and his parents were not able to come to see him off, I explained. She took pity and grabbing his hand said, Come. We went past the two Chinese officials, who looked exceedingly cross. I wondered how I was going to be able to get past them on my return.

We went through immigration to the departure lounge, where a number of conflicting signs indicated which passage to take for BA, Qantas and the other airlines. At this stage my newly acquired Indian friend had to leave us to attend to other business. I gave her my address, which pleased her, and she departed, cutting a swathe through the throngs of passengers.

The departure lounge for BA and Qantas was the same for both flights, although there were two departure gates. Both planes were to leave more or less simultaneously, Qantas back to Australia, BA, on the way from Australia to London.

I took the boy to the counter and asked one of the ground staff to put him on the right plane. She was young, inexperienced and harassed. Yes, yes, she said. The boy was ushered through to the lounge and put in a seat. I stayed outside looking in, wondering if I should wait or stay.

I stayed, and wandered about. Changi now is one of the most efficient airports in the world. Then, it was in the midst of teething problems, particularly concerning the lack of trained, experienced staff. I returned to make sure the boy was still there. He was, although a green light for Qantas indicated the plane was ready for boarding. There was a surge of passengers to the gate, but nobody appeared to be checking them as they walked through the gate to the plane.

The boy suddenly got up to follow the throng, thinking that this was the BA flight. I banged on the glass screen separating us, to no avail. I rushed to the counter. Passengers, mostly latecomers, were milling about, shouting for attention, clucking noisily like busy hens. The poor girl behind the counter was lost, unable to think quickly, unable to control the surge of boarders. I leant over to look for the boy, who had by now disappeared.

Where was he? The green light indicating that BA was now ready for boarding had also lit up, there was another surge of passengers to the other gate. Confusion. Suddenly I espied him, standing hesitantly. I banged on the glass screen; he look around and smiled. I pointed to the BA gate. He waved, and wandered over. He was casual, unperturbed and relaxed: three states of mind that had deserted me for the moment. By the time he reached the gate some semblance of order had been restored; my large Indian lady friend, having returned, surveyed the chaos and restored order.

The boy walked through the gate and was gone. I waved and started back. How was I to leave, avoiding the immigration officials? Fortunately, builders were still on site and I found an opening in the building works which I squeezed through into a corridor which led to an emergency exit. I slid inside furtively and walked briskly along to another door that led into the departure hall. The scene of previous chaos still remained as I slouched out of the hall nonchalantly and found a taxi.

I felt like a drink and told the taxi driver to take me to the Singapore Club. I then realized I had no baggage: I had not yet claimed my suitcases. I got out of the taxi – the driver was annoyed to lose the fare – and walked quickly to the arrival hall. But how was I going to get inside three hours after landing?

I approached the gate and asked the custom officials for their assistance. How was it that my luggage was inside and I was outside, they asked; ticket and passport, please. I handed them over. I was now pretty fed up with the whole episode. One of the officers took my ticket with the bag tags and passport away. I waited. He returned, confirming my cases were in lost property as nobody had come to collect them. Please explain. I tried to make it as honestly plausible as possible. They appeared mystified. Please come with us. I followed; at least I was inside rather than outside.

I was taken to the lost property office; my suitcases were there. I was asked to repeat my story about helping the boy onto the plane and how he almost went to Sydney instead of London. I don't think they believed a word of it, but they were as tired as I was and shrugged their shoulders and let me collect my baggage. It was all much too difficult to understand and no harm had been done. Fortunately, they were Malays and sympathetic.

I had been informed that my next posting was to Kulai Estate in

South Johore. This was a very unattractive posting, although Singapore was not far away.

The estate was all rubber, with a small Indian and Chinese labour force and a large contract rubber-tapping gang, all Chinese, which was not unusual except that it was dominated by a large contingent of ex-supporters of the communist insurgency who had been resettled in a new village nearby the estate. They were good workers but not easy to control. Fortunately, the estate was staffed by both Indian and Chinese conductors, the latter being able to impart some discipline amongst the Chinese workers.

Although it was now over twelve years since the emergency had ended, some of the Chinese staff, junior and senior, reminisced over the part they had played during the campaign. At early morning muster it was quite revealing to see the variety of headwear worn. Old former British regiments were well represented in berets and slouch hats taken after successful ambushes and skirmishes.

They were a hard lot. Many still read, with interest, any news concerning China and Mao Tse-tung's perpetual revolution, forgetting the huge loss of life, 30 million, to achieve the utopian society of equality that they so yearned for. Of course, there was little equality, for fervent, indoctrinated bureaucrats replaced the warlords and their followers and displayed equally cruel, nasty and despotic qualities. Human nature seldom seems to change, the oppressed becoming the oppressors whenever given the opportunity.

Occasionally we talked about the kind of society, which would be most suitable for Malaysia and Singapore to adopt. Most felt a socialist-leaning government would provide for the poor of all races. One staff member who was a diehard communist still felt that a properly conducted fair brand of communism would be the most appropriate for all developing countries. And thereafter all politics should be based on the socialist principles of assisting the poor and the disadvantaged, business and industry being the providers. While supervising in the field he wore a cap pin of the Black Watch Regiment that he had taken as a trophy from a fallen soldier. He treasured it.

Many years later I met up with him again. He had retired and his politics had mellowed, probably because his sons were successful civil servants and his daughter a doctor in Singapore. He smiled cheerfully when I questioned him on his leaning towards socialism. He still felt an affinity towards socialism but also agreed that

121

Malaysia and Singapore had benefited from the right-wing politics of benign successive conservative governments.

He was a very unusual person, principally because he was the only true Malay socialist I ever met.

That does not mean that every Malay was right wing and every Chinese a socialist. As the Chinese dominated commerce, they were only too happy to vote for the moderate conservative party dominated by the Malays, provided they were free to make money.

In contrast some Malays, particularly the young, had very radical ideas. It was interesting to meet them, as I did occasionally. Once when we were about to line up a new rubber planting, recently cleared, I was in the office when the chief clerk entered and announced that a group of Malay students would like to see me. I told him to show them in.

They were from the Agricultural College of Serdang and were seeking paid holiday jobs: would I oblige? As the new planting was quite large and behind schedule, I suggested they first learnt the rudiments of lining the planting points prior to the commencement of planting. This consisted of measuring the planting distance at which the seedlings were to be planted and inserting a peg in the ground at each point. As 450 rubber trees were planted per acre the work was laborious and time-consuming. Once the technique had been mastered, they could start in one block while the usual estate team could start in another.

They learnt very quickly and set off to start lining the field. I visited them and was impressed at the speed they worked, twice that of our estate team. During a break we chattered about their courses, politics, and university life in general. They were articulate, and spoke good English; we conversed in both English and Malay.

The subject most close to their hearts was that any newly independent nation should have fought for its independence. It was not right that it should be the consequence of simple peaceful negotiations only. The meaning was clear. The act of handing over independence in 1957 by the British, once the emergency was over – a subsequent logical conclusion to the pre- and post-war negotiations which had taken place between the natural leaders of the country, the Sultans and the colonial regime, Britain – lacked a trial of strength. There was no bitterness, no animosity and no fighting; Britain had acquiesced to the people's aspirations that Malaya at some stage wanted independence. It was negotiated for, not fought over.

Next door in Indonesia, there was fighting, destruction, animosity, torture, much shedding of blood, when Indonesia gained independence. There was euphoria throughout; the Dutch had been kicked out.

In Malaya after Independence everything went on as normal. The estates continued working, as did the mines. The judiciary administered the law, the civil servants went about their duties. Nothing changed; business as usual. My student workers found this difficult to accept. How could true independence be achieved without a fight? I countered by suggesting that it showed a considerable degree of sophistication to achieve a peaceful handover of power from one to another, without a shot being fired in anger.

They finished the lining after three weeks and came to the office to collect their pay. I had enjoyed our conversations and wished them well for the future. As they departed, their leader turned to me and reiterated his stance that a country, to gain meaningful independence, should fight for it. And, only then could they hold their heads up high and be able to tell their children and the world how they had wrested power from their colonial masters.

I replied by saying that would have meant going around lopping off heads like mine. Was that what he had in mind? Oh, no, he had enjoyed working on the estate and the thought of a bloodbath appalled him; it was unnecessary. But as he left my office, he poked his head back in and smiled and said, 'But just a small skirmish would not have gone amiss.'

As there was very little social life around, or if there was I was not part of it, I tended to gravitate to Singapore, which was only an hour away.

Singapore was a very pleasant city and the new government had opted for complete modernization, which entailed the development of a city state. Out went most things old, buildings and all, while new high-rise apartments, offices, hotels and banks were beginning to be constructed at an amazing speed. Singapore was no longer cheap and a night out on the town necessitated a lot more cash than I was prepared to pay. However, being a member of the Ipoh Club, I could still use the Singapore Cricket Club facilities, which were cheap compared to the restaurants, bars and pubs now springing up throughout the city centre.

I also decided to learn to play the clarinet, which was much easier to carry around from estate to estate than a piano. I managed to find a Selmer instrument in reasonable condition and purchased it, plus teach-yourself fingering exercises and tunes. I also found a Filipino working in a band who agreed to give me lessons once a week. I enjoyed the lessons and practised assiduously back on the estate.

The Filipino played in a band but was the first to admit that learning classical music was much more beneficial than dance tunes. Once you could play the classics, jazz and dance music would be easily mastered. Epi, who was still with me, was impressed, and being very musical would often clap the rhythm, which was quite helpful. Any assistance I received from Epi meant that something was in the air: an advance, time off, a friend to stay, a plethora of excuses or requests. Christmas was now approaching and I was going to stay with friends in Kuala Lumpur, while Epi would be with her children. She wanted to extend her stay until 2nd January. This was out of the question as I had guests coming on 31st December. She was disappointed but appeared resigned to being on the estate over New Year.

I flew to Kuala Lumpur and then returned two days later to Kulai. There was no sign of Epi. There was also no sign of Epi on the 30th or the 31st, which was exceedingly annoying, as I had invited friends to come to the estate for the public holiday. I called around; eventually she was found staying with personages of such high rank that it was out of the question to request her return. I had to do without her and therefore asked the wife of one of the Chinese conductors to help out, who kindly obliged.

New Year turned out to be fun. We ate delicious Chinese food, drank and danced. Epi's presence was not missed.

It was now becoming increasingly obvious that I could not rely upon Epi any more as her past life appeared to be catching up with her again. She remained in demand by a whole range of people who required her presence for some reason or other.

She returned on the 3rd, very apologetic as she always was, and immediately got down to her housework.

My time on Kulai was now almost over and I was to hasten up to Bagan Datoh Estate, which was one of the largest in the company, and take over from Peter Cowling, the manager, who was going on leave.

This was exciting news as Bagan Datoh was in Perak, not far from Ipoh. Equally of note was that my parents, who were on a tour of the Middle East and Asia, were coming to Malaysia at the same time as I would be in Perak. Letters periodically arrived from them as they moved through Iran and then on to India, and I was being kept informed of their itinerary.

I began to realize that it was no longer sensible for me to continue employing Epi. She was just not reliable. As Peter had two old-fashioned Chinese Amahs who looked after him and his family, I asked if they would stay on. They readily agreed, so the time had come for Epi and me to go our separate ways. She did not actually believe me when I told her that she had to go and that I was taking on two other house staff when I left Kulai.

Tears were shed; there was a ringing of hands and cries of anguish. How could I, she exclaimed. I told her I would find her a family to go to. Where, she asked.

I had already been making discreet enquiries around, but found no takers. Then by chance I mentioned her to a family, Tom and Sue Hulton, good friends living in Singapore. I was perfectly honest concerning her capabilities and her imperfections, but they were needing an amah for their children and were quite happy to take her on, although on a trial basis initially.

Epi seemed pleased. She knew Singapore well and had many friends. I think she forgot, momentarily, that she also had to work, and that meant looking after two young toddlers during the day and sometimes at night.

I departed for Bagan Datoh, Epi to Singapore. I heard her news from the Hultons, who, although initially pleased, realized that she was not quite what they wanted, and after a few months she left their service.

I never heard from her or about her again. It was like the end of an amusing and often hilarious story. She was certainly unique and refreshing, but as time went on her antics became exasperating rather than amusing. She had forgotten to remember when to stop.

26

Bagan Datoh

The estate was well managed, principally by two dominant Chinese ladies in the office, a young Tamil girl who seemed to be in total control of the field workers, and the manager of the cocoa factory, who was also a young Chinese lady. It was the only factory in the company where all the workers were women. There was hardly a male of any consequence in sight, except Peter, who patrolled the estate from the air; he owned a Piper Cherokee 150.

Bagan Datoh estate was located close to the mouth of the Perak River. It was hot and humid and consisted of a mix of oil palms, coconuts, and cocoa under coconuts. It was not far from the town of Teluk Anson, the centre of the plantation industry in Perak.

My parents were due to arrive at Ipoh via Penang and Bangkok. My father phoned early one morning to say that the train would be arriving at 1306, and would I please be kind enough to meet them.

I set off to meet them and arrived at the station at 1307, to find the train had arrived slightly early and my father in a telephone booth phoning the estate to find out where I was.

After lunch at the club we returned to Bagan Datoh. Both were tired, having been travelling for at least two months, mostly by coach, but also by train and plane. They were very happy to stay about the house and gardens, and enjoyed reading and lounging about by the riverside under an *attap*-roofed gazebo.

The contractors who did business on the estate were over-eager to take us out for continual rounds of Chinese dinners, hoping to curry favour in return for contracts that might be on offer.

Teluk Anson was renowned for over-generous Chinese contractors who tried to obtain lucrative and long-term projects from the managers. Several managers were definitely open to bribes and handouts, not always realizing that once corrupted, it was difficult thereafter for them to ever say no. Once a Chinese contractor's proffered presents of money or gifts had been grasped by the manager, his grip upon that manager would never be released.

Most of my contemporaries were honest, and, except for bottles of whisky or gin at Christmas, refused any item that could be considered to be of commercial value. It was not unknown for contractors to offer money or cars as presents in order to obtain goodwill and fortune for the future.

One day I borrowed a speedboat from a friend in Teluk Anson and took my parents out to Pulau Rumbia beyond the mouth of the

My parents enjoying the river trip

127

Perak River. The sea was a beautiful blue and the beaches clothed in sparkling yellow. We swam, ate and drank, and my parents snoozed under the shade of palms growing close to the sea edge.

By mid-afternoon it was time to return. The tide would help us back so we set off. The journey was pleasant and without incident until we were a mile away from the estate, when the engine stopped. There was sufficient fuel, the plugs were clean, but the engine would not start.

As the flow of the river was quite strong, we had now drifted past the estate and were heading downstream towards Teluk Anson. We tried to paddle to the shore but the tide provided no assistance. Drastic action was needed, it was too far to swim but ahead I noticed a sampan with a small sail and waved to the boatman, who drew alongside. I told him our predicament; he was sympathetic and suggested he sailed me to the shore in order to get help.

My parents were not in the least perturbed. They were enjoying cataloguing the many different species of sea and river birds which winged their way past. My mother kept her umbrella up as a shield from the sun and they both drank copious quantities of soda and tonic water.

I explained the problem and told them I would sail to shore in the sampan and then drive down to Teluk Anson and borrow a boat to tow them back.

I departed from the ailing speedboat, my parents waving cheerily. On shore I raced to the bungalow to fetch my car. The Chinese house servants were very disapproving that I had left my parents in the boat, clucking their tongues and hissing loudly at me. Then I drove out of the estate and off to Teluk Anson. I wondered who had a boat and could help, and then remembered the boatyard where a Chinese acquaintance built all sorts, from speedboats to junks to landing craft. It was not far and I arrived breathless within an hour. The yard was closed, but the watchman was able to contact the foreman, who lived nearby.

Eventually he arrived. I told him my dilemma and from his reaction he thought my antics totally irresponsible but promised to help. At that moment, midstream, my parents went drifting merrily by. I shouted and waved, and they returned my wave with the umbrella.

The Chinese, fortunately, revere the aged and the foreman immediately was galvanized into action. A boat was found and an outboard engine was bolted to the stern. We jumped in and set off in pursuit of my parents.

It all ended happily. My parents enjoyed the adventure although they were by now very hot and the drink was almost finished. It did not take long to return to the boatyard, and there were many thank-yous all round.

Back at the house, my Chinese servants quickly brought tea and cakes. But for the next week they continued to give me reproving glances, declaring openly how awful it must have been for my parents, alone, drifting downstream without food, drink and only an umbrella for shade. All very bad joss (luck). I said nothing; the episode, according to my parents, had been most pleasant, and they had been lucky to see so much.

The Indian Thaipusam festival was upon us and there were feasts and dancing on the estate amongst the Tamil labour force.

The most fervent and holy of the Hindus walked on red-hot cinders and pierced their bodies with needles to show their complete fidelity to the gods. My mother was surprised they did not bleed when pierced. Once in a trance, they appeared oblivious to the sharp needles which were being jabbed into their flesh, and often very roughly indeed. Especially if by drunken, sadistic bystanders eager to cause hurt.

It was said there were only two planters who had walked on scalding cinders and returned to tell the tale. One was Sam Gaythorne Hardy, who had at one stage been an assistant on Bagan Datoh Estate. As his wife was Indian, he immersed himself totally in all Indian customs of whatever kind, and generally emerged unscathed.

My parents wanted to visit other parts of Malaysia, not just the environs of Bagan Datoh, so I made out a plan of the places to visit and lent them my car and driver.

The east coast of Malaysia was high on their list, being relatively unspoilt with a beautiful coastline and secluded fishing villages, and no tourists. To get there, however, was difficult, and rather than driving from west to east, I decided to ferry them across by plane.

We journeyed down to Kuala Lumpur and I put my parents up

in a hotel. My brother had left KL by now and was sitting in the London office of H&C. I stayed with a friend and sent the driver off with the car to meet us at Kuantan airport the following day. In a plane it does not take long to reach Kuantan, but by road the journey is slow, arduous and hot and can take three to four hours, depending on the traffic; especially the logging trucks which race along, caring for nobody in front nor anybody behind.

The next day was bright and clear. We took off and climbed to 5,000 feet, providing my parents with a scenic view of the mountains and jungle which spread below far and wide into the distance. My mother, a nervous passenger, enjoyed the flight and remarked on how comfortable it was compared to driving in a car.

Approaching Kuantan, there appeared some air activity and I was asked to hold in my present position. We circled again and then again. After about fifteen minutes I asked the tower what was up, but was told to hold as the Yang di Pertuan Agong, the King, was about to leave. He departed in a flurry of good wishes and flag-waving. Then we landed inconspicuously and parked away from the crowded terminal apron.

My parents had an enjoyable time touring the east coast of Malaysia. They stayed in Trengganu with the manager of H&C's sole cocoa estate; bathed in beautiful azure seas and ate satay and prawns and grilled fish. But it was time to leave. I arranged to meet them in Kuala Lumpur and with Pat Baskett, another planter pilot, fly them direct to Singapore for their return trip to the UK.

They returned from the east coast healthy and tanned. The onward journey was uneventful until we approached Singapore Island, when we were asked by control what our routing was supposed to be. As the island was small, what route we took appeared to us to be of little consequence.

By now we could see the airport from over the Straits and flew straight for it. I told control I had the airport in sight and requested approach and landing instructions. They were not pleased; did I not know that I had just passed over a battery of missiles and that Seletar Air Base was now Singapore's Air Command Headquarters. Had I not read NOTAMS (Notice to Airmen) flight information? I had not, nor had Pat. We seldom bothered to read anything concerning flight information, except approaches and runway directions. Nothing else seemed to matter. This was not London Heathrow nor JFK, New York. The controllers were either out to impress their supervisors, or thought that we were not giving their airspace enough respect. However, as we were now fast approaching Payar Lebar airport (now Changi) they had little option but to direct us to land.

We landed and were told not to proceed to the club, located at the far south of the airport, but to proceed to Bay 18, close by the control tower. Pat and I smelt trouble, but my parents were oblivious to the commotion we had supposedly caused and were delighted to have arrived safely and in one piece. I taxied to Bay 18. Changi was now very impressive and smart. Jumbo jets and planes from every nation littered the ground, and ours, a Cessna 172 from The Royal Selangor Flying Club. In Bay 18 a Qantas jet stood idly waiting for the evening.

I parked underneath its wing. It was very hot and it was nice to be under shade, especially for my parents. There were croaks of outrage from the all-seeing controllers, who demanded that we remove ourselves forthwith, but as planes seldom departed until evening there seemed little point. I turned off the radio and we both got out and wandered nonchantly towards the control tower complex.

Two controllers emerged as we sauntered across. Their morning had obviously been spoilt by our presence. They did not like Malaysian club planes flying over their Strategic Air Command Base nor over missile sites. I apologized, and tut-tutted contritely, the only way out, and said it would not happen again. The air controllers could do little else. They could report us, but that would be counterproductive as we were here and the last thing they wanted was for us to remain any longer than necessary.

They walked over to the plane, swearing and spitting, until they saw my dear silver-headed parents, to whom they were introduced. My mother smiled sweetly like the Queen Mother and proffered a hand. It did the trick, they walked back and we taxied onward to the Singapore Flying Club.

On arrival I lifted out my parents' cases and we walked into the club. A red-faced gentleman hurried over and asked me and Pat to come over for a wee chat. He was not pleased that we had violated every code in the book: the Singaporeans were now very sensitive to private fliers prancing around the sky as if they owned it and parking planes under jumbo jets. I told him I had come to Singapore before on many occasions and that I had been always treated extremely courteously and always used the missile battery as a marker.

That was then, now it is different, I was told. Lee Kuan Yew was Prime Minister and Singapore was changing rapidly and developing dramatically. Our red-faced gentleman calmed down a bit and told us that the club had to move as well. An era was over.

My parents departed that evening. Pat and I left the next morning, glad to be away from petulant officialdom.

We didn't read the NOTAMS before we left. You can't get lost flying over Singapore, it is much too small.

27

Back to Work

Pat and I had a good return journey to Kuala Lumpur. My flying hours were building up nicely but I needed to get the odd willing person(s) to pay for my flying; it was exorbitantly expensive and only just affordable. Nowadays it is unaffordable except for well-paid executives and film stars.

Occasionally I was asked by somebody to take them somewhere or to carry out a particular assignment. Flying into jungle airstrips was always exciting. Fortunately, as time went on Robert, the zoologist, asked me to fly him when he went elephant trekking. Which helped, but he was always short of funds and I had to wait for reimbursement. Sometimes it never arrived, but the flying was fun.

I drove back to Bagan Datoh. The house seemed empty without my parents bumbling around. Then I went to the factory to check the stock books. The factory manager was directing operations in her own inimitable style. I asked her a few questions, which she answered coarsely, as only Chinese can; she knew her job and it was a very efficiently managed factory.

I wandered over to the office, where I was presented with some cheques to sign, a letter or two on copra sales and a couple for head office, Kuala Lumpur; all composed by my Chinese ladies, meticulously, meaning nothing, but sufficient to satisfy the gnomes of KL.

As there was no further pressing business to be completed in the office, I drove off to the field. The cocoa was being harvested, the young female Tamil *mandor* (foreman) was hovering around, in control: I exchanged a few words and continued my drive, through the cocoa into the coconuts, my favourite crop. The shouts of the harvesters echoed throughout as their swaying long poles cut the bunches from the palms; then moving slightly they avoided the falling pod of nuts which crashed to the ground. Once, on Carey Island, I saw a harvester's head split open by a falling bunch. Some of the younger harvesters now wore motorcycle helmets, but the older Tamils scorned this protection and relied upon their experience and nimbleness to avoid the falling nuts.

I left the Land Rover by the roadside and proceeded by foot across the fields. Breezes from the nearby river were refreshingly cool during early morning. The workers, it is reckoned, were three times more productive between the hours of 6.30 and 10 a.m. than late morning and midday, when their efforts began to wane.

I wandered on and came to the oil palm division of the estate, Hutan Melintang, once an estate on its own, but now amalgamated with Bagan Datoh. The crop didn't interest me aesthetically, but the oil was becoming increasingly profitable.

Sam Gaythorne Hardy had been assistant on the oil palm estate years past, and had thoroughly enjoyed his sojourn in the district. Sam left H&C soon after me and now lives happily and contentedly in a converted bullock shed in Suffolk. His Indian wife, Grace, works at a local nursery.

28

Reminiscing

I had visited Bagan Datoh a few times before when I was an assistant on Sungei Wangi, which was located the other side of the Perak River, an hour or so by motorcycle, if one knew the short cuts. Murray and I had come over on occasions to visit the assistants on the estate. It was too far to come for the day so we stayed the night, Murray with Sam Gaythorne Hardy and I with Ken Sims.

Ken, other than being a planter, collected wild animals and sold them to zoos; his main ambition was to have a zoo of his own. After many years of hardship, low returns and exorbitant capital costs he has now created an extremely popular zoo at Thrigby Hall in Suffolk.

We all had fun during the evenings eating curried prawns and drinking beer at the fishing village of Bagan Datoh, eventually returning to our respective bungalows. I was about to crash out in the spare bedroom when Ken reminded me not to worry about Horace. Who was Horace, I asked. My pet python, quite harmless but likes the warmth of a bed in the early morning. But he is out at the moment, let him in if you should be awake, Ken said, then went off to bed.

I was too sleepy to give Horace much thought and slept heavily that night. In the morning I got up and went into the bathroom to wash and shower. It was while shaving that I noticed a snake's head emerge from behind the Shanghai jar (a water vessel common to Asian bathrooms). He took little interest in me as he slithered out from behind the jar. But he was very long – his body seemed endless – and I wasn't quite sure what to do. One learnt not to make hasty moves or cause alarm when confronted with wild animals; in other words, keep calm. A friend who met up with a tiger on the boundary of his estate, stopped and lit a cigarette, albeit with a shaking hand, as the tiger approached. Because my friend showed no outward fear or panic, the tiger veered off into the jungle without a second glance. Perhaps it was not hungry.

I thought of this story as I continued shaving. Horace was not interested in me and slid out of the bathroom, and then into the garden at the back, where the Chinese cook threw him a chicken. It was like feeding a dog or cat.

During breakfast I asked Ken if he had any other pets I should know about. He had not, although there was a tame mongoose who was a delight, except while climbing around one's neck, when it would fart copiously.

Ken's passion for animals flourished and so did his collection of animals. It was while I was on Sungei Sedu that Ken asked if he could leave his young crocodiles in my swimming pool for a couple of weeks as he was going up-country on local leave to look for animals. I agreed, and his Land Rover duly arrived. I looked in, so did Epi. It wasn't a pleasant sight, for trussed up were two young, aggressive crocs.

Ken got out breezily and asked me to grab an end, which I did hesitantly, and was flicked on my backside by a scaly tail. Not like that, shouted Ken. I followed his instruction and we bundled them into the pool. Epi stood nearby in attendance.

It was another three weeks before Ken returned to pick up his crocodiles. I did not realize the growth rate of a croc was so rapid, for they now seemed exceedingly large. Ken was in good spirits. He asked me to go into the water and tie up the crocs' mouths and he would haul them up. He was much larger than me and stronger.

I refused; using my swimming pool was one thing but I had no intention of trying to capture his crocodiles. An interested audience of drivers and gardeners had now gathered, so I suggested he do the tying bit and I plus the others would pull them up. He agreed and clambered into the pool. There was considerable threshing about. We all leaned over enthralled. He emerged and handed over the rope. We pulled, and out popped an angry crocodile. My helpers vanished, except Epi, who, surprisingly, seemed to be in her element by telling me which part of the croc's anatomy to grab. I did as instructed. The workers returned and we bundled the croc into the vehicle.

Ken was getting impatient, as he was standing on the other croc's head under water. A line was thrown down and he trussed it up, we hauled, then placed it gently in the Land Rover with its brother.

Ken was in a hurry, he also had work to do, and after a brief thanks hurried away. I congratulated Epi on her croc-trussing capabilities. Oh sir, it was nothing, I once worked at the Royal Zoo in Johore Bahru. Epi's talents never ceased to amaze me.

Ken's hobby fascinated everybody and some of his stories were often hilarious. The most bizarre being when he kept crocodiles on the flat roof of a friend's apartment in Penang. One Saturday evening when a party was in full flow the roof cracked, water flooded down and numerous short stubby legs protruded through the cracks, much to the horror of the guests. They panicked and there was a rush for the door. The house was suddenly deserted except for Ken, his friend and the old cook. Somehow they managed to retrieve the situation.

Ken left H&C and established his zoo.

29

End of a Day

I walk a wide circle around the oil palm plantings and then back through the coconuts. The harvesters have completed their task and are now dehusking, splitting the nuts and removing the flesh (copra). A tractor-trailer arrives to transport the bagged copra back to the driers.

The activities are all well organized, seldom varying from day to day; this daily routine ensures efficiency. I climb back into my Land Rover. What have I achieved? Very little; no momentous decisions have been made, no directives were necessary; today my input has been nil. Has my presence made a difference? Doubtful. I suppose it was necessary that everybody knew I was around. Perhaps, but also doubtful. Introspection is dangerous, and, as old planters used to say, it can lead to drink.

Rather than have a drink followed by a downward slide thereafter, I decide to drive to Ipoh and get some batting practice in the nets. At least all the Indian schoolboys who come to use the nets in the evening will try their utmost to get me out. I am very susceptible to one little Indian boy's off breaks; his demeanour changes from that of a polite, quiet, unassuming schoolboy to a raving demon if he should bowl me out. Which he invariably manages. (He played for Malaysia when only sixteen years old and was indeed very good.)

John Jameson-Black, the manager of Riverside Estate, close to Ipoh, is already at the nets when I arrive.

The schoolboys are bowling their leg breaks, googlies and off breaks, all spun from their slender fingers. A warm evening; they are tireless, praying for a wicket, trying every ploy. Speed is not within their capabilities, but guile dominates their determination to bowl us out.

We enjoy a long net, but as John remarks afterwards, not quite what was required, for Perak are due to play the Australian Air Force team from Butterworth next week, and they have no spinners but lots of fast bowlers.

We retire to the club. John was in the Army in Uganda prior to coming to Malaysia, but still hears from his old regiment; one of his sergeants has recently promoted himself to President. His name is Idi Amin. During his upward ascendancy to the country's presidency he purged 350,000 Ugandans. A blip on the death scale when compared to Cambodia, but still significant.

The Ipoh Club has always been my favourite club. It is no longer as busy as it was before. Many of the older planters have now retired and the European community has long disappeared.

On most evenings the club is sparsely populated. Only the Indians use the facilities, the Chinese and Malays preferring the new golf clubs which have begun to spring up around the town. However, standards have not been compromised and applications for membership are still rigorously scrutinized.

The State cricket captain, an Indian railway clerk, has applied for years to be a member but is continually blackballed. For whatever reason one is not quite sure. When a State game is played the club facilities are used by everybody. But apparently his face does not fit, and it is usually John or me, the English in the team, who ensures the bar boys oblige with drinks.

Of course not all the team are members either, and do not want to be, but for the captain not to be a member is a slice of racism which would not have been tolerated pre- and immediately post-colonial times.

As State games were played over two days, I occasionally stayed the night with the Jameson-Blacks, rather than return to the estate. It was on one of those evenings after a game that my Chinese secretary phoned up and mentioned that Harry Mckay from head office in Kuala Lumpur had telephoned that Saturday morning and asked to speak to me. She had informed him that I was in the field and when he phoned again she told him that I had not yet returned.

He knew I was playing cricket and was checking up on me. He

had been a friend of my brother's, so socially I knew him reasonably well.

I did not return his call until Monday morning. He was not pleased, especially as I asked him what was so desperate that he had wanted to speak to me on Saturday morning. He mouthed some feeble query over the telephone, which I answered.

I knew that all he wanted to know concerned my cricketing activities, so I told him I would send him a calendar of the State's cricket season, otherwise, if I were him, I wouldn't bother to telephone me on Saturdays and Sundays, nor on practice afternoons, Wednesdays and Fridays.

By now he was hopping mad and spluttering down the telephone. Afterwards I realized that as he was being groomed to be a future chairman or for some other senior position, I had not done my career aspirations much good.

Like most office wallahs, he had a long memory. For in the Kuala Lumpur office one day during the mid-1970s when dishonest staff were being exposed every minute, he jokingly but half seriously mentioned that all managers were making money on the side, and by inference this included me. I was absolutely livid and told him that I could be accused of many things but not that.

Being on the acting circuit, I knew exactly who was honest and who was dishonest. He tried then to wriggle his way out of this unfortunate breach of protocol. His remarks have always rankled and it showed how head office personnel could be so officious and antagonistic in their dealings with the planting fraternity.

After one State game that finished early, the then engineer of Selaba Estate, located close to Teluk Anson, asked if I wanted a lift back in his plane. Although he had passed his flying test he still preferred to be accompanied by another pilot. I didn't know then the reason why.

The weather was clear, and we took off and climbed to 4,000 feet and set course for Teluk Anson. It was a lovely evening and we chattered about H&C, a subject close to our hearts and one which never failed to trigger outrage and wrath concerning HO's antics.

As we neared the Jenderata airstrip, I was surprised that my friend showed no inclination to descend. He was, however, correct to proceed over the strip to make sure that it was devoid of planes, people and tractors. It was clear, so he started to descend, then, realizing that he had a lot of height to lose, made steep turns at an incline which could not be described as standard practice.

We joined the approach still too high and went into an even steeper descent. I then by chance glanced to my left and noticed that his eyes appeared to be glazed as if in a trance. I nudged his shoulder and pointed out that we must reduce speed and start thinking of applying flaps. I didn't want to appear bossy, but flaps are needed, usually.

The subsequent landing was smooth and he taxied over to the hangar. I got out and he motored inside.

His wife was waiting and I sauntered over to her. He joined us and without either embarrassment or hesitancy thanked me for tapping him on the shoulder. I looked for a reaction from his wife. There was none, so I asked him if he always snoozed when coming in to land. He laughed and said oh no, he wasn't asleep but occasionally suffered short minor mental blackouts if the descent was too steep. A sudden rush of blood to the brain, he described it. That was why he always flew with somebody who could wake him up, although it was only necessary in steep turns and when descending sharply.

I, needless to say, was quite taken aback and asked if he had ever discussed this mental aberration with a doctor. Heavens no, he replied, for if I should consult a doctor that would be the end of my flying. They then drove off, his wife at the wheel, as always, and I returned to Bagan Datoh.

30

Lower Perak and Flying

It was an enjoyable district to live in. I was posted from Bagan Datoh to Selaba, where the resident manager, Alec Chalmers, an enormous bear of a man, at least six foot seven inches, presided over a small, efficient estate, along with the flying engineer, Brian, who managed the oil palm mill. Being in the same district meant continuity. This was very welcome after the continuous moving around from one side of the country to the other that I had been experiencing.

The estate was all oil palms, flat, boring and without any agricultural excitements or excitements of any sort. It was close to Teluk Anson, which had plenty of excellent Chinese restaurants but little else.

The local Planters' Association was quite active and meetings were held frequently. Guest speakers were varied, some radical. One was particularly offensive toward the white planters, his main complaint being that in the old days British Government Representatives made the Sultans sit on the floor while they sat in chairs. It was pointed out quietly by a manager that Malays much preferred sitting on mats, or on rugs, just as Arab potentates still do. And Western people prefer chairs because of their long stiff legs, which are difficult to position elegantly on a mat.

He didn't like us anyway. At the time anything Western was being looked at askance, even education and particularly the use of English. All textbooks should be translated into Malay, the newspapers raged. Not many thought this was a good idea except a few MPs from rural Malaysia who could not understand why, as Malaysia was now an independent country, English should continue to be used as a medium of learning and communication.

Nobody wanted to argue with these sons of the soil as they were the backbone of the party and did not understand that English was the key to development and advancement.

The standard of English, unfortunately, did begin to decline dramatically. And, it was nearly ten years before more emphasis was again placed on improving the standard of the language. It was such a waste, for the standard of English in the 1950s and 1960s had been very high.

I wandered around the field most days, and had long chats with Brian, the engineer. He had proudly bought himself a BMW car that was always giving trouble, unlike the modern BMW that goes on for ever. At that time, Germany, industrially, was only just climbing back after total obliteration during the war.

As Germany emerged as the industrial giant, so Britain declined. When I first arrived in 1961 every shop sold only British manufactured goods, whether it be cutlery or china, generators or lathes. Everything had been manufactured in either Birmingham or Sheffield. Ten years later, the cars were Japanese and the power plants German; to find British-made goods was difficult. As Brian quipped, only planters and engineers were now made in Britain.

The demise of British manufacturing could be seen throughout the country. It was only five years before that a very good friend and a manager of Wearne Brothers, which marketed British-made cars, mentioned that Japanese or Korean cars hadn't a chance in Malaysia. He wasn't being particularly complacent but didn't understand the industrial might of Japan just across the water, nor their ability to mass-produce at affordable prices.

I never bought a Japanese car. In those days there were terrible stories of soft bodies and poor steering. Accidents abounded. Always Japanese cars were the cause. I couldn't afford a new car so I purchased second-hand ones. However, the problems of quality were soon ironed out and the market became swamped with Toyotas and Hondas.

Likewise heavy equipment, such as graders and excavators. The once-dominant Priestmans and Aveling Barford lost ground to makers of inferior but cheaper products. Selaba Estate, being flat, necessitated a lot of drainage work and required a new excavator. The best, Priestmans, were currently unavailable, but please wait six months and one will be delivered. We could not wait, so a Komatsu was purchased. The old Komatsus were quite awful but Priestmans were not able to deliver on time and lost the business.

143

It was a sorry state of affairs, and sadly British goods were either priced out of the market or were just unavailable when they were wanted. And, of course the quality of Japanese goods improved out of all recognition as they began to capture the business.

31

1971–1973

I seemed to criss-cross the country repeatedly. It was no longer fun. Now that Esah was married and ensconced in a small eating shop, my only companion was my red pedigree Dobermann dog, Hara. He loved the estates, especially the jungle fringes where he encircled and trapped monkeys by running around the trees wildly and barking furiously. This made the monkeys dizzy and they climbed down, to be snapped up by him as they descended. He was a tremendous friend and as he grew older became battle scarred from fights with wild cats, monitor lizards, other dogs and the occasional wild pig.

I was flying regularly with Robert, who had now perfected his transmitter system for receiving signals from elephants which he had collared and earmarked for special attention. It was quite simple, in that an elephant was shot and stunned with an anaesthetic dart. A collar with a transmitter attached would then be fixed around the elephant's neck as it lay snoring on the ground. The receiver, which Robert carried in the plane, would then pick up the signal from the transmitter through the antennae tied to the wing.

Robert had a number of elephants, all collared, in various parts of Malaysia. As the elephants moved around in the forests the signal could be picked up and the animal's location fixed on a map.

A number of families were in the Taman Negara National Game Park, a huge area of jungle in the middle of the country. The park was ruggedly mountainous, with steep sheer slopes and ravines. Dense forest covered the mountains from foothills to peaks and from the air it presented a daunting landscape.

When learning to fly we were taught how to survive in the jungle, what to eat and what may be poisonous. One piece of information that had always stuck in my mind was that provided you had sufficient water, you could survive on just leaves, roots or berries for thirty-two days. Water was fortunately readily available from streams or from the plants themselves; for example, a cut vine contained a plentiful supply.

We were also taught in our survival lessons that if you had engine failure, never flutter down in a slow uncontrolled glide. You must be positive, search around as you descend for a clearing, or two dominant trees growing close together, and then aim the plane towards the space in between the trees. The impact of the wings hitting the trees would slow you down and as they sheared off with the impact, the fuselage would continue, minus the wings, and slide slowly down through the mass of canopy and branches, sinking gently to the forest floor below. Whereupon you opened the door, hopped out, took a few deep breaths, retrieved your survival kit and compass from the wrecked carcass of the plane and set off, whistling a happy tune, in the direction of the nearest settlement, which could be a hundred miles away.

When we flew over Taman Negara searching for elephants I was continuously looking out below for those specific two dominant trees. There were many. When I married Julia and we flew across the mountains, she also searched for likely spots to land in an emergency, or for two large trees which might be suitable for a crash landing. One pilot I knew, each time he flew across the mountains prayed furiously beforehand for a safe journey. I always felt slightly vulnerable in a small plane crossing dense forested mountains, especially if there was turbulence. I couldn't help remembering the demise of my instructor whose wings came off in severe unexpected turbulent conditions.

Robert appeared not to be that concerned and always exhibited a happy and unflustered exterior. The elephants did not make flying particularly easy for us as they often appeared to be in the most inaccessible places: deep ravines and cul-de-sacs that were a nightmare, requiring horrific steep turns to get out of them as Robert wanted to get as close as possible to the signals. Mountains loomed large as we skimmed the treetops. Robert looked at his maps, fixing locations, while I scanned the terrain, praying the elephants were not feeding in the furthest indent of a ravine.

146

Robert barks instructions: left, straighten slightly, now right, down, do go down, Robin; where are those bloody animals? Left, turn left, for Christ sake. Got them! Let's get out.

How? Mountains all around, I veer sharply left and climb vertically. Stalling speed, should just miss the tops. Robert is happily poring over his maps. I am just trying to lift this horrible little underpowered plane out of the valley.

We are over; I breathe a sigh of relief. Robert is content, the wings are still attached, the elephants are marked on the map. Robert wants to be put down on the national park's grass airstrip at Kuala Tahan, constructed in the shape of a banana. At one end of the strip is a conical hill; most pilots come in from that end. I

Landing at Kuala Tahan

147

prefer the other, although it means that if I overshoot I fly straight into the hill. The approach, however, from my preferred end is without obstacles except the trees, and one can approach at a lower level.

The strip comes into sight and I fly just above tree level. Robert prefers the other end and tightens his harness. I land with a touch of flaps and brake sharply. All is well. Robert grimaces and asks, why do you always come in the wrong way? NOTAMS specifically say Kuala Tahan should be approached from the conical hillside, not the other way. I tell him what he can do with his bloody NOTAMS. The tension is released. A group of aboriginals have arrived and stand around watching us curiously. We take off the antennae and he lifts out his rucksack. He stays with the park rangers when he comes to Kuala Tahan.

After a few sodas I say farewell and take off in the direction of the conical hill, then veer to the right. The air is calm; I should be back in Kuala Lumpur by evening.

Robert, having found his elephants through the transmitter, sets off to find out all about them, what they are eating, what they are doing, their habits, numbers and all the other data needed for his PhD and study of the Asian elephant and its habitat

Out of the jungle, he enjoys an extremely hectic social life in Kuala Lumpur, where he shares a house with an American and a Malay. Life is humming; a social mix of all races, and an exotic free and easy lifestyle pervades all corners of society. Racism is a word never, or rarely ever, heard. It did not exist as far as my contemporaries were concerned.

Although Malaysia was developing socially, industrially the country's economy remained fixed upon logging, plantations and mines and the commodities that were produced from them. There was still little industrialization; the electronic industry was a long distance away, while tourism was just beginning to make an impact.

Of course there were only twelve million people in Malaya, a million and half in Sarawak and less than a million in Sabah. The country thus was able to sustain itself on its primary commodities of timber, rubber, oil palm, cocoa, tea, copra and tin, principally because half the population, the rural Malays, lived a subsistence

148

way of life and were not big consumers of anything manufactured. Their habits hardly changed for another ten years.

I frequented the flying club whenever possible, not to read the latest NOTAMS, but to see if anybody wanted my services. Flying costs had increased and I could not always rely upon Robert's infrequent handouts.

Occasionally I would be asked to give a lift to somebody who wanted to go to some inaccessible location where there was a strip: a surveyor, a logger, an occasional 'somebody' without a name or emblem. John Mackintosh on Prang Besar phoned me when I was acting on Carey Island and asked if I would go and bail out two of his rubber scrap lorries which had been impounded by the police for being overweight. They were at Bentong, could I go as quickly as possible – the rubber would be deteriorating fast.

I booked a plane and took off for Bentong, which although not far from Kuala Lumpur nestled amongst the foothills of the main mountain range. The only place to land was at an army camp just outside town.

It was a pleasant journey. As I had departed in the early morning, there was little turbulence and I landed at the army camp in good time. The major in charge was happy for a chat and allowed me to call a taxi to take me to court.

Arriving early, I hung around outside the court. Since I was to plead guilty on behalf of the lorries and Prang Besar, I hoped it could all be completed amicably behind closed doors. It should not be necessary for me to appear, although I would if required.

The magistrate hadn't arrived by 10 a.m. but the clerks were busying themselves and I entered the clerk's office at the back. Please may I pay the fine and go, I requested. Certainly, said an old clerk but the magistrate would have to determine the amount. Usually in these cases 50 to 70 ringgit should suffice. We waited. The magistrate arrived, and I was called into his office; the law books were scrutinized. The magistrate was a young Malay and obviously eager to impress. He and the clerk whispered together. That will be 400 ringgit, I was told. The clerk looked very apologetic. I asked, couldn't he put it down a bit, I had only brought 300 with me. Wanting to appear magnanimous, the magistrate agreed and I handed over the money and received a receipt.

My taxi was waiting outside and we drove off to the police compound. They, as always, were very courteous and the lorry drivers were called. The sergeant, however, reiterated that the lorries were still overweight and couldn't be released. By how much? At least a ton and a half on each, he answered.

The taxi driver, who smelt business, suggested that he call his brother's wife's aunt, whose husband had just the right size of lorry to accommodate the excess and which he knew was available. Off he rushed when I agreed, and within ten minutes a small three-ton lorry appeared. I hired it to take the rubber and paid the driver 70 ringgit and, after loading, all three lorries departed for Prang Besar Estate. My taxi driver then dropped me off at the army base and I went over to the major's office to report.

After a cup of coffee he asked if I would give a lift to a soldier who had recently arrived after an exercise in the jungle. I agreed, of course, and after saying my farewells went out to the plane to check it over.

An army Land Rover drew up and a very pale, drawn, tired soldier got out. He was English and although hatless had the look of special forces. We took off. It was now turbulent and I climbed to 5,000 feet. My soldier passenger slept throughout the journey and only awoke when I was landing; he requested me to taxi to the RMAF section of the base and drop him off by the control tower.

I noticed as I approached the tower a Land Rover standing by. I stopped. He thanked me, and as he got out I asked him where he had come from. Thailand, he replied. Did you walk all the way, I asked, thinking he must have got an occasional lift by helicopter. All the way, he said in thirty-three days. I light-heartedly mentioned that it should be in the *Guinness Book of Records*. He did not answer at first and then said, no, the record was thirty-one days.

It made my so-called Tamil-passing effort appear very insignificant indeed. Walking down the mountain spine of Malaysia in thirty-three days was definitely a very, very superior undertaking.

The Bentong court episode was just one of a number that I was involved in. Usually it concerned me, myself, for speeding or driving an uninsured car, and for other minor offences. Planters were frequently waylaid when returning home after a night out. The

150

police could be over-zealous or forgiving or just amused by our high spirits.

On one occasion I was stopped for speeding in the RMAF base on my way to the flying club. As the base was a built-up area with barracks, offices, aircrew messes and hangars all dotted around, it was very difficult to speed at all, so I was surprised when I was waved down by a policeman who presented me with a speeding ticket for 35 m.p.h., 5 m.p.h. over the limit. I thought this particularly unfair and told him so; 35 m.p.h. is over the limit, I would have to pay the fine, he argued.

As my life was still one of continual movement and I was never quite sure where my next address would be, I hoped that the summons would not catch up with me. For six months it did not, and, then one afternoon sitting in the Nordonal Estate office in Johore, where I was acting, far away from Kuala Lumpur, a policeman walked in with a summons for speeding and a warrant for my arrest for not appearing in court on three separate occasions.

This was a surprise, and I told the policeman that it was probable that my summons had not caught up with me because I was travelling a lot. He was not impressed and asked me to come to the police station. There I explained my problems to the inspector and he said another summons would be issued immediately, please attend or else. It duly arrived; I was to appear at court in Kuala Lumpur. So off I went on the designated day.

I appeared at court in front of a young attractive Malay magistrate straight from the Inns of Court in London. I knew this was going to cost me dearly; she had that look.

She hardly bothered to glance up when my case was called and said I was to be fined 200 ringgit. What, I exclaimed, 200 ringgit for 35 m.p.h.? That was just not fair, for on one occasion in Perak I had been fined only 21 ringgit for speeding, no tax, without insurance and an out-of-date driving licence. How, possibly, could she fine me 200 ringgit for just one offence? Well, she said, as 21 ringgit had been a totally inadequate penalty for the four offences, I was extremely lucky to get away with 200 ringgit. I did not have that amount on me, I told her. Then change a cheque at the Weld supermarket and return with the cash, she countered.

I left the court moaning to anybody and everybody about young Malay female magistrates overcharging respectable law-abiding citizens for offences which hardly deserved a penalty at all. All commiserated, wondering what penalties they were going to be asked to pay.

The Weld supermarket, the alternative bank for planters, changed my cheque and I returned to the court, which had just adjourned for lunch. I felt thoroughly peeved. The 200 ringgit was approximately one-sixth of my monthly salary and losing it because of 35 m.p.h. was not pleasing.

As I paid the clerk of the court, the magistrate sauntered out, probably pleased at the amount she had amassed through fines, for there were others standing around just as disgruntled as I was.

Having paid, I walked out to the parking lot and was about to get into my car when she walked by. That was a very steep fine for 35 m.p.h., I said. She turned and said yes it was, but the Government was short of funds at the moment and every little bit helped. We chattered a bit and I asked if she would like to have lunch at the Selangor club often referred to as The Dog. She said she would and we drove off.

We both ordered. The waiter asked if it was separate bills. I said definitely separate and she agreed. It was a pleasant lunch and after a dessert of ice cream, she got up languidly, thanked me and prepared to leave. Was she not going to pay her bill, I asked. How ungentlemanly of you, she exclaimed; of course I would pay my bill if I could, but I am not a member. And out she walked.

Carey Island - my home on South Estate

The ferry plying between Carey Island and the mainland

The bund breaks at Sungei Samak

Swept away in the flood waters

A beach near Lumut, Sitiawan

A wedding party, Sungei Samak

My bungalow at Sungei Samak

Doris Fraser, myself and Lian with the badminton team at Sungei Samak

Rubber on Welch

The jungle and lower slopes of Mt. Ophir

Sunset at Welch. Mt. Ophir in the background

Burns Night at Seremban. Julia sitting between myself and Duncan Blincoe

Julia at Burns night, the Dixons welcoming guests

The waterfall near Welch Estate

32

Lanadron and Nordonal Estate

I stayed on Lanadron and Nordonal for a few months before moving on to Welch Estate, where I became permanent manager. My acting circuit days were drawing to a close, and not too soon for me. Lanadron estate was all oil palm, with good crops, there was little difficulty settling down; the estate ran like clockwork and the assistants and conductors kept a grip on the labour force.

The estate was quite close to the towns of Muar and Batu Pahat, from which keen teams of runners emerged twice weekly to take part in hash house harrier cross-country running. The sport was popular throughout Malaysia and entailed a paper chain being laid which the runners had to follow. Intermittently, the paper chain would disappear and the runners then needed to find it again to resume the chase. 'On On' means 'Let's go' – a call made by the runners, and the name used for the party after the run. They were great fun, especially the festivities (the 'on on') afterwards that were either held at a participant's house or at a restaurant. I was approached to join, and being far away from any sporting centre I readily agreed.

Every Wednesday after work and on Saturdays we trotted off to an arranged venue. Most runs were held in the countryside amongst the villages or in secondary jungle where logging roads provided reasonable access, and occasionally on estates which were ideal locations.

For each run different hares set a paper trail. Some of the runs took only one and a half to two hours to complete, others over three hours. Once I arrived back at 7 p.m. having lost my way. Every trail differed and provided a different challenge; some were long but easy, while others over hilly terrain were short, limiting the running to a glorified scramble.

I was asked if I would lay a trail and use my house for the 'on on' afterwards. I readily agreed, provided they supplied the beer and I the food.

At the time I had taken over the previous manager's house staff, Abu and his wife Salimah, who had been exceedingly well trained, as most planters' staff happened to be. They later followed me to Welch, where they remain to this day.

Robert Olivier was also in the district and loved the hash. Once he learnt of a hash taking place on Nordonal I knew he would soon turn up. As was the case, for early one evening I heard the familiar rattle of his VW Combi as it trundled through the estate in the direction of the house. It arrived steaming, Robert beaming; a good time was on offer. He had been tracking an elephant on foot and was in immediate need of sustenance.

Robert was always welcome and by now knew most of those planters strategically located close to where his tagged elephants were to be found. Periodically he emerged from the jungle, pale, drawn and underfed, gasping for a beer, sustenance and a bed. Planters' wives doubled the amount of food being prepared for the evening once his Combi was sighted or heard rattling its way through the estate to their homes.

He was good company and enjoyed the effortless hospitality of the planting community, who not only fed him, but often repaired his vehicle, fixed or modified the wing antennae and provided refrigeration for the many samples he had collected to analyse. These often comprised of undigested food, parasites, sometimes worms, and once Julia found elephant's turds in her fridge, which she thought were leftover portions of a stew. Nobody minded this intrusion and everyone was happy to assist.

Having now arrived at Nordonal, I invited him to lay a trail. As he wanted to run the race, he asked to be excused and stayed in the house and relaxed. Instead, one of the assistants volunteered to lay the trail. He was fit and strong and I knew that he would lay a difficult run. After telling him the approximate area, I left him to it.

By early afternoon a seething mass of runners had arrived at the starting point, the factory on the other side of the river which divided the estate. As nobody knew where the end was, it could be anywhere, the first check laid confused everybody as it had been placed on a small pontoon in the middle of the river, which, meant a lot of crossing and recrossing before the new trail was found. It was a good start, everybody was wet, hot and irritable. And this was only for starters.

The runners, all experienced, quickly got into their stride and soon were finding the checks and new trails without too much difficulty. Then halfway through the run, the trail veered away from the estate and entered a small village. There it petered out and everybody started to hunt high and low for the paper trail. It could not be found. The assistant and I were also running but well to the rear; Robert as always was in the front. As we entered the village we came across most of the runners searching frantically for the paper trail, while the less energetic were sitting around eating durian fruit.

I asked the assistant where the trail was. He trotted off behind some village dwellings and returned saying the paper had disappeared. Children, I said, where are the children? I shouted to everybody, find the village children and you find the trail. This turned out to be correct, for amongst the coconut and durian trees small figures were seen scurrying hither and thither picking up the trail of paper. The race leaders howled 'on on' and raced after the children. The trail was found again and off everybody galloped.

As we neared the end of the course, my house, I caught up with Robert, having taken some short cuts. He was amongst the leaders, but flagging. I drew up alongside and he slowed to my pace. I then suggested that he and I had a race to the finish line, my home, with the loser agreeing to pay my bar bill at the Rex Hotel, which was many months overdue. He readily agreed, being confident that he could easily win, and aware that he had unashamedly been using my account at the Rex for the past year or so. I did not mind, as he usually paid his portion, but this time the bill was over 120 ringgit, of which at least eighty per cent was his.

Although not as fit as he was, I was faster over 100 yards. Thus as we approached the garden of the house, which was built on the side of a hill, I raced up the slope at top speed, beating him quite easily. My win did not spoil his evening, but towards the end of the party he looked fairly sombre at the prospect of having to pay the bill at the Rex.

* * *

The Rex Hotel was perhaps the most famous bar, restaurant and house of ill repute in Malaysia and Singapore. Probably Asia too.

The madam was known as Molly, a short, rotund Chinese lady who in her youth had been considered a beauty. She had a soft spot for planters, her business having depended upon their drinking habits and desires for many years. Molly was universally well known, and it caused great sadness when she died quite suddenly.

There was a funeral, attended by many, the great and the good and, of course, many planters. Wreaths were piled high upon her coffin and everybody mourned her passing away. The Rex would never be the same again.

I learnt of her death while on leave in England. I had gone to a party with Robert's sister Katherine and her actress friend, Pamela Salem, who lived together in a flat in Earls Court. The party was quite fun. There was a sprinkling of showbiz personalities, the odd well-known singer, the usual riffraff of hangers-on, and others, like myself, without allegiance.

It was while chatting, as one does about nothing, that a guest came over and said that he had overheard I came from Malaysia, and that his law firm had an office in Kuala Lumpur; he was a barrister. Had I heard, he asked. What should I have heard, I replied. Molly had died quite suddenly. I had not heard this news. We stood in silence. He then moved away, saying he knew her well, his firm had acted on her behalf on many occasions. Molly indeed was well known everywhere.

Robert paid the Rex bill, eventually, which I had not expected. Molly had always allowed planters considerable leeway in settling their accounts. She only had to get in touch with the various companies and settlement would be immediate; everybody knew that it was not only thirsty planters who frequented her bar, she also supplied a whole range of services to a mixed bag of personnel from judges to directors, brigadiers to lawyers. She had many tentacles, nobody could afford to be on the wrong side of Molly. However, she in turn could be kind, generous, discreet and hospitable, and would never let her clients down.

Because her children had been sent away to expensive schools and universities, none were willing to return to the more menial job of running a bar. Fortunately, not all was lost. A young nephew took over and managed to run the establishment as well as could be expected after the demise of such a charismatic personality.

Luckily, all the bar boys stayed on, which ensured a reasonable degree of continuity. The Rex continued to be frequented, but it began to lose its allure as the clientele grew older and people of my age, female and male, began to patronize hotel bars and clubs rather than the less salubrious bars of old. After all, one couldn't take one's wife or girlfriend to the Rex, it was just not the sort of place one went to with a lady on one's arm. Anyway, it would have been like taking coals to Newcastle, as one planter quipped.

33

Welch Estate

I left Lanadron and Nordonal for Welch Estate. Murray Milne was managing the property and was being moved to another estate in Negri Sembilan.

It was nice going to an estate that had been managed by a friend, for you knew the take-over would be brief and simple. Once, I took over from one manager, who requested that I count all the pencils and pens, every fertilizer sack plus make a complete inventory of the estate's rolling stock. When he returned from leave he did the same, counting everything. The whole process took ages.

With Murray it was over in an afternoon. I learnt the safe combination, checked the accounts, counted the petty cash, inspected the stores and read the last visiting agent's report, which was satisfactory, and then waved farewell to Murray as he sped away later that evening.

I had acted on the estate before, so I knew the fields and the problem areas, which were many. Welch was very hilly, with a road system designed by the manager before Murray, who had no idea how to construct roads up hillsides. In consequence many of the roads went vertically up without any attention paid to the suitability of incline and degree of slope. In consequence crop transportation was a nightmare. One hill with a vertical road became known as Read's Folly, named after the previous manager.

The manager's house was perched on a hill with a magnificent view of the estate and the jungle beyond. Close to one boundary was Mount Ophir, 3,500 feet high and covered with jungle.

In the garden was a small swimming pool and, dotted throughout, mango trees, mangosteens and avocado pears, all of which provided a seasonal supply of fruit.

As already mentioned, I brought my house staff, Abu and his wife Salimah, with me. They were well trained and could cook European as well as Chinese and Malayan food for whatever number of guests might suddenly appear.

The manager's driver, Hamdan, was a rogue but very likeable and energetic; while Rahman had been thirty years a gardener, and loved to be a waiter whenever a party was arranged. For although a Muslim he imbibed discreetly. The signs soon became visible as he used to enter into conversation with the guests. Knowing some English, he was very happy to chat whenever an opportunity arose. All the planters liked him, and would often seek him out to learn the latest gossip. Rahman was always most happy to oblige.

Hara, my Dobermannn, was in heaven: lots of colobus monkeys on the boundaries to chase, a whole range of fauna amongst the oil palms, and a reasonably cool location to rush around in. There were few other dogs around as the estate workforce was a hundred per cent Malay.

Having a complete labour force of Malays was very unusual, and the history of this anomaly went back to the time of the communist emergency. In those days the labour force was Chinese, but as the conflict became increasing bitter, they responded by becoming ever more difficult to control. It was therefore decided to purge the estate of all Chinese and bring in a Malay labour force from the surrounding villages.

Although Malays were not experienced in working on estates, they soon adapted to the discipline and even began to enjoy the regulated community lifestyle associated with plantations.

The Chinese did not appear to mind very much either as there was plenty of land around and they could carry out their own market gardening, which included the raising of pigs, an activity the company would not allow on Welch. One or two also went and joined their brethren living in the jungle, banding together in order to fight the government forces arrayed against them.

Once the Malays were in residence, it was necessary for management to instil a work ethic. As the majority of rural Malays were farmers, it was not difficult to teach them the principles of tree crop establishment, which were rubber and oil palms, nor the husbandry practices required to keep the crops in optimum productivity. They soon learnt, and over the years a work ethic was quickly established.

On my arrival, the estate was very much like any other H&C property. Standards had been set and were being maintained, costs were low and rubber production was as good as on any estate, even those located on more favourable soils and terrain. Welch was suitable for rubber, not oil palms or cocoa, but because of the high price of palm oil, H&C decided to plant up half the area of Welch with oil palms.

This was a mistake, as everybody soon realized. Oil palm enjoys deep fertile soils, flat terrain and high rainfall. Welch possessed none of these agronomic requirements. The estate was extremely hilly, the rainfall low and the soils stony. By the time I arrived some harvesting of the oil palm had already started, but the crops were poor except in the valleys and ravines, where harvesting was difficult to perform and the fruit heavy to carry out to the roadsides.

Close to Welch was the small town of Jementah, which was one street long and possessed a flyblown market, a small Anglican chapel, a few shop houses and a hardware shop which was also the local workshop, transport company and petrol station, all belonging to a Chinese businessman, Mr Tan of Ghee Hup Guan Ltd. He owned probably most of Jementah and its surroundings. He was likeable, friendly, inquisitive and generous. Not a high-flyer in the business world, although he certainly had lots of fingers in many pies.

His premises were not awe-inspiring; they were a bit ramshackled. Tools of every description littered the store. Every kind of screw, nut, bolt, lock; paint of every colour, cement, glue; bags of this and that, protruded from every corner. It was a nightmare to find anything but somehow the Chinese lady who ran the shop knew where everything was, and I was amazed that whatever I wanted was there, and soon found.

Ghee Hup Guan, Mr Tan, or as we irreverently called him fatty Tan, also had the oil palm fruit collection business. He possessed a collection of vintage trucks that whizzed around the estates collecting the fruit bunches and transporting them to local factories.

His trucks were not especially reliable and were always breaking down, but somehow each would immediately be replaced by another, albeit equally dilapidated. However, Mr Tan invariably managed to get the fruit away by evening, and this small contract, by his standards, provided him with what he called his pocket money for the week.

I became very fond of Mr Tan, who spoke good English, although it was often interspersed with foul language picked up from planters, which he thought was quite permissible to use in any circle, polite or otherwise.

In the back of his workshop-cum-store, he would entertain his friends and business acquaintances. There were a few broken-down chairs, but one usually sat on a heap of tyres or a box or anything which was flat. Although this small room could hardly be called luxurious or even pleasant, the sumptuous Chinese food served was the most delicious I have ever tasted. And his enthusiastic generosity was afforded without any desire to profit from his hospitality.

But of course he did gain from his kindness, for whatever the standard of his work we usually forgave him. The thought of Welch operating without Mr Tan was unthinkable. He was very much part of the estate.

There was no doubt he was rich, but not excessively so. He owned a fleet of logging lorries and possessed at least a dozen bulldozers. But, for all his wealth, he was a simple, unsophisticated man.

I took him flying once; he was thrilled and took control of the joystick. We went up, down, sideways and almost stalled on several occasions. When at last we landed he said in his gravely voice, we will go to Singapore next week and have good time. I will show all my friends this proper way to travel.

An evening out with Mr Tan plus friends would have been riotous but I knew the plane was not available and this provided me with an excuse not to go. Travelling by car from Jementah to Singapore was not for me.

He also had second thoughts, for it was a few weeks later that he arrived at my office and said that he and two friends had now decided to go to Singapore and find some white girls to sleep with. He then pulled out from his shopping bag, which he always carried around, a girlie calendar with the usual scantily dressed buxom ladies featured each month. He liked April and showed me. She was indeed attractive. Are all white girls like this? he asked. He had obviously not met too many. Some are, I replied, but most are not.

The purpose of his visit to my office then became apparent, he wanted an advance, pocket money, he called it. I asked how much; 5,000 ringgit, he said, enough for a night out. He was obviously going to have his night out in style. I did not have that much, but I gave him what was available. He signed for his pocket money and got up to leave. Mr Bryant, he said, looking a little embarrassed, do all white women smell of cheese? A friend of his had told him they did.

I have not noticed, I told him. As far as my experiences are worth, no, white women do not smell cheesy. Good, he said, because he had eaten cheese and did not like it. And the worst cheese of all to eat was Stilton. He could never sleep with a woman who smelt of Stilton.

It was many weeks later before I met up with him again. He arrived at the office late afternoon, which was surprising, and got out of his Mercedes and bustled in. He had a look about him which I had not seen before: he was troubled, from what, I could not imagine.

He shook my hand and sat down. I asked him politely about his weekend in Singapore. Was it fun? Oh yes, he said. No, white women don't smell of cheese, he confirmed.

However, he had not come to recount his escapades in Singapore, instead he invited me to come for a meal at his shop that evening.

I arrived at his shop and walked through to the rear. He was with another Chinese man, who sat on a beautifully carved camphorwood chest and appeared to be quaffing large amounts of VSOP brandy. We were introduced. He spoke little English, so we conversed in Malay. The food arrived and, as usual, it was delicious, especially the river prawns. We all ate and drank, conversing disjointedly, not normal for such evenings.

After a while and much belching, the Chinese gentleman got up and told Tan he was going outside to urinate. Tan then leant over, looking very troubled. Very bad man, he said, wicked man. Why, I asked. He seemed pleasant enough. Tan hoarsely repeated himself as he often did. He has just murdered his mother-in-law and does not know what to do with her, he added.

I was once told by a Chinese girl of good pedigree, never get mixed up with the Chinese when there is trouble about. I certainly could smell it very distinctly at that moment. How did Mr Tan know that this Chinese man had killed his mother-in-law? Because he showed her to me, he answered. Where, I asked. She is in the box, look and see. No, I said very firmly, I was certainly not going to open the box; dead mothers-in-law were not for viewing. She is packed in a large polythene bag, the kind you use in rubber factories. Very thick, good quality, he said, and began to reflect eloquently upon the quality of the bag, when the Chinese man returned and sat down upon his mother-in-law's temporary abode.

I really at this stage did not know what to do. Lots of married couples say that they would like to strangle their mother-in-law. Few ever do; it is a criminal offence. Did that apply to the Chinese? I had no idea. I also doubted that the Malay police sergeant in Jementah would particularly thank me should I go along to the station and tell him what I believed had happened. Tan then leant over and asked what should be done, the secret was out, how could they get rid of mother-in-law? His Chinese guest also seemed eager to know. Surely she should have a funeral, I suggested lamely, but then everybody would ask how she died; she was not that old either, he replied. Anyway, he said dismissively, she's in very small pieces.

I realized then that I had nothing further to contribute and got up and shook hands all round. Mr Tan came out with me, obviously somewhat distraught. I thanked him for a most enjoyable evening and drove off back to the estate.

It was another two weeks before I met up with Mr Tan again. He was parked by the roadside talking to one of his drivers. I drew alongside and got out. Had the problem of how to dispose of mother-in-law been solved? I asked. He looked as though he didn't want the subject ever broached again. Yes, it had been solved, he said, and left it at that.

He then turned to me and asked, those big polythene bags the ones used in the rubber factories, the good quality ones, like the one used as a receptacle for mother-in-law, where can I buy some.

I need them urgently for transporting cow dung to the garden of a new house that I am building for my family. I told him where he could go and buy the bags.

Better for transporting cow dung than ex-mother-in-laws, I thought. Or, possibly for both, I guessed.

34

Social Events

There were numerous estates in the district, and the biggest area of rubber and oil palms belonged to Dunlops.

The Dunlops management system was very different from H&C's. Whereas H&C followed a 'hands-off approach and were very willing to permit managers a considerable degree of responsibility and initiative in managing their estates, other companies such as Dunlops and Guthries appeared to keep their estate management on a very short rein, and, visits by head office personnel were frequent.

Their managers and assistants were generally very pleasant people but hardly exciting, mostly good plodders, working within their meagre capabilities. Generally it was considered that their managerial acumen was well below that of most H&C planters. However, the social life of the district revolved around the Dunlop estates' facilities, the club, golf course, swimming pool and tennis court. All were used frequently and with great pleasure.

Going to the club followed a routine: wives sat around gossiping, while their husbands played dice on the bar, or card games. All looked forward to retirement, a thatched cottage in the country with bamboo furniture and dogs, usually yappy small ones, or the favourite of country people in pastoral England, Labradors, faithful and un-questioning.

Being country people, they dreamed of busying themselves in the garden, playing with their grandchildren, pushing trolleys around supermarkets, whenever possible meeting up with other retired planters who lived not far away.

The reality would be forced jollity, with many wishing they were back in the tropics. As the pensionable age was fifty-five years, a couple on returning to the UK had another thirty years to look forward to before death relieved them of the tedium of retirement.

*   *   *

In our district, parties were frequent and generally boring; the same people, the same conversations, the sameness of everything. The main topic of discussion was servants, followed closely by their children, food and of course the heat. How they longed for bright, frosty mornings, forgetting that mornings were often damp, misty and murky, and, in the suburbs, most gloomy.

Fortunately the district was alive with cricketers and a planter's team was soon organized.

Every cricket team needs a Peter Bonner. He was the secretary, the manager, the kit man, the groundsman on occasions, and the wicket keeper. Without him the team would just not have functioned, and because of him we had weekly fixtures as far afield as Singapore to the south and the Selangor Club in the north.

We had a strong side which could beat most other teams, including the Singapore Sunday XI, which came once a year to the district. We played them on one of the Dunlop sports fields, especially prepared for the game.

As we didn't have our own pitch most of our games were played away, which suited us. It was nice to get off our respective estates and enjoy fresh surroundings. The Malacca Club was one of our favourite grounds and the evenings were always most pleasant and convivial.

The highlight of the season was playing Singapore. They would come on the Saturday evening and stay at the various planters' homes. Many had never been on an estate and found the labyrinth of roads difficult to negotiate before arriving at the manager's house.

I organized a party for both teams and most of the district turned up as well. Abu cooked satay, Rahman and Hamdan served drinks. Tom and Sue Hulton came and stayed. Tom was in the team and the principal organizer of the event.

The party went on into the early morning. Some of the Singapore team could not find their way back to their respective beds and returned to Welch and slept on the floor.

In the morning most of the planters were up bright and early. They seldom ever had hangovers and normally woke early. The Singapore team, less adaptable, slept late and all complained of hangovers. The sun was out; it was going to be a very hot sweaty day. Tom spent most of the morning trying to locate his team, while Sue lazily swam in the pool, praying that she would not be needed to score.

Peter, as usual, was organizing everything and in dribs and drabs we turned up for the 11 a.m. kick-off. Bleary-eyed Singaporeans arrived, many feeling that there had been a gigantic conspiracy by the planters to get them drunk. But there hadn't, planters were naturally hospitable and lived isolated and often lonely lives. A party was to be enjoyed until it stopped, whatever time that was. The longest I ever attended lasted three days. In contrast, the shortest party ever was all over by 9 p.m., everybody having got completely drunk on schnapps and a crate of sixty per cent proof vodka, which somebody had managed to procure. People collapsed by the poolside, one walked through a plate glass window, another was found lying head down in the swimming pool hoping to die. It was certainly an experience rather than a party and one that was never repeated.

We were now two teams. We tossed, and Singapore elected to bat, hoping that their first four batsmen would make all the runs. As one of the batsman was an Australian Sheffield Shield player and another played for Kent second eleven, we realized we could be in for a long day in the field.

The wicket was slow, but provided no turn for the spinners. It was a nothing wicket. However, it did have one flaw that could flummox the most experienced batsman: a slight indentation at one end, on a good length, that had been treasured by the groundsman under Peter's direction. Should a slow ball hit this indentation, it would skid underneath any bat. If the ball was bowled fast, it would rise precipitously from the indentation, which although unnerving never got anybody out and could easily be hit. All the slow bowlers in the know aimed for this spot, but as it was a mere abrasion in the wicket it was difficult to direct a ball there consistently.

The game started with Ross Dixon bowling. He was by his own admission the slowest fast bowler ever, but he managed to swing the ball off a good length and always picked up a couple of wickets. However, he was bowling against two ex-professional batsmen and his first over went for fourteen runs. I bowled from the other end, without much success either.

The score rose rapidly and both batsmen were looking very confident. It was then that Ross bowled an even slower ball, which did as it should, skidding under the bat but missing the stumps. The Australian Sheffield player looked at the pitch and searched for the offending spot. He patted it, remembering where it was, and waited for Ross's next delivery, which was even slower than the previous one. The batsman jumped out of his crease and thumped it high into the air. It must be a six, we thought. We lost sight of the ball. There, it was still going up. Having reached its zenith it started to descend.

Far away, waiting on the long-on boundary, was my assistant Balan, a bright young Tamil who loved cricket but was not very good at the game. He suddenly became the focus of our attention, for the ball was falling in his direction. Balan had been ruminating about life under the shade of a very large mango tree which adorned the boundary, when we shouted a chorus of *Balan*. He looked up and noticed this red globe descending towards him. He watched, he moved slightly to the left then back to the right. We were mesmerized. If he dropped the catch was it a sackable offence? The ball thudded into his hands. He gripped it. A catch, the first this season, in fact the first ever for him. There was loud applause, cheers. He was in heaven.

In those days cricketers were undemonstrative in their feelings when a wicket fell. Balan waved, threw the ball back to the square and returned to the shade of his tree. No embracing, hugs, kisses or loving pats. Not like nowadays, with sickly congratulations all round.

Although I was captain I had completely forgotten about Balan, so I was doubly pleased that he had caught a catch in a position which he shouldn't have been in.

The game started to swing our way. We had the State fast bowler in our team, Navaratnam, who was exceedingly quick and whom I brought on once the pitch became responsive. However, a particularly stubborn batsman was giving us problems, so we reverted to a plan which never failed and that was to bring on Balan to bowl his donkey drops. He could be expensive but it was necessary to try anything to dislodge this player.

A conference was held on the square. Peter as wicket keeper came up to the stumps. Another player was positioned close to the square leg umpire to chat at the appropriate moment. All was in place.

Balan bowled. The first ball went for four, the second for six.

Oh dear, this *was* going to be expensive. The third was unreachable and then came the fourth. Balan bowled the ball; it snaked high in the air and landed on the indentation, whereupon it slid under the bat of the advancing batsman. He was out of his crease, the bails were whipped off by Peter, the umpire was chatting to square leg. There was a huge appeal. Peter looked ferocious. The umpire saw the batsman out of his crease, the bails were off; was the ball in Peter's gloved hands? It appeared to be, he must be out. Up went the finger. There was silence from the Singapore crowd, for the bails seemed to have come off before the ball had even reached the wicket. In fact the ball seemed to have been lost in the euphoria of the dismissal.

Balan was deliriously happy, so was Peter, Singapore resistance thereafter crumbled and they were all out for 170 runs.

Lian, a Chinese assistant, opened the batting with Ross, who was patience personified. Lian was a good golfer and tennis player and possessed a very quick eye. If Lian was in form then every ball would be hit out of the ground. He hated running between wickets, especially as he suffered from stones in the kidney.

After taking stock of the bowling he then unleashed his talents, and while Ross defended stoutly, Lian raced ahead scoring quickly. But on thirty-five runs he was out, caught. I then went in and sliced and glanced another twenty or so. We had good batting to come. Duncan Blincoe, a very good player, stroked the ball effortlessly around the ground. We were well on course for an easy victory.

Then as more often than not a batting collapse occurred. We needed twenty-five runs to win. The next man in was Balan. Peter was batting, pushing and nudging a run here and there, a scampered two. Balan's time had come. Play your natural game, I told him. What's that? he asked unassumingly. I was not sure either. We all held our breath.

Peter's innings progressed slowly. It always did, and as long as he stayed in we had a chance. Balan had hardly faced a ball, but now he was at the crease, the bowler was quick. The delivery arrived. He swished. Another ball, another swish. Suddenly the ball hit the spot at speed. Balan knew all about the indentation, he waited as it rose and then slashed it through the covers. Balan had hit a four. They remained together for the rest of the innings. Balan hit his highest ever score, but Peter was the mainstay.

After the game, we stayed behind on the ground. The Singapore players had enjoyed the game. The critical phase was Peter's stumping off Balan. Nobody knew where the ball was except Peter, who knew but was not saying. After all, it was their umpire who gave him out. He should have been watching instead of chatting.

Murray Milne, the other umpire, knew but had not been consulted. As Peter said, it was all because of his treasured indentation. Cricket needed players like Peter and Balan, they weren't the best but they often won matches.

35

Visiting Agents

Visiting agents inspected an estate every six months. The visit could last a day or even a week, depending on its size and the existing agronomic and productivity standards of the estate.

Welch was approximately 3,200 acres and unless a VA was particularly keen, a day and half was sufficient. On Bagan Datoh, which was 8,000 acres and with three crops, one of which, cocoa, required particularly intensive management, a visit could last for five days. When I was on Bagan Datoh the visiting agent, John Leach, walked to every corner and inspected almost every tree.

While I was on the acting circuit, John Leach, as luck would have it, had been my most frequent visiting agent so I got to know his habits quite well. Now that I was on Welch, I was unfortunate to be visited by a previous manager who, having just been promoted to the position, was enthusiastic about starting his new career by visiting his old estate.

Although he was industrious and a good walker, his knowledge of plant agronomy was sadly limited, and arguments arose as to what was best for the crop. Like many of the older visiting agents, he had a fixation concerning weed control practices and hated to see vegetation growing anywhere close to a tree. Competitive, he said; costly, uneconomic, I answered. Balls, he cried. Every visiting agent wanted pristine conditions whatever the cost.

The visiting agents and research officers formulated agricultural policies. H&C had excellent research establishments at Prang Besar for rubber, and, at Banting for oil palm. The directors of both stations were considered the best in the business. Certainly Ron Shepherd, head of the Rubber Research Institute at Prang Besar, enjoyed enormous success in all aspects of rubber plant breeding. In consequence high-yielding clonal material was planted not only

171

on H&C estates, but was also sold throughout the country and the rubber world to smallholders and estates alike. It was a profitable business.

Visiting agents being ex-senior managers, were more practical in their approach to estate agricultural and management practices. This sometimes led to friction when the committee's mix of research personnel and visiting agents came together to discuss agronomic policies for implementation.

However, at the same time it was recognized throughout Malaysia that agronomic policies engineered by H&C's agricultural committee were at the forefront of estate development. Other companies, and the huge agricultural development schemes that were being established up and down the country, adopted many of H&C's agronomic practices and husbandry procedures.

A VA's visit was an essential ingredient to the estate's husbandry and maintenance progress. The principal purpose of a visit was to energize management, to ensure that all policies and directives from the company were being implemented.

As growing tropical tree crops could not be considered 'high tech', except for cocoa, which required considerable attention, all field agronomic practices, crop production and processing procedures were well documented and simple to execute. Thus a visit was regarded as a chance for a VA to inspect the fields and ensure that standards were being complied with as per H&C directives.

A visit was a walking tour of inspection. Up and down hills, into the valleys and ravines, and then up again. As field inspection was the essence of a visiting agent visit, they were very fit as a breed. Most were fitter than the planters, who soon felt the rasp of an agent's tongue if they could not keep up.

The first visit I experienced on Welch, by this previous manager, was not dissimilar to any other. He walked, made notes, discussed and continued from field to field.

He was not especially displeased with anything; neither did he feel that Welch, in his eyes, had made great strides since he had left a few years ago. On his last day we went through the visiting agent's questionnaire together, much of which I had completed

172

before his arrival. After a one-night stay he departed the next day after lunch.

I cannot say I waited with bated breadth for his report, which was not slow in arriving. It contained many gripes, few compliments and endless verbiage that could have been written in a sentence. The covering letter from the company agent in Kuala Lumpur was fairly terse, bringing to my attention those points, which required my immediate attention.

I had learnt from my brother, when he worked as an agent at HO in Kuala Lumpur, that one-liners, short sentences and just noted, were far better received than endless excuses and ramblings. I followed his advice and instead of answering with explanations and mitigations, wrote against the various sections requiring a response; noted, no comment, agreed, in hand, now ongoing, completed and many others. It all amounted to a page and a half.

It did not please the VA, while the head office agent, Bill Croggan, replied that although he approved of brevity my reply was inadequate. I therefore duly added the occasional sentence and my reply was now a full two sides.

After this incident, Bill Croggan, realizing I was not the most communicative of planters, kept correspondence to a minimum, unless it was of extreme urgency. This happy state of affairs went on for all the time I was on Welch. And, probably I have the 'lack of communication' record of all H&C planters, for during one period I did not write a letter to HO for two months. This must have been the ultimate in communicative silence.

After this initial visit, the visiting agent changed and James Gilbert, one of the most senior visiting agents, took over the Welch slot.

He did not know Welch, but knew me, for he had acted for Peg-leg Harvey on Sungei Wangi. Being a Scot, he regarded all English as effete snobs, which was of little consequence to me, but he was equally harsh about his Scottish contemporaries, whom he considered lazy, talkative and incompetent, especially the engineers.

I liked Jimmy; he was fair, fit and loved a good gossip. Prior to his visits I completed all entries of the visiting agent's questionnaire and even wrote up some of the report myself. Completing the report saved time and allowed him to be off early to play golf with his friends at Dunlops. Thus my half yearly VA visit was reduced to one day only.

He never really liked staying on Welch; it was a little too spartan, with no air conditioning and noisy fans. Although Abu tried his best, I never really gave him enough money to buy the kind of food Jimmy was accustomed to when visiting estates. Thus he would leave as soon as possible to find more convivial surroundings.

He regarded visiting Welch Estate as one of his least onerous duties and wrote reasonably laudatory reports that required few comments either from me or from the agent at head office. Which pleased everybody.

36

The Director and a Dog

Managing Welch was a very happy experience. The junior staff, especially Das, Rocky and Rafiah, were excellent and the *mandors* (foremen), particularly Abang, were intelligent and had good labour control.

During my four years on Welch there were five different assistants, all very good except one, and all reached high positions in H&C or joined other companies where they did equally well.

Balan, the cricketer, although the most casual, was efficient and calm in the way he carried out his duties, and likewise Lian, my Chinese assistant, who eventually took over Welch when I left. He always displayed an unhurried temperament and was self possessed and diligent.

I had only one Malay assistant, Tahir, who was a thoughtful, moderate Muslim, enjoyed a beer, but never over-imbibed and would discuss during the evenings the relative merits of Christianity over Islam, and vice versa, plus the country's religious future. He was not far wrong.

Tahir was small, eager and keen, and when in later years I managed to contact him again he fortunately had never become tainted with the dogma of fundamentalism, although he stopped drinking in public, as most Muslims were forced to do.

The estate worked like clockwork and operated equally effectively whether I was on or off. Rubber crops increased, costs went down; Welch operated frugally but efficiently.

Visiting agents' visits were never prolonged affairs and we were seldom visited by anybody from H&C; the occasional research officer came to decide upon fertilizer recommendations, an engineer called once a year.

175

Looking for root disease

On one occasion a director from the UK came to Welch and was rude about tapping standards in one particular field of young rubber. Especially, wounding of the tapping panels, the cuts being far too deep and ragged, which was unfortunately rife, but the tappers had already been replaced.

When told that the offending tappers had been removed, the director then went around the whole field criticizing whenever he found a flaw in tapping standards, particularly concerning the amount of bark a tapper should sliver off while tapping.

By this time it was evident he had not read the latest circulars on bark consumption. So as he was measuring a tapping panel in one row and pedantically calling out the measurements, as if he was auctioning steers at a market, to the accompanying agent, who was writing them assiduously down, I interrupted the proceedings gently and politely during a pause and reminded the director and agent that if they had read Policy Rubber Circular R-11 they would be aware that all trees were within the new limit.

Company directors all over the world don't like being corrected by their subordinates. Neither do agents, who feel their position neutered when some young upstart of a manager corrects them concerning the contents of a circular that they had been partly instrumental in composing.

Both looked at me as if I had bad breath. I smiled sweetly, rather like my mum in Singapore, but without the same effect. The director was not pleased; he was hot and sweaty and, like most deskbound city slickers, was wearing long trousers, as was the agent, rather than shorts – the planters' garb. I had not done my future much good. The situation was not retrieved either by Hara, my red Dobermannn, coming over to find out why we seemed to be glued to this one spot. Realizing that we were not about to depart, he cocked his leg and peed against the same tree that the director was in the process of measuring and upon which our discussion was centred.

Hara was a splendid animal, battle scarred, and always gentle and affectionate. Unfortunately, his physical splendour was seasonally marred by an enlarged scrotum, brought about by mango fly which favoured the tender tissue of Hara's testicles as a site to lay its eggs. Because the eggs developed into maggots I had to squeeze them out daily, which Hara didn't mind, but a landscape of scars and holes remained. It was not a pleasant picture.

City guests usually uttered cries of disgust on learning the reason for his big balls. And, when I mentioned the best antiseptic was vodka, no more would be drunk that evening.

In the face of such genteel sensibilities, Hara was not the kind of dog that would win a prize at Crufts. His fur was patchy and streaked, his legs grazed, and an enormous scar across his nose after a fight with a monitor lizard did not enhance his looks. But I loved him dearly and although not good-looking he had masses of character. All the workers loved him too, principally because he did not slobber over them or lick them, and in the early morning would go around the rubber hoping that the odd tapper would throw him a handful of rice or a dry biscuit.

177

However, at this particular moment Hara was not popular with either the director or the agent. Both uttered cries of abhorrence. Hara, come here, I cried. Disgusting, shouted the director. What a foul beast, uttered the agent. No discipline, said the director. What kind of dog is he, sniped the agent. Hara gazed into the distance, looking for something to chase, totally unconcerned at the furore he had caused.

There was silence, I poked the ground with my stick, and the director did the same. I wondered what was passing through his mind. I glanced sideways at the agent, who was looking at the tree canopies overhead.

These trees have got root disease, he cried; look at the leaves, they are turning yellow. Oh, ho, cried the director. A position had emerged from which I could be slapped down. They looked around. My God, they said, root disease is rampant. Indeed, a slight yellowing was evident. The director started to dig around the base of a tree with his walking stick. Both bent down to look for the telltale signs of the disease. They dug a little deeper. A penknife was produced; the agent knelt on the ground in his long trousers. Bits of earth were tossed upward. This activity attracted Hara, who wandered over to see what all the excitement was about, pushed his wet panting nose into the small hole and then started to scrape away the earth as dogs enjoy doing. Clods went flying, left, right and centre. They sprayed the director, who was concentrating on his digging. A wet dirty muzzle slobbered against the agent's white shirt. Pull the bloody dog away, he cried. I pulled Hara away from the tree.

They got up. There it is, they exclaimed excitedly, a diseased root. I looked down. Perfectly healthy, I replied. Look at the leaves, they exalted. I breathed deeply, I think it may have slipped your minds, I said, that rubber, being a deciduous tree sheds its leaves annually. It is now the very beginning of autumn. Leaf fall is about to start, hence the slight yellowing.

Silence. Oh, how they hated me at this moment. The agent got off his knees; the director brushed away bits of earth. Nobody said anything. Shall we go and have lunch, I asked.

We departed to the bungalow. I prayed Abu had cooked something special. He had, prawns. I cannot eat prawns, said the director, I come out in a rash. Fortunately, there were other dishes he did like. After a few beers the director mellowed and the afternoon passed more convivially than the morning. However, I longed for them to go. Eventually they got up and their driver was called.

You must get a grip of the estate, Bryant, said the director. Yes, you must, said the agent. I saw much too much weed in the interrows, said the director. Good tapping though. I am pleased you read the circulars. Just trying you out, you know, wanted to see how you young planters are managing. A limp hand was offered. The agent realizing how the wind was blowing, muttered a few non-committal comments under his breath. Saw some lalang (a noxious weed) in field 19, should remove it, he harrumphed. You didn't, I replied. We went nowhere near field 19. A look of puce sourness returned. That was not very diplomatic of me, I thought. Oh well, they can always send me to Borneo again.

37

Elephants And Robert

Robert's visits became more frequent as he collared a number of elephants in the jungle near New Rompin, which was not far from Welch.

On one occasion, as one of the transmitters was only operating intermittently, Robert decided to track the elephants by foot and change the transmitter. I got a plane and we landed at a small airstrip not far from where the elephants' last position had been fixed. We then entered the jungle. Robert and his rangers, uncannily, soon located the herd. Although the jungle was lowland and therefore difficult to penetrate, a swathe left by the moving herd was easily followed and soon we caught up with them as they lumbered slowly along, foraging from the luxuriant vegetation.

Robert did not want to disturb them unduly. First he had to identify the elephant with the collar, then stun the beast with a dart, remove the transmitter from the collar and replace it with a new one.

We followed the family closely, peering at the animals through the dense foliage. Eventually they ambled into a small clearing. This was Robert's chance. He waited gun in hand, with a dart inserted. Suddenly there was a tremendous commotion; it sounded as if an express train was charging towards us. I dived behind the closest tree as the noise rushed past us. I thought my time was up and that the family of elephants was charging.

After a few minutes I looked up to see Robert and the head ranger standing in the middle of the clearing. It's all right, he said, it was only a herd of wild pig that we disturbed.

The elephants, fortunately, were not too agitated and Robert quickly took aim and fired his gun. The herd trumpeted in annoyance and set off into the jungle. We followed. It wasn't long before we

Robert tying on a radio transmitter

caught up with the elephants, one of which was wobbling unsteadily on his legs as if blown by a stiff breeze. It then began to descend slowly to its knees, toppling gently on its side as it came to rest on the jungle floor.

Robert and the rangers rushed into action and started unscrewing the collar. The amount of drug needed to anaesthetize an elephant depended on the guesstimated size and weight of the animal. Robert always erred to the least necessary, as he was concerned about how much antidote should be injected to wake the elephant up after attaching the collar. Tragic consequences can occur if too much antidote is applied.

The elephant, meanwhile, was not sleeping heavily. Although

immobilized he was still awake, and Robert noticed an eye opening. Cover the eye, he ordered. So I pulled out my grimy handkerchief and put it over the eye. The elephant blinked, and the handkerchief fell off. Hold it over his eye, sit on it, keep it firmly in place, he commanded. A new transmitter was being screwed to the collar. It worked; the familiar beep was heard on a portable hand receiver he had brought along.

Robert then administered the antidote and after a while the elephant drunkenly got to its feet, took his bearings and ambled off after the rest of the herd. We followed in order to ensure there were no side effects from the antidote.

After a while the elephant stopped by a stream and, realizing that he was being followed, turned around to confront us. Robert was taking photos but wanted some close-ups, so he asked if I would use his other camera while he took up a different position.

I moved slowly closer. The elephant did not like what he saw and advanced towards me, trumpeting loudly. At this stage, he probably also had a sore head from the effect of the antidote, and was annoyed and felt threatened. I retreated. Robert called, don't drop the camera, seemingly little concerned about what happened to me.

The elephant, realizing that I was no threat, turned about and shambled off into the jungle to find his loved ones. I backed up to where the rangers were watching and sitting on their haunches smoking, completely unconcerned but mildly amused by my nervous antics. Robert was also sitting down, playing with his portable receiver, from which regular beeps were now clearly heard.

You nearly dropped my camera, he said. And I was nearly trampled upon by an angry elephant, I retorted. Don't be ridiculous, the animal was young and only intent upon showing us how brave he was by demonstrating threateningly. He meant no harm. You mustn't be so noisy, Robert continued, they get frightened most easily.

By early evening we were back at the airstrip and took off to get an exact fix of the elephant's position. He was easy to find and after circling above the forest pinpointing his movement, we headed back to Segamat, the closest airstrip to Welch.

Robert was also learning to fly and when with me he often took

182

control of the aeroplane. All he needed was to get a licence; he really didn't require any instruction.

As there was a little daylight left he asked if he could do some take-offs and landings. I agreed, and we changed seats, which was against the rules, but he was hardly a novice.

His take-offs and landings were good and he suggested that the next morning we should find the elephant and then do some more landings and take-offs on our way back. There was also another strip at Gemas, which was extremely short and used only in emergencies. He wanted to land there as well. I agreed, but said I would have to be in the left-hand seat.

Next morning we set off, and after finding the elephant and making sure the transmitter was working satisfactorily we departed for Gemas. Although the approach was easy, its length meant there was no room for error. However, we landed safely and managed to stop short of the rough at the end. After another couple of circuits we changed seats and left for Segamat.

It was a lovely morning, ideal for flying. Robert took control as we approached Segamat airfield. Height and airspeed were correct, but on approach I noticed from the 'windsock' that there was a gusty crosswind blowing. This was not unusual for early mornings. We touched down too heavily, with a skew-off bump, so I pushed on power and immediately went round again. I then landed the plane.

Unbeknown to us, sitting in the small pavilion which served as a waiting room were a team from the Civil Aviation Authority, who had chosen this particular day to inspect the airstrip at Segamat. Out of the pavilion stalked a Sikh gentleman. Good morning, he said. I greeted him in return. Who is the captain of this plane, he asked. Me, I replied. Who landed the plane, he queried. Me, said Robert. No, me, said I. Well who, he asked. I was in control, I said. Oh no, exclaimed Robert, trying to take the blame, the bad landing was my fault.

I realized the Sikh gentleman, however courteous, was not on a casual visit to Segamat. I asked the reason for his questions. CAA, he replied. Who was sitting in the left-hand seat, he asked. Me, said Robert. Oh Lord, that's torn it, I thought. Do you have a licence? Only a provisional, Robert replied proudly.

The Sikh turned to me. Commanding the plane from the right-hand seat is against the rules unless you are an instructor or hold a commercial licence. You must know that, he said. Good heavens, I answered, we were only practising take-offs and landings, no harm has been done. But it is against aviation law, surely you read NOTAMS, queried the Sikh. All the time, I replied. Then you know the rules, he retorted.

Look, I said, going on the offensive, I bet you have broken rules when flying, everybody does, minor ones. Yes, of course I have broken rules, on many occasions. Well then, that's that, I said. No it isn't, he replied. Sitting in the pavilion are another two officials from the CAA and they also watched the aborted landing and take-off. They also have broken rules while flying in the past, we all have, but you have been seen breaking the rules by all three of us. That is the difference. He stalked off. Robert was apologetic. I was annoyed because Robert had been trying to be helpful and this now would cost me my flying licence. I would be grounded for at least three months.

When a licence is about to be suspended a hearing has to be convened before the Flying Committee. I was duly summoned to Kuala Lumpur.

The chairman, a Chinese Squadron Leader, went through the issue quickly. What did I have to say in mitigation, he asked. I replied, nothing, it was my mistake. Then you are suspended from flying for four months, this being your first offence.

Why not three months, I said. After all, I am sure you don't consider this a big issue. It's very minor stuff. Oh I know, replied the squadron leader chairman, but the problem is that you were seen. I suggest that next time when you pay little attention to the rules, you do so when there are not three CAA officials looking on. Good evening gentlemen.

I was not pleased. Robert was suitably apologetic. I told Mr Tan what had happened, and he said very bad luck, he would get his mother to look at her cards to see what could be done. Fortunately, it was the beginning of the cricket season so there was plenty to look forward to. But I missed the flying and four months was a long time. However, suspension from one club didn't mean you couldn't fly elsewhere. There was no stamp in my logbook; I just could not take out a KL club plane.

Thus one weekend I decided to go to Singapore and stay with the Hultons and do some flying from there. I called up the Singapore Flying Club and was told I would have to be checked out first before going off on my own.

It was very pleasant staying with the Hultons and we ate delicious but expensive Chinese food. Not as good as at Mr Tan's, but different and more exotic, better suited to the more discerning palates of Singaporean Chinese.

Singapore was changing dramatically. New highways were being built, and shopping centres to attract tourists were springing up throughout the City State. The old drinking havens of Bugis Street and Colyer Quay were being tarted up, the old character lost for ever. The only places seemingly untouched were the Singapore Cricket Club, the law courts, theatre and cathedral. A different breed of members now inhabited the Cricket Club. Smartness was in; casual wear was discouraged. Somerset Maugham wouldn't have liked it.

On Sunday morning I took a taxi to the Flying Club. It had moved to Seletar – temporarily, I was told. I had booked a plane, so on arrival I went to the instructors' office to find someone to check me out. I was allocated an Australian female instructor who had a commercial licence but no work; she was desperate to find employment. Unfortunately, there was a surfeit of pilots in Australia, and it was becoming a highly competitive career in Southeast Asia. She did not like instructing and also did not like small planes. She found them horribly fragile and vulnerable but needed the salary she was paid as a professional instructor.

A Piper Cherokee 150 had been allocated for me to use. I was not completely familiar with this make of plane, although I knew it required more runway to take off from, having a low wing base compared to a Cessna.

I did the checks and we got in. Clearance was given and we lined up for take-off. There was little activity, except over Changi, so after taking off I veered off to the right and over the City State.

She was not relaxed at all and spent all her time peering behind, left and right. I asked what was wrong but was told in no uncertain fashion to concentrate on my flying.

We were now over the straits separating the island of Singapore from Johore Bahru. We had arranged to fly into Malaysian airspace and do some short strips landings at Mersing and then at Labis Estate.

Neither was far away and we soon reached Mersing town. The strip was below us, by the sea. Having passed overhead, I lost height and approached downwind, and then lined up to land. Aren't you too high, she asked. No, I always approach at this height because of the sea breezes, which can be tricky; allows me more height to play around with. What speed are the winds usually, she asked. No idea, I replied, but by the feel of the plane, fifteen to twenty knots.

Silence. Have you made enough allowance for the wind, she asked. Should be all right, I said; I was beginning to wonder who was checking who. You're coming in too fast, she responded. Put your nose up. Why no flaps? I only put on five to ten degree flaps in these windy conditions, I said. She shuffled in her seat, not at ease. You are too fast, raise the nose more, and apply flaps now. We bumped about in the turbulence. Christ, what are you doing, she cried. You said put on more flaps, which I have done. Power, put on power. Abort. Go around again – no, let's go to Labis instead.

I turned to her. Mersing is an easy strip, I have done it three times before. The only problem is the wind from the sea and today is calm compared to other days. No, you were too high, with too much speed, go to Labis. So off we trundled to Labis, where the strip was long and grassy. We landed safely and I taxied over to the wooden shack that served as a pick-up point. We got out and she wandered around smoking a cigarette. She was hardly the kind of instructor I was used to.

We took off again and started back to Singapore. Cloud had begun to thicken and there was rain about. A squall hit the plane, rocking it. She looked out. Which way are we coming in, she asked. Over the missiles, I said, it's the only way I know. Oh God, not over the missiles, we will be grounded. They won't fire them, much too expensive at half a million a pop, and anyway they would miss us at this height, I replied jokingly. We were now 1,500 feet downwind and descending. I joined the circuit and then made sure the landing was my very best. It was, and I taxied up to the club pleased with myself.

That was the most dangerous flight I have ever had, she said. I was flabbergasted. What are you talking about, I asked. At Mersing you made every mistake possible; at Labis your approach was too low, and taking-off you just missed the factory. And now you have

186

just flown over the missile base. Who the hell taught you to fly, she demanded. The RAF, I replied. Silence. Who? she queried. I was taught to fly by RAF personnel seconded to the Malaysian Air Force. The best, I said, the very best. She uttered an expletive. I continued, the problem with you, Brenda, you have no idea about how to fly cross-country in small planes, nor how to approach and land on small, rough air strips. I was thoroughly annoyed by now. I have been to Mersing three times, I know the strip. Labis is a doddle. I flew low over the Labis factory to let the manager know I was in the vicinity and would be dropping in for a beer later this evening. We always use the missile base as a marker for joining the circuit; if the Government doesn't like us using the base as a reference point, tell them to move the bloody missiles. As for you, learn to fly cross-country in small planes. I got out of the plane and stomped off. And park the plane yourself if you can, I shouted back.

I went to the club and signed in. I needed a beer desperately; I called the bar boy as I filled in my logbook. I have never been spoken to like that before, she said, having entered the clubhouse. I turned around and so did everybody else; I suggest you never try to instruct at the Royal Selangor Flying Club, you would be laughed out of the business. If you think I am dangerous then go and fly with some of the other pilots up there. I am considered a rabbit compared to them.

I finished my beer, got up and left. That was the last time I ever went to the Singapore Flying Club. They were happy to see me leave.

I returned to Welch, stopping off at various estates along the way. What a waste of time, I thought. Bugger Robert for his honesty. Oh well, I will just have to serve my sentence and trust that I can get lots of flying in once my suspension is lifted.

38

The Staff Strike

During the early 1960s the National Union of Plantation Workers caused the estates considerable problems and disrupted the generally harmonious relationship between management and workers. However, once an agreement had been reached all workers benefited considerably, particularly in terms of wage increases, hours of employment, and accommodation. Nonetheless, there was a price to pay, for to accommodate the higher wages and increased capital expenditure of housing it was necessary for management to reduce costs. Worker numbers were cut and mechanization was adopted whenever possible. Contractors were now carrying out work performed previously by resident permanent labour. Thus by the early 1970s most estates had cut costs to a bare minimum and at the same time had managed to improve efficiency.

Workers were generally happy with their new terms and conditions on the estates, which had improved out of all recognition, especially accommodation. On all H&C estates house building programmes were initiated and soon all workers were being provided with semi-detached bungalow units. A general air of stability reigned throughout.

Whereas the NUPW were instrumental in improving the working conditions of their members, the Junior Staff Union had been asleep over the past twenty years. Now with a more vigorous and belligerent leadership, the Staff Union began to flex its muscles. There were many anomalies that had to be ironed out. For example, some oil palm harvesters were making more money than the staff. A new agreement was urgently needed.

Although it was generally agreed that estate staff salaries and benefits had long been left behind compared to those of other industries, it was also necessary that the employers and the union sit down and work out a package acceptable to both sides.

Unfortunately, the union leadership comprised a team of young hotheads, all Indians, mainly Tamils, who had no idea of the protocol involved and whose only desire was to cause the employers as much trouble as they could. There was an excellent case for improving all aspects of staff employment, but it had to be negotiated sensibly and without rancour, and preferably not by a bunch of upstarts.

The negotiations did not go well and a series of walkouts, usually locally organized, were instigated, and these eventually culminated in a nationwide strike of all junior staff members. Most staff were not happy about leaving their posts, but had no option. On Welch all the staff apologetically returned to their homes to await the outcome of the negotiations, and instructions from their union.

As managers were well aware of what was going to happen, most had prepared themselves prior to the staff walkout. Managers, assistants and the foremen took over the positions vacated by the staff. On Welch, Balan, who was the assistant then, took over all bookkeeping duties in the office. Ratna, the check roll clerk, took over the duties of storeman. The *mandors* were seconded into more elevated positions than they had hitherto experienced. Welch continued as before.

Throughout the country the impact of the strike was hardly felt, except in the factories where the proportion of staff to workers was much higher than in the field. Fortunately, engineers melted into those positions previously occupied by the staff and most factories continued to operate.

Union headquarters soon realized that generally the strike was a failure and a newfound pragmatism replaced the previous belligerent approach.

After a few days the strike was called off, but some managers had not heard officially what the next step concerning staff re-employment was to be.

On Welch, I delayed taking the staff back because they were represented by a particularly nasty, officious, local union representative. As much as I liked them, I explained, I had to get confirmation from H&C first. Of course H&C did not know anything and I was told to follow local procedures. Which were, nobody knew. The union representative came to my office angrily demanding that I permit the staff to return to work. Of course, I replied, but I have received no official document stating that the employers have agreed that the staff should return to work. There was uproar. We want our jobs back, they cried. Then I must get official confirmation first, I answered. Balan and I were quite content with the way things had gone; also I had paid the *mandors* extra for their increased workload. The union representative was livid and I made it known he had very much aggravated the situation by his belligerence.

It was not long before a telephone call from H&C came through. Whatever was I doing, the agent Bill Croggan asked. Nothing, absolutely nothing I said, just waiting for you lot to let me know when I should re-engage the staff. Oh, he said, I thought it was obvious the strike was over. Not officially, I countered. Well, most managers in the company have now re-engaged their staff, he replied. Why not you? Nobody down here has re-engaged yet, I answered, we are all waiting for official confirmation that the strike is over. Surely we should not be following religiously what the staff union demand of us, without reference to our employers' representatives. We are only playing by the rules.

How extraordinary, said Bill. What is extraordinary, I enquired. Why, for the first time ever, you lot have decided to follow the rules. The line went dead; he had hung up.

39

Leave

Contracts had now been reduced to eighteen months only, at the end of which we were allowed six weeks' leave. This allowed continuity on the estate, with an assistant, usually, requested to take over when the manager departed. The acting circuit thus became a thing of the past.

The disadvantage of six weeks' leave was that it always went too quickly and one seemed to be continually travelling.

For my leave in 1973 I decided to go to Kashmir and ski. Few ever went to the Himalayas to ski, facilities being minimal and travelling there difficult. Tourism in Srinagar had developed over the years centred around houseboats on the lake, carpet making, intricately carved wooden artifacts and metal work, and, of course, hiking holidays in the mountains. There was no religious animosity then between the Indian and the Muslim populations.

I stayed one night in Srinagar and then went to find the agent responsible for the Gulmarg resort. He inhabited an upstairs room above a carpet-making establishment. It was intriguing watching the young boys weaving their elaborate patterns so skilfully and deftly.

The agent had received my letter and booked me into Nadu's hotel at Gulmarg. There was, I think, only this one hotel, but the agent happily promoted the area as a ski resort of the future. I asked how one got there, as it was far away in the mountains. Too far to walk, he joked. All I had to do was to catch a bus to a rendezvous point in the foothills, then take the transport that the hotel would be providing.

I left immediately and went to the bus station and found a dilapidated bus, which was indeed going in that direction. The journey seemed to take for ever, probably an hour or two only, then the conductor told me I should get off. I looked out of the window; there was just snow, mountains and forest, no sign of life. I got off the bus and tramped across the road to a small track that had been opened up by a snowplough. I presumed this would be the pick-up point.

As the sun was out I did not feel too cold, but I imagined in a few hours the temperatures would drop dramatically. I had warm clothing but it was hardly suitable for outdoors at night in the Himalayas. I wondered what to do next. Was I expected to walk up the track? To where? Possibly it was not even the right track. Just as I was beginning to entertain the idea that this was not the right place anyway, I heard the sound of a vehicle coming towards me, and rattling down the track was a tractor-trailer with a snow blade attached. It drew to a slippery halt on seeing me and the driver got off and asked if I was the guest coming to Nadu's. I affirmed that I was. My bag was slung into the trailer and I was asked to sit on the bench which had been fixed to the trailer sides.

Up we went, higher and higher, and although the track had been cleared initially by a snowplough, the driver still had to use his blade wherever the snow had slipped in from the drifting sides. It was a long haul up to Gulmarg and by late afternoon I felt very cold.

The hotel was a low, long building made of wood. Inside, it was beautifully warm and comfortable. The owner, a delightful middle-aged Indian gentleman, welcomed me with a hot toddy from the bar. We chatted amicably as I unfroze and he told me that I was the only guest for the moment but a further six were on their way from Hong Kong and an Indian film crew were arriving later in the week to film a sequence of action shots for a movie. Demand from the Indian public for such movies was ceaseless; once one was completed another was started.

After a delicious curry I went to bed and in the morning hired some ski equipment and went out to survey the scene.

Such beauty could not be surpassed, I thought. The sun glittered on the mountain peaks that stretched far into the distance, 18,000 feet to the left, 21,000 feet to the right. Forest-clad hillsides and sparkling white snow. It was captivating and awe-inspiring, never had I seen such grandeur.

I trudged over to the ski lifts. Are they working, I asked. Oh yes, a nodding head asserted. The ski slope went vertically downhill and an army of labourers were beating down the snow to provide a run. Good morning, came a voice behind me. An army colonel, judging by his insignia, had approached. Are you staying, he asked. Yes indeed, I replied. Are you? He pointed to a number of cabins dotted about the hillsides used by Indian Army officers as holiday rest and recuperation hostelries. We chatted and then skied down the one slope. It did not take long to reach the bottom. We then held onto the ski rope and were pulled back up. I wondered if this was going to be sufficiently exhilarating for my two-week stay. However, there were alternatives, the Colonel explained, which included a 32-kilometre run down to Srinagar, then a hike back. The Indian Army does it as a training exercise, he explained.

It sounded like fun, except for the tramp back, but no doubt I could hire a snowplough to give me a lift back to the hotel.

I was awoken next morning. Time, sahib; time, please sahib, time. I got out of bed and opened the door. A bearer was outside. Army waiting, he said. I had forgotten we were going skiing so early in the morning. I dressed quickly and found the Colonel in the dining room finishing his porridge. We have to walk at first, then we just ski down to Srinagar, he told me. I hoped the walking was not going to be a long march.

After breakfast my boots and skis were handed to an army batman and off we tramped through the snow. Fortunately, a track had been well trodden by the advancing skiers, providing easy access as we wound our way upward.

It was a glorious morning and as the sun rose we started to shed our clothing until all I was wearing was my shirt and my father's old mess jacket. My anorak, scarf and jersey were deposited into the arms of the accompanying porters, who were perspiring freely behind us as they laboured uphill.

After every one and half hours of marching we stopped for a rest, and on a charcoal brazier, kept alight and carried by a porter, tea was brewed and handed around. After the refreshment we continued our journey; higher and higher we trudged.

At midday we stopped for lunch, naan bread and mutton. One could not help feeling intoxicated by the grandeur and quiet stillness of the mountainside. The only movement was a breeze and the moving clouds above. Nobody chattered; we all seemed in awe of our surroundings, as if in a cathedral; the solemnity and tranquillity embracing us all. We watched, waited and thought our own thoughts, without intrusion.

A sergeant barked orders and we fitted on our skis. Instructions were issued and the first wave set off, followed by the second, with the Colonel and myself last. Bringing up the rear were the batmen and the porters, who seemed to manage, without fuss, to drape and tie all the gear around them and ski effortlessly at the same time.

The snow was deep powder so I was thankful that I could follow the tracks as we sped downhill. Turns were difficult, but gradually I managed to remember instructions from years past. It was exhilarating. Through forest, contouring mountainsides, on and on; down steep slopes, rounding rocky outcrops, through entangled copses of trees. All the time downward.

The Colonel was a better skier than me, being in continual practice. His legs didn't ache like mine, nor his back, but the full enjoyment of skiing without human obstacles hindering our descent, ensured an uninhibited freedom which the organized skiing of Europe could never match.

By mid-afternoon, the slopes' incline lessened and eventually we drew up in a sheltered valley where a number of wooden cabins showed life, with smoke rising from their chimneys.

The army skiers milled around. We sat down to take off our boots. My feet were trembling pieces of white flesh. Hot tea was brought round. I drank eagerly, tired but content, and sat on a rough chair breathing in the cold but soft air.

A snowplough had been organized to take us back to Gulmarg. Most of the skiers were continuing downhill and with shouts and whoops they resumed their journey.

We arrived back at the hotel at night. It had been a long return journey, although not as long as the downhill run. The manager eagerly awaited us and we dragged ourselves into the bar, where hot toddy was served. The Hong Kong contingent had also arrived and were enjoying the wood fire and drinking whisky with lemon.

There were a couple of pretty girls who worked as secretaries in the Colony, obviously spoilt by the abundance of eligible European men, although disappointed that so many of them had Chinese girlfriends. They were reasonably pleasant young ladies, spoilt and arrogant but good company in a vibrant, demanding manner. So unlike their Chinese counterparts.

The other group was a young family, the father on contract to an engineering firm. They were keen skiers and I wondered how they would enjoy the one ski lift.

The next day featured the arrival of the film team, which livened up the hotel considerably and filled all the rooms. Also present was an Australian 'hot dog skier', Ted, who toured the world showing off his acrobatic skills whenever there was demand. At Gulmag there was no demand for his skills but he had just come from Darjeeling, where the resorts were more developed and he had helped out at a ski school.

He was great fun and was staying at a small hostel down the valley, which was cheap although not very clean, and so he came up to Nadu's every day to eat and drink.

The film crew, which included a very glamorous leading lady, were to stay for a week. The actress's boyfriend, also an actor, was coming midweek. Both Ted and I made a beeline for the star, but she was waiting, although it appeared to us with a definite lack of enthusiasm, for the arrival of her actor boyfriend.

Chess was played most evenings, especially by the Indian Army contingent, who arrived nightly for drinks, food, conversation and a game. I was, therefore, extremely pleased when one day the actress asked if I would teach her to play, much to Ted's chagrin.

Unfortunately nothing eventuated from our evening sessions, to my disappointment, particularly as her boyfriend, when he eventually arrived, turned out to be a weedy young man with pimples, although I understood him to be an excellent actor. However, the subsequent filming was of great interest to watch. Ted had already been asked to perform in some of the skiing scenes, as he was the best skier around. Then by accident the villain, who could ski, while the hero couldn't, suffered a badly sprained ankle and was only just able to hobble about.

The producer was frantic. Who could fill in and perform the skiing shots? The army would not release any of their soldiers unless paid an exorbitant sum. Also the resident ski instructors wanted more than the producer could afford to pay; the two stars, being well known, commanded huge fees.

Hesitantly the producer's eyes lighted upon me. Would I play the villain during the skiing scenes? Of course, I agreed. How much, he asked. For my bar bills only, I proposed. He was delighted; all was not lost and filming recommenced immediately.

My part was simple. I had to ski down the mountain slope to the villain, who was waiting below to perform the close-up acting parts. I would then stand off camera to await the next skiing take.

Ted was the hero and his accommodation was upgraded to Nadu's, one of the bedrooms being immediately vacated by a hapless lesser-known actor. He didn't deserve a room anyway, pronounced the director. Ted was happy and I was thoroughly enjoying myself. My part was completed in a day and a half and for the rest of the time I milled around with the rest of the filming contingent. The actress sang, pouted, danced and fought her way through the scenes. It was hard work, morning to dusk. After filming we all raced for the bar, which was soon crowded with actors, Ted, me, three or four army officers and the Hong Kong contingent.

Time passed much too quickly. It was one of the most enjoyable holidays I had ever had and certainly the most memorable. For one could not fail to be impressed by the grandeur of the Himalayas and Nadu's oasis of hospitality in the wilderness.

I reluctantly packed my bags and went to pay my bill. The film crew had also just left, having kindly settled my bar account before departure. I said farewell to the staff and went to the manager's office. Are you going back to England, he asked. I replied in the affirmative. Could you do me a favour, he queried, I am going to England at the start of the horse racing season, but owing to foreign exchange restrictions in India it is difficult to change rupees into foreign currencies. Would it be possible for you pay your bill with a cheque in pounds sterling that I can then credit to my account in London? I confirmed I would be most happy to oblige. How much, I queried. He was making odd calculations and then crossing them out. The total amount for the fortnight will be £45, he said. I hope it isn't too much. Indeed it was very little.

Arriving at Srinagar airport I noticed the Colonel standing around.

196

We chattered and I mentioned how much I had enjoyed my stay. Marvellous hotel, he said; then commented, it was built, you know, by Nadu himself. They say, he whispered, he goes each year to England to bet on the horses. Very good at it, I understand.

The film *Yesterday, Today and Tomorrow* was a success. I went to the cinema at Segamat to see whether my skiing part had been erased by the director or was still in. The film was very long; I waited with bated breath. Yes, I was in the film, a few glimpses only. I told the Welch staff. They went to the film en masse but were disappointed that my appearance was so brief and that they couldn't really distinguish me from anybody else. For me it was a thrill, for them a minor disappointment. It was a pity I was not more visible, they said, especially as they had told all their friends and relations that their manager had a lead role.

At least the local cinemas appeared to have benefited from my presence on the big screen, even though it was for barely a minute.

The remainder of my leave was spent in the UK. I travelled up to Ardmore on the northwest coast of Scotland and stayed with the adventurer John Ridgeway, who I knew. He asked me to help out on a course as one of his permanent instructors had an emergency at home to attend to. I loved the wild country, and the daily trekking, sailing and orienteering, helped to improve my fitness. I would have liked to stay on, but I had to return to London. My leave was disappearing too quickly.

I left and drove south. As I wanted to visit a friend at Hereford I had to journey cross-country. Motorway construction was still in its infancy and except for the M1, major road construction was ongoing rather than completed. Fortunately, though, traffic throughout the country was not heavy except around the major cities. Outside the urban areas, although the roads were narrow, there was little congestion and driving in the open country was still pleasant and unpolluted when compared today.

I arrived outside Hereford in the evening. My friend, who had been in the Malayan Field Force during the 1960s, lived in a beautiful old mill, ramshackle but cosy. He was in his late thirties, and although he had lots of girlfriends, was not really the marrying type; his soldiering had probably precluded a long-term relationship.

It was a thoroughly enjoyable evening. Some other friends joined us and we stayed up until early morning. I wanted to be away at first light so after a couple of hours of sleep, started my drive home.

I now had only a few days left of my leave, so I drove on to my parents' house in Kent. They were a little greyer, although my father was still active and very fit, always gardening in his spare time, which he enjoyed. Because of the garden's size, extra help was continually needed, especially for grass cutting; this seemed to be a never-ending chore during the summer. Gardens so often become a burden for the elderly to maintain and both my brother and I knew that at some stage our parents would not be able to cope, even when extra help was employed.

40

I Return to Welch

On my return, the estate appeared to be in better condition than prior to my departure. I was superfluous to requirements. It seemed Welch ran like clockwork without me.

I enjoyed estate life; the workers were generally content and the staff had settled back into their daily routines, although there had been changes to their working hours. In the past, most staff seldom worked to a time schedule; they carried out their duties until such time as they were completed, whenever that might be. Now there were fixed hours, but as Welch was a small estate, it was easy to arrange their working habits to fit into the hours laid down in the agreement. However, as time went on, the field staff soon reverted to their previous timetables, which although longer, they could adapt to the needs of the day.

Planting was not a job but a vocation. It was therefore very difficult to make an estate function well on an hourly routine basis. Similar to farming, hours of work were difficult to assess and count. You cannot stop milking a cow once started. Likewise a conductor could not just discontinue measuring a tapper's latex, should his hours for the day be completed. Flexibility was essential and most staff realized that an eight-hour working day was not realistic, while a programmed eight hours within a day was. Thus the regulation number of hours, initially agreed upon, soon got lost in the labyrinth of activities that were performed daily on an estate. Staff input schedules could no longer be followed if the estate was to work satisfactorily. At the same time the manager had to make allowances for his staff, ensuring that their daily inputs could be performed with a reasonable degree of flexibility, but were also fair.

Of course, on some estates staff union members stuck rigidly to the agreement. Which meant new staff had to be recruited to fill in the gaps once a staff member had returned home after his eight hours. Thus causing considerable inconvenience.

On Welch such problems did not exist, and life continued as before, although the burden of increased salaries and allowances meant that estate expenditure had to be scrutinized even more rigorously to ensure profitability. None of us wanted to return to those days when estates were sold and management and staff laid off.

We had now developed quite a skilful football team. I enjoyed playing very much, usually at centre forward because I could head the ball. I certainly was not very skilful but would hustle and bustle in front of the opposition's goal – which they generally found disconcerting – particularly when playing against another estate team. Because of my position they would be reluctant to tackle too hard or foul me, wondering always what retribution would be heaped upon them if I was kicked or tackled over-zealously. Referees seldom had control of the game and repeated fouling was prevalent throughout the eighty minutes.

We played in a league and most of our opponents were teams made up from the various branches of the civil service, for example the police, the public works department, health and others.

Jementah town had a team as well and the game between Welch and Jementah was a spectacle that the local population very much looked forward to, especially as Welch was all Malay except me, and Jemantah primarily Chinese. However, it was generally played in good spirit and there was always much betting on who was going to win.

Mr Tan cheered on Jementah and then me, in turn, and at half-time one could hear the rasping hoarseness of his tongue as he exhorted the town team to greater efforts. Then I knew his money was on Jementah, which spurred us on. The games were hard fought as both teams were evenly matched.

Once, when an obvious goal by Jementah was disallowed, having supposedly been scored from an offside position, the town supporters erupted with unconcealed anger. How could the referee adjudge the goal to be from an offside position when he was still ambling about at the opposite end of the pitch? And the linesmen, who consisted of an adolescent who spent most of the time chatting with his friends or eyeing up the girls, and an old man who could hardly walk let alone run, were nowhere in the vicinity of where the purported offside took place. Jementah felt hard done by and it was only Mr Tan and other town worthies who managed to calm down their supporters.

The game finished a draw; we were happy but not particularly pleased with our efforts. Some of our team who had worked a full day in the field were also now quite tired after their exertions. It was bad luck that after a hard day's work digging drains or harvesting oil palm fruit, they had to play a game of competitive football.

Some estate football teams were almost professional, the team members being allocated plenty of practice time. On Welch this was impossible as we were not sufficiently large to be able to hide a contingent of players in easy jobs. We just had to make do with the player resources on site.

Gradually we moulded a better team. My position was now in jeopardy as it was abundantly clear to most that my scoring capabilities had become eroded with time. And whereas once upon a time a manager or assistant playing in a team would throw the opposition into confusion and doubt, just by their presence, this no longer applied. Those days were going, if not gone, and instead the opposition would very often target any senior staff member playing, who soon felt the over keen robustness of their tackling whenever an opportunity arose. I was no longer an asset; the picture was fading fast.

Too rapidly, for when a team was about to be picked to play a local estate, Tangkah, managed at the time by Ken Wallis, the Welch captain and vice captain came to my office and standing embarrassedly presented the team list to me. My name was not included. I felt quite put out, but realized that the centre forward who was replacing me was indeed probably much better. Perhaps I had hoped that I would be at fullback, but no, I had been excluded.

I watched the game. I was not missed. We won quite easily and the team was jubilant, for Tangkah was considered a much stronger team than Welch. Perhaps my game playing days were drawing to a close; I was now thirty-four years old, which was hardly old, but I was no longer in my prime.

* * *

The thought of pursuing more sedentary pursuits filled me with gloom. Even flying had lessened considerably as Robert had now obtained his flying licence and no longer required another pilot alongside.

At the same time, the flying club committee was now discussing at length new rules concerning flying for monetary gain by pilots not holding a commercial licence. The days of carrying out 'odd jobs' were over, as I knew very well the committee hoped to be able to acquire for themselves those jobs that I and pilots like myself had performed in the past.

The club's easy-going ambience was also changing. Nearly all the RAF pilots had gone, leaving behind a residue of RAF maintenance staff only. Also some of the local older RMAF pilots had disappeared from the scene, having been elevated upward to more exalted positions.

A new breed had taken over the club, expatriates and local. Checkouts had become more rigorous; cross-country flight plans were scrutinized more thoroughly, new flying rules were introduced. Red tape, unnecessary rules, checks, instructors not agreeing to a flight plan because the strip was too short or bumpy, or the grass too long, or principally because they did not like short strip landings themselves, all this dampened my enthusiasm.

Flying was losing its fun and I did less and less, and only when Julia arrived on the scene did it become enjoyable again.

41

Brightman's

It was during a cricket match while I was bowling and Murray Milne umpiring that the idea of starting an exclusive society of hand-picked friends was first mooted. By my fifth over we had mulled over membership procedures, rules (very few), venues and how many times a week or month or year we were to meet.

The most important theme which ran through our mutterings was how to limit membership to those persons we both actually liked, and that only the two of us would be able to choose who could become a member. In other words, if I liked Joe Bloggs and Murray did not, then Joe Bloggs, however much he pleaded to join our select group, could not become a Brightman. Although the aim was to admit, initially, those only from the planting fraternity, anybody could apply, and once word had got round, this would include ladies as well. We had no intention of Brightman's just being a male preserve. There were many female lawyers, media personnel, models and executives who would easily meet the selection criteria, whatever they were, and gain admission.

I stopped bowling, and in order to concentrate on our earth-shaking musings I went to field in the outfield, for by now it was a foregone conclusion that the game was as good as won and I wanted to tie up Brightman's constitution as quickly as possible.

I wrote up the memorandum of membership later that evening and owing to its importance, sent a bearer with the documents for Murray's appraisal and comments. We were all set to open the most exclusive club in Asia.

Of course nobody had ever heard of Brightman's, so the most important next step was to spread the word to promote the society, hoping people would start enquiring who was Brightman's, have you heard, etc. We expected to hear the name soon on everybody's lips.

It would be untrue to give the impression that there was a sudden rush of interest with people clamouring for membership. There was indeed initial interest, usually from the more undesirable elements of planter society who hated the thought of being left out of anything.

As time went by we gradually were able to select a coterie of persons who fulfilled our selection criteria. Sam Gaythorne Hardy and Grace, his wife, were included in the first batch. Robert also. Pat Baskett another. Faridah, a KL lawyer, was our first solo lady member, followed closely by Isobel Tan, a clever, attractive Chinese high-powered media executive.

We had to be careful that the floodgates were not opened too wide, thereby permitting an influx of undesirable types from entering.

A meeting of all members was convened and we met at the bar of the Equatorial Hotel, which was one of the first of KL's modern hotels to be built. The purpose was firstly to enjoy ourselves and then explain the purpose of Brightman's and the reason for its exclusiveness. All of which hinged upon its members being the cream of society, who would at some stage reach the top of their chosen profession. Of course, we had to make sure that an appropriate clause was built into the constitution, which would then allow us to evict anybody whose behavioural standards fell by the wayside, or who could no longer be regarded as the 'cream'.

The evening was a resounding success and we agreed to meet monthly. A new society/club was born, which at all times would remain under Murray's and my control.

Membership became international when Tom and Sue Hulton from Singapore became members; Dicky Doyle from Papua New Guinea, who owned a cocoa estate in New Britain, also joined. The privileges of overseas membership, we hoped, would become universally sought after.

Dicky was an Australian who periodically visited Malaysia to keep abreast with the crops' agronomic practices. He usually stayed with a fellow Australian, Denis Pager, who sadly died while managing an oil palm scheme in West Kalimantan, up river, living on a houseboat, surrounded by Dayaks, the indigenous headhunters.

Both were good fun, although Denis used to occasionally suffer from fits of depression and then would spout the whole of the

Rubaiyat of Omar Khayyam off by heart and without a pause. He lived a lonely existence on an isolated plantation and, being a naturally gregarious individual, found the imposed 'splendid isolation', as he called it, not easy to cope with.

Dicky was equally affable and would quaff huge quantities of beer, which seemed to do him no harm, except that he would become totally disorientated. Once when dancing at the Penang Club he relieved himself on a potted plant that inhabited a corner of the dance hall, not realizing that he had yet to reach the toilet. Having peed and buttoned himself up, he wandered back to our table and continued as if nothing untoward had happened. The band needless to say did not miss a beat.

Robert invited most of Brightman's to his birthday party, which was to be held in one of KL's smartest hotels. A room was reserved, but knowing Robert's parlous financial status, I wondered how he was going to pay. Probably everybody else was also curious as to how he was going settle the bill when it arrived.

The party was a great success, the food was delicious and there was plenty of drink. Towards 11 p.m. some of us thought of going on to a club before returning to our estates. The bill had to be paid and Robert was also eager to leave for another venue. As we waited for the girls to exit from the ladies', the bill arrived and was given to Robert. He opened it and blanched. We carried on conversing, unconcerned, and slowly wended our way out of the room and into the hotel's main hall. We stood around nonchantly, a gathering of happy people together, waiting for the ladies, relaxed.

There was a small cough behind us; I have a small problem, said Robert. Silence; another embarrassed cough from him. The bill is a little larger than expected, in fact much larger; the situation is a little complicated, if you understand what I mean. No, we haven't a clue what you are getting at, said Sam with a stutter. A pause. I am afraid I have no money, said Robert. Well, not enough. How much do you have, enquired Faridah. Only forty ringgit. I didn't realize that the cost would be one hundred and eighty, pleaded Robert. Surely you realized a party of this size would be expensive, certainly more than forty, I exclaimed. Oh, I realized it could be, but I hoped it wouldn't be, he replied. So now you know it is, what happens next, I asked. Well, if I could borrow the balance, it would be quite helpful. I will pay it back of course. Of course. Of course, everybody chanted, knowing full well that reimbursement could take a long time, if ever.

Robert looked thoroughly unhappy. It was his birthday, after all. Of course we would pay. The money was handed over to the head waiter, who was hovering nearby, knowing that a party like this always necessitated everybody paying up. He wasn't concerned, he had seen such happenings many times before.

The party broke up and we departed, Robert still looking embarrassed. Virginia, a model, looked concerned, wondering how he would ever be able to afford to pay back such an amount. But of course he didn't and nobody ever mentioned it again.

Brightman's went from strength to strength, and the membership, including wives, rose to forty-three. Amongst the members were a bevy of attractive lawyers and businesswomen and media executives; Faridah was the first to join, Naomi another, Ratna, Isobel Tan, all educated overseas, mainly in the UK. They brought not only a touch of Asian femininity and fun to the gatherings, but also a soft gentleness which smoothed over our occasional outbursts of rude behaviour; they were a good influence upon us.

At the same time they championed the emerging advancement of women's rights and the desire for social equality, which in any Asian society was difficult to achieve as male domination was embedded so firmly in the culture of the country and therefore difficult to disrupt.

Many educated women, such as they, certainly had no wish to lose their femininity and allure, but at the same time energetically campaigned for the betterment of the uneducated and the poor, insisting that a woman's life should not just forever be that of beast of burden, especially amongst the rural communities.

Of course, women's advancement took a step backward when Islamic fundamentalism started to penetrate throughout the Muslim communities of Malaysia. Although initially moderate in dogma, it soon placed pressure upon both women and men to change their attitudes concerning all aspects of life. Sexual apartheid became the norm in some eastern states of the country where Islam was followed more devoutly than in the more progressive States, for example, Perak and Selangor.

The genteel codes of behaviour adopted over the centuries by the Islamic communities soon dissolved as the more strident dogma of fundamentalism, so often misinterpreted, usurped the current less forbidding and popular modern persuasion. Although never promoted as objectionably as Christianity in the fourteenth and fifteenth centuries, it became all-pervasive. It appealed particularly to the ill educated among the urban and rural poor, who had gained very little from the social and commercial progress made since Independence.

Just as the familiar codes of behaviour, so equable and friendly, became eroded under the imposition of stricter rules of worship, dress and habits, the people's natural goodwill, grace and genius, the fun and jollity that had permeated all strata of society, slowly disappeared as new laws were enforced. Happy countenances gave way to unsmiling masked faces of dourness. Out went colour, in came dowdiness, unfamiliar, unnatural but now, unhappily, widespread.

I was once asked to express an opinion on what was the greatest threat to stability in Southeast Asia. At that stage (1966) communism was regarded throughout the Western world, and those countries which were affiliated to the Western approach to business and government, as the principal antagonist to a Western-inclined way of life. For this reason I repeated the usual dogma that communism was the major threat.

I was also influenced by the huge strides that Russia was making in trying to penetrate the Malaysian business and commercial world by introducing at discounted prices tractors, ploughs, lathes and heavy equipment. There were also Russian fairs showing off their latest consumer goods, and circuses toured the country providing high-class entertainment, quite opposite in quality to any of their engineering products on show.

It appeared to some that such commercial expansion could be a prelude to the more sinister promotion of their own form of hard left-wing socialism. However, as it turned out, my so-called interpretation was quite wrong and the real concern was the march of Islam, the sleeping giant of all religions, which was gradually awakening. Communism was given another twenty years before its creed ran its course and thereafter was of no consequence. It was a youthful religion and could not compete with either Islam or Christianity in the long run.

To many it was difficult to comprehend how this new strict code of Islam, which had created no new surprises or enterprises, was responsible for no new ideas, thoughts or knowledge, should be the product of a religion which once upon a time dominated the world of science, mathematics, architecture and art. And upon which so much of our own modern world has been based.

The fact that some far-sighted experts could see beyond communism's demise to the advent of a new religious dogma was all the more riveting. Particularly as the perpetrator of fundamentalism, Ayatollah Khomeini, remained lying in wait in Paris; while in Iran, where it was all about to happen, the Shah was still in residence, enjoying a lifestyle quite out of keeping with the faith to which he belonged.

It is difficult to understand how a change of emphasis in a belief could so effectively shatter the world's peace and stability.

Brightman's also eventually became a victim of Islam, as Malays no longer felt that they should be members of a club created by infidels for pleasure and fun only, their new religious masters having now outlawed both.

Murray and I, the founding fathers, also departed from the scene, I (with Julia) to the Solomon Islands and Murray to Australia. It continued but half-heartedly, and became even more depleted as other members left the country for pastures new; including Robert, who returned to Kenya with his glamorous Sri Lankan wife, to immerse himself in other animal conservation schemes.

However, in the 1970s it flourished and the last member to join was Julia, my wife.

42

Julia

Jimmy Gilbert, the visiting agent, asked in his usual inimitable way when was I going to marry. I hadn't given it a great deal of thought as I was fairly content with the way of life I was leading and enjoying the company of an attractive female accountant.

I liked being on Welch although it could be sometimes boring. However, I could have left as I had been offered Giram Estate, which I had declined as it would not have been the most scintillating place to live as a bachelor.

Because I had turned down Giram, Jimmy thought that my decision would not have done my planting career prospects much good. Refusing an obvious promotion would be looked upon by the gnomes of KL as a distinct rebuff; being a bachelor was of no consequence to them.

Probably, in hindsight, I should have gone, for during my next leave I met my future wife, whose companionship would have alleviated any possible loneliness.

But at that stage marriage had not entered the equation and I was very much enjoying life. Then along came an Indian fortuneteller who walked into Welch to ply his trade. All Asians love having their fortunes told and soon all the staff had their palms read and their future life recited. The Indian soothsayer then latched on to me. I was not at all keen on having my privacy intruded upon by a semi-naked fakir and told him to leave the estate and not hang around any further. He paid no heed and was obviously determined to divine my future; for me the price would be ten ringgit, double that paid by the staff. In return, as he explained, I would get a typewritten document with all aspects of my past, current and future life written in bold print, while the highlights and conclusions of his observations would be printed in italics. Whereupon he introduced

Reading my fortune on Welch

me to his ancient typewriter, which he had placed on the veranda and to demonstrate its virtuosity and accuracy, he slowly and methodically, with years of experienced dexterity, typed my name, date of birth, favourite colour and which precious stone I liked the most.

I was still firmly against any further commitment but unless I was overtly offensive, I realized that he was not going to take no for an answer.

So I succumbed, and he set about reading my palm while I watched and listened, and replied or commented upon his many queries. It was, I admit, fascinating, but equally absorbing was a large dewdrop stuck to the tip of his nose, which wobbled but refused to drop. I had always associated dewdrops with cold climates rather than the tropics. However, there it was suspended, immobile, and ready to drop. Watching it, I wondered which palm line it would splash onto.

The divining took much longer than I had originally supposed. I was now becoming impatient, and sitting cross-legged on the veranda floor was not at all comfortable. Eventually he stopped. I will write it up for you, he said. I got up and told him to carry on and walked down to the office.

It was teatime when I returned. Abu brought the tea and then enquired whether the soothsayer should also be served tea. I said, of course, and continued reading my post and newspaper.

By 6 p.m. it was finished. The document was complete. He asked if he should remain and explain it to me. No, that would not be necessary, I said. I handed over the ten ringgit and after numerous salaams he departed into the evening dusk.

The document was well typed and grammatically correct. Much of what he had written was worthless verbiage, most of which he had gleaned from me. However, he mentioned other things as well, which included that I was soon going to marry.

The woman who was described would very closely resemble Julia, and that we would have three children, and all the other bits and pieces of information which come with palmistry. I read it all, intrigued. Could it possibly be true? Then on the last page I realized that it might be, for smudged on the final paragraph was a small damp mark. The dewdrop had fallen, a moist stamp to seal approval.

Immediately after Jimmy's one-day visit, now reduced to three-quarters of a day because he wanted to go and play golf and I had more or less written up the report anyway, including his appraisal remarks, Hamdan drove me up to KL to catch the flight to the UK. I was going on leave.

Subang airport was a scrum. Although I had a full-fare ticket and BA had arranged a sort of business class section on their planes, it was no more comfortable than economy class, except that one got on and off a little quicker.

BA in those days had not been privatized, and although having excellent routes the airline was let down by a casual and indifferent in-flight service. On the plane I was asked to fill in a questionnaire, the final question being why did I fly BA, which I answered in two parts. One, I had little option, two, the service was so desultory I could sleep throughout the journey without ever being disturbed by a steward.

We stopped at Calcutta and Rome. It was a long flight, and there were no films, so one slept and read and hoped that a drink would be served sometime.

I stayed initially at Pamela Salem's flat in Nevern Square. She was currently in a TV series and also working on a film with Sean Connery. I then went by train to visit my parents, where once again nothing seemed to have changed.

While at home, a good friend called Harry phoned up and asked me to come and stay at his parents' country house. I hesitated, then agreed as he sounded excited about something.

The purpose of his invitation was not just to renew acquaintance, but to gain advice on how to court a girl he had become very much infatuated with; a girl he had met in London, who enjoyed the same kind of music, art and theatre that he did. Harry didn't actually talk about being madly in love but certainly their relationship, if you could call it that, was more than a mere passing fancy, certainly from his point of view. Would it be possible to jolly this girl along into his clutches, he asked. He would be very grateful if I would present him in the most attractive way so that the scales of indifference would fall from her eyes and she would fall madly in love with him.

Harry was organizing a play reading at his flat in London. Would I come? Of course, I agreed, intrigued with what was going to unfold.

I arrived at his flat quite late; everybody was there, including Julia, whom I was supposed to jolly along in Harry's favour. Julia was slim with deep blue eyes and was very pretty. She was serious, but when she smiled it was enough to whet one's appetite for more. Probably the party was not quite to her liking as play-reading can be quite a tedious form of entertainment. But I thoroughly enjoyed it, and another attractive young lady, also invited, the daughter of an H&C director, was amusing company.

Eats and drinks were served and by midnight everybody was exhausted and began to depart. I had hardly said anything to Julia, who certainly never gave the impression that she found anybody remotely attractive, least of all my friend.

In order to get the process going I asked if she could give me a lift to Nevern Square. No, she said abruptly. Chelsea Bridge, I asked, brightly. No, she said. Could you drop me off at the tube station? No she couldn't.

Harry, thinking that we were absorbed in some deep meaningful conversation about him, sidled over as she was putting on her coat and I was getting ready for a long walk back to Nevern Square. Did you know, asked Harry, that Robin plays the clarinet and wants lessons. There was a flicker of interest. Oh, yes, I said. How much do you charge? She looked me up and down. Five pounds for half an hour, she replied. That seemed a bit steep and I wondered if this could be included in my Harry's matchmaking expense account. However, it would be nice to have some lessons from such a pretty person.

The lessons were not a success; Julia lived in a house in Brixton inhabited by a very musical crowd whose idea of fun was not listening to me playing scales. Still, I enjoyed the visits, although jollying her along into Harry's arms had now been forgotten.

Harry, however, was persistent and suggested we all fly down to the West Country for lunch. This was agreed as Julia lived in Cornwall, and the idea of flying to Land's End seemed a very agreeable plan.

I hired a plane from Biggin Hill airport and we set off for Devon. I had not prepared the flight very well and, having lost my map, brought along an AA road map. Unfortunately the road map was very old and neither Heathrow nor Gatwick were marked. Luckily I had been checked out at Gatwick the previous week and the fourth member of our party, Simon Michel, fortunately knew which direction Devon happened to be.

It was a bad start for I lined up for take-off on the wrong runway. I was asked by the control tower, hadn't I read NOTAMS. Oh yes, I replied, very sorry. They let us go and we took off for the West. Turn right, said Simon, and then straight.

Flying in controlled airspace was certainly a new and different experience from landing on short strips in the jungle. There was a continual cackle over the radio, giving flight levels, QNH readings and stacks of other information. Suddenly, I was asked what my routing was, which owing to the fact that I had had a late night and was without a map did not make the question easy to answer.

However, noticing that I was overhead a roundabout and that it appeared to be full of traffic, Simon thought we were not far from Reading. This information was relayed to control, who then requested us to call again overhead Newbury. Newbury, Newbury, Harry exclaimed excitedly. I know a really nice little pub at Newbury. Let's drop in for lunch. Everybody thought this was a good idea, so I told control I was going to land at Newbury, to which they replied we were now clear to Land's End.

My experience of flying in England was wafer-thin and I have to admit that I had no idea where Newbury happened to be, and only once had I been west of Taunton. As far as I was concerned I was passing over virgin soil. There it is, shouted Harry. There is what, I asked. Newbury racecourse, he cried. I told control that indeed I was routed for Land's End but via Newbury. Roger, they answered.

I descended and landed on the racecourse. We left the plane and trudged off in search of the pub. Harry had now forgotten its whereabouts but it did not matter, for there were plenty of others and we had an enjoyable lunch. Nobody seemed to care whether we went to Land's End or not, but as it was getting late I suggested either we continue now, hoping to arrive before nightfall, or return the way we came.

Harry, who was a good cook, suggested we return to Biggin Hill and he would cook us all dinner. So our trip to the far west of England was aborted and we took off, just missing the main spectator stand. Air traffic controllers were a lot less fussy than they are nowadays and I managed to get flight approval to return to Biggin Hill. Probably they were thankful that there would soon be one less plane in the sky to deal with.

Simon flew the plane back. Harry tried to cosy up to Julia in the rear seat, who steadfastly looked out of the window.

At Biggin Hill we joined the circuit and were number eight to land. Our approach and landing had to be up to scratch as there were another four planes behind.

We landed without a hitch. Harry by now had given up trying to cosy up to Julia and was asking what we would like for dinner. I folded up my road map and put in my pocket.

After parking the plane we got out and walked over to the club. Were you the unidentified plane flying in Heathrow airspace, the club's chief instructor asked me. Absolutely not, we were well clear, I replied. Oh well, it must have been someone else, he said, because apparently a light plane was off course and was coasting along on the fringes of Heathrow. Couldn't have been us, I replied, as we had no exchanges with London control except when taking off from Newbury and landing here.

I signed off and we said our goodbyes. Oh, by the way, the instructor added, I found your map in my office, you must have left it behind last time you were here. I was wondering what you were using today. Got a spare one, have you? We left without answering, hoping he would question us no further.

We got into Harry's car; I sat in the back with Julia. This is much nicer, I thought, than trudging around the skies navigating with a pre-war AA road map.

43

Back On Welch

I had a few more clarinet lessons and then it was time for me to return to Welch. I suggested to Julia that if she had nothing else better to do she could always spend Christmas in Malaysia. She would think about it, she replied.

I arrived on Welch to find the estate in excellent condition. Everybody was pleased to see me back, only in so much that I had become a permanent fixture, whether on or off, and Malays, being very conservative people, did not like change.

Similarly, after returning from previous leaves, I found the estate hardly needed my presence. However, I still enjoyed the daily rambles through the rubber, especially in springtime when the sweet perfume of the rubber flowers proclaimed the arrival of the new leaf flushes. It was the best time of the year to be on a rubber plantation and I never got bored walking down the long avenues of trees stretching upward and swaying inward, resembling a cathedral's nave, cool, high and domed.

Hara thrived. He was middle-aged now but never missed his daily routine visits to the field. He often went to early morning muster, and lay in front of the small field office, panting furiously, while the staff called out the names of the workers. He would then slope off into the field, following his favourite workers or *mandor*, going from one gang to another until such time as I would arrive on the scene. To find out where he had gone, all I had to ask was in which direction he was travelling. Eventually I always caught up with him sitting near a group of tappers or field workers taking a mid morning rest.

Nobody minded Hara, he never licked anybody or disturbed them by barks or growls or a snuffling nose, which many found repugnant. He always kept outside the circle, never within, and always minded his own business, never seeking attention, which a Malay would be reluctant to supply even if he should want to.

Have you seen Hara, I ask one morning. He has gone to field nine, probably he will be in Abdullah's task, I am told. I walk to Abdullah's task. Is Hara around, I ask. Oh, yes, but he left half an hour ago, he should be with Abu Mansoor now.

Sure enough, Hara is found lying down a few yards away from Abu Mansoor. Occasionally a handful of rice is thrown to him, which he gobbles up. Abu, my cook, feeds him well, but Hara seems perpetually hungry and when he goes whoring for maybe three or four days, or in search of monkeys, he returns thin and exhausted. On seeing me, he gets up and with a lolling tongue walks over to the Land Rover and jumps into the back. He steadies himself as I drive away.

Brunch is served at about 9.30 a.m. By the time I arrive Abu has prepared the table and I sit down to bacon and eggs or whatever he has cooked. Kippers are my favourite, but they can only be found in Kuala Lumpur or Singapore. I provide Abu with meagre funds to play with, so visitors or friends never regard his cooking as the ultimate experience in haute cuisine, the only exception being when I have a party and satay is prepared, the best in the district. Abu is certainly capable of cooking to the highest standard if the ingredients are available.

I throw Hara some bacon rinds, which he swallows. He sits in a heap waiting, his scrotum large and distended; the mango fly season is with us and the tell-tale signs of feasting maggots can be seen.

After breakfast I drive down to the office. Hara enters, and slumps in a corner on his back, his legs erect against the wall. A curious but cool position that many large dogs adopt.

Raffiah has opened the estate mail; there is nothing from head office, which is satisfactory. There is, however, amongst the pile, a letter from Julia. I tear it open. If the invitation is still on offer I would very much like to come to Welch over Christmas, it reads. Good. I reply immediately and tell her to let me know dates and times.

As I write, Mr Tan arrives and I tell him a young English lady

217

is coming out for Christmas. He is suitably impressed as he thinks that everybody should marry at an early age and have dozens of children. I beg to differ, but it is of no consequence, as he has come to extract money from me and not to chat about marriage. He is working on a huge neighbouring planting scheme and is doing all the felling and clearing work. The costs are enormous and it requires considerable financial resources for a contractor to keep a fleet of bulldozers and chainsaws operating day in, day out.

How much advance do you want, I ask. He says a figure. Impossible, I tell him. It is more than his current contract is worth. After half an hour of haggling, I write a cheque for him to cash, the amount being approximate to what the estate owes.

He is relieved and shows it. When you coming to Singapore, he asks. Have a good time before new wife arrives. I am not getting married, I interrupt him. Yes, yes he says, but soon. Come to Singapore, we find good-looking Chinese women, have a good time. There is a long pause; he looks over my head as if into the distance. Marriage, he says, very good but very, very expensive, especially to white women. All my friends say white women too expensive. Why not get Chinese? Chinese very nice, good cooks, take off your shoes, give you drink. Everything done for you. White women too bossy. Try Chinese. Try both, he urges. Much better have two wives, one fat European, one thin Chinese girl. Good cook, very important, and he pats his stomach.

Having imparted these words of wisdom, he gets up and shuffles towards the door. Anyway, come to Singapore, we will have good time before your new missus come. He departs with a throaty cackle and speeds off in his latest Mercedes Benz, full of good humour.

Who's the bird, Robert asks, while drinking beer on the veranda. Which bird, I ask. The one whose coming out at Christmas, he replies. How the hell do you know anybody is coming out for Christmas, I ask him. Everybody knows, I was at New Rompin Estate and it is common knowledge. I thought it was my sister at first, then I heard it was a clarinet teacher.

News in the tropics has few constraining influences. A sentence quoted becomes a story to be embellished, latched upon, regurgitated and amplified for a larger audience. Tittle-tattle, wives are happy

Waiting for Julia at Christmas on Welch Estate

to expound and digest. At last something new to gossip about. What will she be like, they ask themselves.

What's she like, asks Robert from beneath the foam of his beer. Tall, pretty, blue eyes, slim, I reply. Sounds all right, continues Robert. I wonder what she will think of Welch and the planters, Robert contemplates. A slight difference from teaching choral scholars at King's College, Cambridge, to conducting the Batu Enam singers (a musical group of planters started up by Ross Dixon's wife), Robert chuckles. Oh well, she should not have any trouble joining Brightman's.

I remain silent throughout Robert's monologue. He is quite right, teaching choral scholars is one thing, conducting the Batu Enam singers is something else altogether. Anyway, probably a few weeks on Welch will be enough and, London, its music scene, that haven of artistic talent, will never be absented from ever again.

The roar of a vehicle coming up the hill to the house interrupts our musings. Out jumps Duncan Blincoe and his lovely Danish wife Karen. What's this we hear, he cries. What's what, I ask. Oh, don't be so perverse, who's the bird we hear is joining you for Christmas? Robert smirks into his third beer. Abu treads softly into the room, his very large left toe flapping agitatedly on the floor. He awaits drinks orders. Hara yawns and licks his scrotum. Why don't you do something about that dog, asks Karen, he's revolting. What do you mean, I ask. Everything is now down to size and he is in excellent shape. Don't change the subject, Duncan commands.

Robert, who loves a gossip just as much as anybody, probably more, because he spends so much time in the jungle with his elephants and lacks news, now starts to regale everybody with the physical and mental attributes of Julia.

They eagerly listen. I help Abu with the drinks and tell him to prepare more food. This is going to be a long evening.

It is early morning before Duncan and Karen leave. Robert has long slouched off to bed, exhausted after the drink, food and jungle trekking. In which order I am not sure. I go to bed and sleep fitfully and then wake up. Hara has already gone to muster and I get in the Land Rover and drive down to the main office.

Early morning in the equatorial regions of the world is the most agreeable time to be up and about, so beautifully cool, misty and still. Night-time sounds of crickets and frogs can still be heard. I listen to the loudening activities in the distance, the muffled cries of workers talking and calling as they prepare to go to work.

The staff come into the office, bringing their muster chits showing which fields the labour are working in.

The sun glows faintly in the East, just peeping above the rubber. Another day has started. I wonder what can be better than this. Probably, teaching choral scholars at Kings.

44

Christmas

Air travel is still very expensive and Julia catches a charter flight which commences from Brussels. Unfortunately, owing to bad weather, the connecting flight from Heathrow is cancelled, thus necessitating all the passengers to flock down to Dover in order to catch a Channel Hovercraft and then a train to Brussels. Chaos reigns and the flight, needless to say, is delayed.

I meanwhile go to the airport to meet the plane at the appointed time. Of course there is no plane and no Julia. I stay in Kuala Lumpur for another day, and as telecommunications are so desultory I have no idea what is happening.

That evening I return to Welch. On the third day Julia telephones from Kuala Lumpur to say that she has arrived. Where are you, she demands. Here on Welch, I say. You are late.

Fortunately, a family has invited her to stay with them until I arrive, so Hamdan and I speed off back to Kuala Lumpur to meet her. After three days of travel she is tired and bedraggled. What a start to her holiday in Malaysia. But she soon settles down at Welch and sleeps late in the morning.

Christmas is fun, there are lots of parties, and everybody wants to meet the community's latest entry.

Mr Tan comes up to the estate to view my 'new acquisition' as he calls her; for him there is little difference between acquiring a wife and a car. He likes Julia and invites us down to his shop for Chinese *makan* (food), where all the other Jementah hierarchy turn up to view this new white woman who has suddenly arrived in their midst.

Time goes racing by and Julia's holiday is short. Her flight back is from Singapore and so I book a club plane and Robert flies it to Segamat, where his VW Combie meets him. We take off for Singapore. Our routing is via Johore Bahru and the missile base, but there are no complications this time. We stay in Singapore at Simon Michel's brother's house; he is Jardine's representative for Southeast Asia.

As Julia's flight is next evening we decide to fly to Mersing and have a swim. It is a beautiful day and the flight is not far. We land and leave the plane by the pick-up point. An elderly Malay agrees to guard it as little boys soon gather round to play; clambering over a plane when left unattended always provides an amusing diversion to their usual quiet and unhurried existence.

We walk to the sea through a paddy field and a fishing village. It is idyllic, the real Malaysia, unspoilt by encroaching urbanization and commercialism and their attendant problems.

We swim and then walk to a nearby village and eat fish and rice. Time goes quickly and by mid-afternoon we have to leave. The old Malay is still there in attendance. Little boys, wide eyed, play close by. I hand over some money to the old man and we prepare to leave.

It is a funny flight, for after taking off I set course due north instead of south. Is the sea supposed to be on our right or left, asks Julia. Left, I say. Then why is the sea on our right, she asks.

I turn 180 degrees and set course for Singapore. My father would not approve of your navigation skills, Julia comments. Can't you read a compass? As Julia's father and grandfather and great-great grandfather were all in the Royal Navy, they certainly wouldn't have approved of my flying north when I should have been going south.

After landing we hurry back to the 'Jardine house', where we change and Julia packs her bag. We have decided to eat at the Singapore Club and then go on to the airport.

We arrive at the club and settle down to dine. What time is your plane actually departing, I ask. It is leaving at 10 p.m., she replies. As the charter airline has recently become defunct, for some reason or other, she has been rebooked on Qantas.

Julia draws out her ticket from her handbag and inspects it: 2000 hours, she says. As I can see, it is indeed 2000 hours. Your plane departs in one hour's time; 2000 hours is not ten o'clock, it is eight o'clock. Surely as the daughter of a naval officer you should know that. Oh, my God, she cries, let's go. The food hasn't arrived and I tell the waiter I will be back. We rush out and grab a taxi. The airport in fifteen minutes, I say to the driver. Not possible, he replies, half an hour the earliest. Go, I say, as fast as you can.

We arrive at Changi airport breathless, the driver exhilarated by his own driving expertise and the speed of his old taxi car, a Hillman, which he compliments as being the best on the road.

We rush into the terminal and to the Qantas counter. I am afraid the gates are closed, say the airline counter staff. Well open them, I demand, the plane hasn't taken off yet, there is another fifteen minutes to go. That is quite impossible, they say. Julia is worried, she starts teaching the day after tomorrow.

Can we use this ticket on another airline, I ask. The clerk looks at the ticket. You can try, she says. We rush over to the BA counter. Julia takes command. I have just missed the Qantas flight because we got lost over Malaysia in our little plane and have now just arrived. Please, please, can you help, I have to get back to the UK to start work.

They are sympathetic and impressed. Tickets in those days could readily be endorsed with another airline, but Julia's ex-charter flight ticket is not so easily endorsable. However, the staff are kind and phone up Qantas, who now appear less tetchy. They agree; Julia is relieved. Let's go and have something to eat, I say. We go up to the restaurant and eat ravenously a mix of Chinese dishes, synthetic, typical airport food.

It is not long before BA calls up their passengers and we go to the departure gate. I express the hope that Julia will return; she seems doubtful, but thanks me for a wonderful holiday. She goes through the gates. I leave the airport for the Singapore Club to pay for our aborted meal.

45

Marriage

Julia agrees to marry me and although my feeling is that the tiny Chinese Anglican chapel in Jementah is sufficient, she has other ideas and insists we marry at Penberth, Cornwall, where her family have always lived.

I take a week off. H&C agrees that it may be deducted from my home leave and I depart on Aeroflot, via Moscow, that being the cheapest airline to travel on.

It is 1976, a beautiful May day, and Penberth could not have looked lovelier. An uncle of Julia's conducts the service and after a stand-up reception, instead of today's sit-down bun fights and discos, we depart for Dartmoor and a three-day honeymoon.

Julia has a lot of organizing to do, for having just started teaching at Eton College she has now to give in her notice, which is highly embarrassing.

Our return tickets are via Singapore. We stay a night at Raffles, now transformed into a luxury hotel. Then it was a rambling old building cooled by huge whirling ceiling fans.

Hamdan comes down to meet us and we drive into Malaysia and back up to Welch. It is a long journey but pleasant. The car's air conditioning is working, which is a relief for Julia.

We arrive early evening and find that we have a guest; it is Robert, slouched on the veranda, with a beer in his hand. He greets us and hands over his wedding present, a visitors' book, with his name already prominently entered on the first page. Very appropriate, we think, especially for our first night on Welch as a married couple.

Hara completes the family picture. He has risen from his snoring slumbers and brushes a moist muzzle against my hand and then saunters over to Julia, sniffs and retreats to his corner.

Abu and Salimah are delighted and thankful that a woman is now in residence, somebody whom they can confer with rather than me, and that the days of soft under-boiled eggs being thrown at them are over. Abu longs for more money so that he can exploit his repertoire of recipes, which to date has seldom been utilized.

We sit and talk. Robert has been staying at the bungalow, from his visitors' book entry, for the past two days and appears in no hurry to move out.

The evening is warm, although a breeze from Mount Ophir keeps the temperature pleasant. We drink gin and tonics, Robert a beer. Abu has cooked a delicious feast of fish and prawns. Our first day in Malaysia as a married couple draws to a close.

46

In Residence

When a woman takes over a bachelor household, changes soon follow. The first was the sudden absence of Abu and Salimah on Sundays.

I had never given much thought to the working hours of my house staff, for if I was at home I expected them to be there as well. When one was off for a day or days, they in turn could have time off.

There was no need for rules, nor times on or times off. There was no need to specify who did what, when or how. All that was necessary was a routine agreeable to both parties. Abu and Salimah's days off had always coincided with my own departures from the estate, and these were more than sufficient to keep them both happy.

But no, each had to be given a day off, Sunday. They are Muslims, why not Fridays? Everybody's staff has a day off every week, said Julia. But ours don't want a day off, they are very happy working and when I am away they can relax accordingly. This logic was lost. Neither Abu nor Salimah knew what to do on their day off. They just sat around outside looking thoroughly bored and unhappy. My Sundays were now disrupted, tea was absent at 7 a.m. and therefore I had to go and make my own or wait for Julia to get up. I had become used to everything being done for me, but the household worked as Julia admitted, like a four-star hotel, and in a happy state of mutual contentment.

Julia thought I was extremely spoilt, and when Pat Baskett, Robert and I were drinking by the swimming pool one weekend, she said light-heartedly how difficult it was to understand how we could behave so often like juvenile schoolboys but at the same time appear to have so much responsibility and authority. She had not come across this phenomenon before. It did not exist in the UK; how could it, the whole code and way of life was different.

It was necessary, said Robert, to be able to relax. Plantations were huge commercial assets, for which the planters were responsible and accountable. He was being nice, but it was true, and a comparison was sometimes made with industry in the Western world, organized and run by a team of managerial staff, while a plantation was managed by a planter, a couple of assistants and a bunch of junior staff, many of whom had worked up from the ranks with little to no formal education, and how well they had adapted to the responsibility.

It was a comparison much quoted by planters. For a planter was responsible for all agronomic aspects of the estate, its productivity, revenue and capital expenditure, processing and profitability, not forgetting the employment and control of hundreds of workers and their families, residing on and off the estate.

There were no labour-intensive industrial commodity crop plantations in the First World, so it was difficult to compare. However, without a doubt a manager of an estate had to be considerably more versatile than the manager of an industrial complex in Europe. There was also nowhere to hide when the chips were down and certainly nobody to blame except oneself when things went wrong. You were responsible and that was that.

How different to nowadays when nobody accepts blame should something go wrong. And, the premise that it is always somebody else's fault, never one's own, indicates how management is willing to deftly evade responsibility in times of crisis.

47

The Jungle

A visitor arrived one day. He was a friend of Robert's who had spent the last four years of his life trying to capture a rhinoceros in order to collar it and then track its movements. He had built a number of traps, as stunning rhinos could be physically harmful and was not recommended. One rhino had actually entered a trap but failed to trigger the rear door mechanism. He was a patient American and still hoped that one day he would be successful and have a collar tied onto a rhino. He was now going on leave.

We both listened intently to his stories and asked where the rhinos were meant to be. One area was behind Rompin Estate, a large tract of jungle which stretched to the east and was referred to as the Endau Forest Reserve. He showed us on one of his maps where the closest trap happened to be. We will go and have a look for you, I said. It's not far and there are plenty of tracks; better take a tracker from the village though, he advised.

We left one weekend and drove to the village, which he suggested was the best take-off point. There were no guides available at the time, but if we waited one would be found. We did not have time to wait. It could be days, as many of the villagers, who were aboriginals, had vanished into the jungle to follow their many hunting and gathering pursuits: a lifestyle that had been passed down from one generation to another.

Julia and I set off with compass in hand. It was a stiff climb and we stopped frequently to drink what little water we found, having deposited most of ours on the jungle floor as it was too weighty to carry. There were usually many jungle streams to drink from, but alas many of these had now dried up, for the country was experiencing an exceptional dry period.

I have always had a minimalistic approach to jungle survival, probably due to the influence of the survival lessons that I used to attend. Survival was simple; one could exist quite happily in the jungle with a pocketful of dried fish, some rice and the edible leaves of ferns, which generally grew prolifically throughout. However, the purpose of a weekend trip into the jungle with one's spouse was not to find out how much she, or we, could endure without food and water, but to enjoy ourselves and experience the wonders of the forest environment. We had enough food, but as we climbed up so our water supply diminished rapidly without being replenished. Luckily, the air became cooler and less humid the higher up we scrambled, resulting in open, pleasant conditions for walking. As the forest tree canopy became more impenetrable and dense, less ground vegetation hindered our progress beneath the towering trees and we almost felt as though we were walking in a giant parkland.

We walked briskly and found a track made by hunters and animals. Tiger spoors were seen, and also those of deer and wild boar. Eventually the tracks converged and then petered out. We continued on compass bearings, walking steadily along a ridge with a panoramic view of the jungle, which stretched into the far distance, a myriad of mixed greens, browns and dark yellows. Occasionally a Flame of the Forest was seen, or other flowering trees which provided dashes of red, yellow and orange at the same time blending exquisitely with the endless foliage greens which flowed far and wide as the breezes swept the horizon of canopies.

By late afternoon we realized that we must have taken a wrong path for we seemed to have been walking for hours without any tell-tale signs of the trap or camp.

Julia was fit and walked well. However, as evening approached it was obvious that it would be foolish to continue; a wrenched ankle or leg sprain would not be helpful.

We found a small flat terrace on the mountain side and unloaded our light rucksacks. Not far away was a tiny spring and we drank thirstily from it and filled our water bottles. We had a groundsheet, which we spread over the leaf-strewn earth and lay upon it, our backs propped up against our rucksacks. We watched the dusk approach, rising from the valley below and through the trees, embracing the landscape, and us, enforcing a stillness, a silence;

those few minutes in the tropics when nature briefly quietens. Even the wind, which had been rustling the leaves and billowing the canopies like sails at sea, turning the leaves inside and out as its turbulence swept through the forest, suddenly calmed, as though it had enough for the day and was satisfied with its efforts.

These brief moments of silence can be breathtaking, for it is almost as if the forest has stopped talking to itself. It is only momentary, for blackness soon settles in and the noises start again; different ones, louder, as though the trees and animals have become brave once more.

We sit and listen in the blackness. A few stars sparkle above, scuffing sounds nearby, probably a wild boar, followed by a snort, a hoot and a bark of deer, a plethora of noises which startle Julia, but do not disturb her. She is enjoying it as much as I am.

We have some sambal (a prawn paste), a little dried fish (*ikan billis*) and rice. We are not hungry but have to eat, though we do not need much. We drink from our water bottles, which I go and refill. The spring, I am sure, will be a popular meeting place for the animals during the night. Should we move? No, but I will light a fire to keep any marauding animal at a distance.

The evening passes slowly and comfortably. It grows chilly but that is refreshing. We both put on light jumpers and lie down. It is serenely tranquil.

Morning arrives. We both go over to the spring. There are numerous hoof and footmarks, but none of rhino or tiger. They have not come near us during the night.

After breakfast we decide to continue on another track, which we hope will lead us to the trap. We descend into a valley and then up the other side. Vegetation in the valley is much thicker than on the elevated terrain, but there are more discernible tracks to follow. We march on and stop for lunch by a small stream. Julia decides to lie in a pool to soak and rinse the sweat off her body. It is idyllic and she closes her eyes and slumbers. Do you think we will find the trap and his camp, she asks. I have a feeling not, I answer. Actually I have no idea where we are and it would be best to follow this stream downhill, as it is sure to lead us to a river. Where there is a river there is habitation.

We are both tired and it is late afternoon. Let's stay here, I say, and we can set off tomorrow morning. Will anybody miss us, asks Julia. I doubt it, I reply, a couple of nights away from home is hardly going to excite comment. But if we are lost, continues Julia, rather like Winnie the Pooh, won't anybody know that we are lost? It is very doubtful that anybody will know that we are lost because nobody actually knows where we are. And, if they don't know where we are, then how will they know we are lost, I tell her. Oh, I see, she murmurs, watching the scudding clouds flee across the sky. Of course if we are here long enough somebody will notice the Land Rover and perhaps enquire of our whereabouts, but I shouldn't worry because we are not really lost, we just have temporarily mislaid our position, I say.

It is a beautiful time of the day and we prepare to spend our second night in the jungle. I feel confident that as long as we follow the stream we will soon reach civilization. However, I am quite happy to be where we are for the moment.

The next morning we set off, walking slowly along tracks which meander through the trees and vegetation. We expect each hour to arrive at a river or settlement, but none appear and time becomes shorter, as it always does when you want it to be longer. We are both tired, Julia more than me, for walking in the jungle is new to her, but having been brought up on the cliffs of Cornwall she is very fit, even though London has recently reduced the muscle of her slim figure.

Then suddenly the scenery changes; the primary jungle gives way to secondary forest, in which a durian tree is seen and then an old, old rubber tree. We are not the first to have walked this track.

The descent is less steep and we see more durian trees, then a small grove of mangos, and at last a wisp of smoke ahead and a woman squatting, sifting rice in a wicker tray basket. We quicken our pace and walk towards her. She looks startled, but calmly surveys our entry into her life and continues her task.

Julia is relieved. I am as well but wonder where we are. I have a horrible feeling we are a long way from our Land Rover. The old lady calls a boy, who trots off and after a while returns with a youngish man in tow. He joins us by the fire and asks where we have come from. That is difficult to answer, because I do not know, but I tell him that we have left our Land Rover at a village close by Rompin Estate. That's very far, he says, you must have lost your way in the jungle. I ask where the nearest road is and whether or not I could find somebody to drive us round to find our vehicle.

He consults the old lady and after a while says yes, he can help. So Julia and I get up and follow him down the trail.

It is another hour before we reach a vehicle track, which we continue along. It is now nightfall and we have no lights to guide us; Julia and I trip and stumble step by step. Fortunately, we notice dots of light ahead, and sure enough a small village comes into view: houses, bicycles, a shop. We stop. Would you like a beer, I ask Julia. Oh yes, please, she cries. I go into the shop and ask for two beers and a Coca-Cola for our guide.

The owner, a Chinese man, is interested in our whereabouts and offers his son to take us to our parked Land Rover. He has an old car at the back of the shop we can use. We are very grateful, and after paying for our drinks set off in his car to find our vehicle.

At last, at last, after winding around hills, smallholdings and estate land we eventually come to the Land Rover. I did not think that I would ever see it again, says Julia. We have only been out three days and two nights, I answer. You can last thirty-two days without food in the jungle, I repeat. I actually don't want to survive thirty-two days without food, Julia retorts. Two days is enough.

I thank the driver and offer to pay him for his time and petrol. No, no, but sometime I hope we shall meet again, he replies in impeccable English. We had up to that point been conversing in Malay.

We are not satisfied with our trekking expedition as we had not found the trap or the American's camp, and a couple of months later I send Hamdan to arrange for a tracker to lead us there.

So, off we go again, this time with a tracker leading the way. It is so much easier following somebody who knows, rather than somebody who does not, comments Julia, as we march along.

Indeed, that is the case, and by mid-afternoon we approach a clearing deep in the jungle where an *attap*-roofed house is set amongst the trees. We offload our rucksacks and the guide then takes us further on to where the rhino trap, a stockade constructed with tree trunks, stands unused and uninhabited. It is operational,

Looking for rhinos in the jungle

one can see, and the tracker points to some animal footmarks at the threshold of the trap. I ask what if an animal is trapped; what happens next if there is nobody at the camp? He assuages our fears; there is always somebody who comes past, and if there should be a rhino inside, he comes to the village and phones the American or his associate. Nobody has much hope though; there are few rhinos and only brief glimpses are ever seen of these elusive animals.

We spend the night camped in the *attap* house, which has a raised bamboo sleeping platform. We are both awoken by sharp coughs.

233

The aboriginal tracker is fast asleep by the fire, undisturbed. The coughs can easily be heard coming from outside the camp surrounds.

In the morning we tell the tracker that we heard coughs during the night. Oh, that will be a tiger, there are plenty around. You have to keep your feet well inside the house or they may be nibbled. However, it could be a spirit of the forest, their sighs often sound like distant coughs, he explains.

We spend one more night at the camp. The tracker cooks a delicious meal of dried fish, rice, fern leaves and chillies crushed into a paste. The evening passes into night and we sleep early. Julia tucks her feet under her sarong; I lie awake listening to the sounds of the jungle. A wisp of smoke spirals upwards into the forest canopies. We are too high and chilly for mosquitoes to be a nuisance.

We will have to return tomorrow, which neither of us looks forward to, but we cannot go on looking for invisible rhinos; better they remain invisible, then they will never be caught or killed, for there are apparently only thirty left in this huge expanse of jungle.

I then wonder how does one know that there are only thirty rhinos when none are visible. Even the aboriginals, let alone the American and his trackers, hardly ever see them. How is such a figure extrapolated? Perhaps there are more; I hope so. Possibly less, though. Who knows? How does one count an invisible animal? Spoors, I suppose; spoors... I drift off to sleep.

Welch tomorrow, a VA's visit next week, cricket on Sunday. Unlike rhinos, all very real and visible.

48

Musical Adventures

Julia's musical adventures started with the Batu Enam singers. Each week we gathered, a group of us, to sing. Most of us found singing difficult; others, like Duncan Blincoe and Karen, were musical, and Ross also possessed a good voice.

At schools or when conducting choral works, Julia had never embraced such a motley group as ours. This was definitely a new experience for her to savour. And, to be conducted by a professional possibly aided those with ability, although certainly not the majority. However, her presence provided a new interest for us all.

It was enjoyable, and the fruits of our practising culminated in a Christmas concert at the Segamat Catholic Church, featuring us as a choral background to the Christmas service rather than a solo musical interlude. A performance which could have undermined the whole festive season.

Needless to say, Julia was hardly content with our weekly singing get-togethers and soon trotted off to Kuala Lumpur with Hamdan to find out was going on musically in the capital. She returned with a whole range of initiatives to explore, the most promising and demanding being to play at a British Council concert for resident musicians, local and expatriates, and to be an accompanist at the University of Malaya's musical production of *West Side Story*.

Unfortunately, it meant a lot of travelling, but necessary, 'to keep my tiny mind active', she explained.

She chose for the British Council concert a difficult clarinet piece, *Sonatina*, by Malcolm Arnold, which also necessitated finding a competent piano accompanist. Duncan Blincoe was recruited, but admitted that to get the piece up to scratch he would have to practise rather more assiduously than he was prepared to do, nor did he have the time. After some careful soul-searching he thought

235

it better Julia found someone else. As the piano accompanist for *West Side Story* was an extremely accomplished Chinese pianist, Julia asked him if he would accompany her. Soo Ghee looked at the music, found it not too demanding and agreed to perform with Julia.

The concert went very well. Julia and Soo Ghee received a tremendous ovation and we all went out for *makan* in the evening. The Blincoes came with us as well. Julia had quickly entered the musical scene.

West Side Story was also a success, containing a number of highly skilled performers. I watched the performance twice and could not help feeling that it was just as enjoyable and as professionally performed as the production I had seen on the stage in London.

Julia agreed that the performances were high-class and the leading roles were of an excellent standard. However, it was totally beyond her comprehension how the rehearsals could be so unprofessionally lax, offhand and unpunctual; the performers seemed to turn up at any hour during the evening. It was a director's and conductor's nightmare, but as most of the participants were Chinese, as was the conductor, nobody seemed to mind. It was all very relaxed. On the other hand, everybody seemed to peak at the right time, and Julia was happy to concede that although the build-up was fraught the end result was most satisfactory.

I still played my clarinet, badly. Julia tried to improve my playing, free of charge. Unfortunately, I was not receptive to her instruction, and she was pretty critical of my technique. Not the sound but the beat.

It all came to an end when she stopped me and said Mozart had not written the music at that speed. I replied that probably if he had thought about it, he would have. Julia did not find that at all amusing and complained that if that was my attitude, there was little she could do to help me further.

I was no longer enjoying playing, and squeaking jazzy solos from my veranda, with the moon peeping from behind Mount Ophir, was a thing of the past.

I gave up. Julia was disappointed, because I was, in her words, her only failure. This she found annoying, for like all music teachers she hated failures and thought I could have done a lot better had

I tried. However, as I pointed out to her, it was not me that had failed, it was the composers who never could get the beat quite right. Especially for musicians like me.

49

Dressing Up

Each year one of the major events of the social calendar, celebrated by Europeans and Malaysians alike, was Burns Night. All the Scots dressed up in their kilts, while the rest of us wore evening dress. On this day large pink planters were transformed into handsome, elegant and debonair toffs, and the ladies, how they dressed and groomed themselves so that even the plainest became desirable, especially as the champagne flowed and inhibitions were drowned in the extravagance of the night. Of course there were some who were already extremely attractive anyway. Doris Fraser in her dashing Highland outfit was always glamorous, so also were Karen Blincoe and Julia. Some wives were unrecognizable, having spent days dolling and tarting themselves up. And the men in their varied clan kilts, which had been hung out to dry to get rid of the mould stains and moths, also had concentrated many hours upon their appearance.

Julia and I were guests of the Dixons and so we attired ourselves in evening wear. The many Malaysians who came were equally resplendent in evening dress or in their national costume. It was a fun evening and continued until early morning when breakfast was served.

Most guests returned eventually to their own estates or houses. This contrasted to Burns Night celebrations held in Kuala Lumpur, when it was more than likely that you would find someone in your car whom you did not recognize and who wanted a lift anywhere, or somebody you did know but it wouldn't have been prudent to give a lift to, or somebody you would have very much liked to have taken away, but would have had your head chopped off in the process if you had.

On one previous Burns Night, a planter friend, as the revelries were drawing to a close, got in his car and set off for home. While driving along he looked into his rear mirror to see a slim hand emerge from the back seat, then a head that emitted a sigh of desire. Good heavens, thought my friend, what have we here, and drove ever faster home. Soon they arrived and a beautiful female emerged from the back seat. He offered her his arm and they walked into his house.

After his ablutions he got into bed to await the lovely lady, who in the early morning light joined him. She indeed was beautiful, he sighed, what luck. However, his luck soon turned to ashes, for the lovely lady turned out to be a man. There were no histrionics. He got up, dressed, called for his driver and told him to take this beautiful lady back to Kuala Lumpur.

The driver was mystified, for the lady was indeed very attractive, as only such men can be and drove her back to KL, she reclining languidly in the back. Probably her night out had been much more amusing than my friend's.

As the celebrations were a great mix of races and personages, it was not unusual to find oneself dancing with Malay film stars or celebrities. Sultans and their wives, sons and daughters, cousins plus entourage were invited and invariably stayed all night.

When young and single I and some other bachelors, guests of one Scottish planter, made a beeline for a couple of attractive *Ungkus* (princesses). However, it was difficult to get them away from the eagle eye of those chaperoning them.

As I was acting on Bagan Datoh Estate at the time, I suggested they came back with us for an early breakfast. When, they asked. Now, we all said. Can't, said they. Next week then. It was agreed. But would they, could they? Next week arrived and the week after. Then John Leach, the VA, drove up for his six-monthly visit. My mind had to concentrate on his visit.

On his last day as we were returning from the cocoa factory to the bungalow, we noticed under the house porch an old, elegant, beautifully polished Jaguar car with a driver lounging nearby. Upstairs were my Chinese amahs, twittering nervously, and reclining gracefully were the two *Ungkus* plus a brother and a hanger-on.

John Leach offered a hand, I also. What excellent taste and timing, said John Leach. Just as I am about to leave. What a pity. He seemed most put out.

He needn't have been, for they did not stay long having come to apologize for their absence two weeks earlier. Their brother asked hesitantly if I could loan him some cash, his father always kept him short of funds. As I was in a continual state of penury, I couldn't, I replied. He didn't seem to mind. Probably he thought it worth a try although unlikely to succeed. Planters, I explained, especially those employed by H&C, were always penniless. The prince sighed; he understood perfectly. H&C sounded rather like his father, both behaving miserly towards their children.

50

Waterfalls

The year 1976 was very dry in Malaysia, the rainy season hardly appeared and was generally intermittent. There was barely 1,000 millimetres of rain instead of 1,700. Not enough.

So we built a reservoir, to be fed by streams, firstly with the aid of Mr Tan, who completed a most extraordinary structure which was supposed to hold one million litres of water to be used in the factory. However, as the work was of such poor quality we knocked it down and built another using our own plans and labour.

Mandor Abang was in-charge of the construction work, which he and his workers performed meticulously. Mr Tan was not happy to see his reservoir plundered, but eventually realized that the subcontractor who had been in charge of the job was just a drunk and an imbecile and only interested in getting away with doing as little as possible for maximum return.

The reservoir was completed and Julia duly opened it. At the onset of the rains the reservoir soon filled and provided more than an adequate supply for the factory, workshop and some of the staff houses.

At the weekends, should there be no cricket or other pursuits, Julia and I would go off to a waterfall on the upper slopes of Mount Ophir, behind Tangkah Estate. A stream running down the mountainside fed an adjacent Dunlop estate. It was beautifully, clear and cold.

We would climb up above the natural catchment area nestling in the foot hills, past the waterfall, then further up where there were many crystal-clear rock pools in which we would lie half submerged as the stream cascaded around us, contentedly looking up into the green canopies above, listening to the daytime sounds and dreaming.

It was ideal, with the sunlight percolating through the forest canopy and glancing off the rushing water, the spray sparkling as it careered downhill from rock to rock. It was a magical location and although others swam in the lower pools of the stream, they seldom ventured up to the higher elevations, for it took an hour and a half to reach and was a scramble rather than a walk.

Abu would make a picnic for us, chapattis, curried chicken and prawns wrapped in banana leaves. We lugged up beer and a bottle of wine which we kept submerged in a pool, with any leftover drink hung from a branch of a tree away from prying animals and insects, to be drunk another day.

We stayed lounging about and reading, only starting our downward trek when daylight began to fade and the jungle noises changed from their usual shrill cacophony of mixed sounds to the more mellow chirping of crickets and night birds about to awake.

How quickly the light faded as we hurried down hill. And how soon the evening grey filtered up towards us, darkening the night sky to a charcoal blackness, which only the tropics can harmonize to the natural hue of a night-time sky.

An aboriginal once said, the blacker the sky the more stars to lighten the way. For me the blackness was overpowering and enveloping, especially as the stars had yet to lighten the sky and one could scarcely see a yard in front.

Evenings were barely a prelude to the long nights ahead, for daytime suddenly stopped as the sun settled below the horizon. Then a short break of half an hour would elapse before the fast fading evening light was extinguished as though a black sheet was being drawn across the sky. The sudden awakening of the stars gradually provided a speckled glimmer but insufficient to lighten one's way.

By the time the evening light had faded away we had generally managed to reach the Land Rover and throwing in our rucksacks, drove down the hill to the catchment area below, then through the rubber bordering the jungle and onto the main road.

The Blincoes lived at Tangkah and sometimes we stopped for an evening drink. Karen, a graphic designer, was tentatively looking for opportunities to exploit her talent in KL, but usually we drove straight back to Welch, where Abu would be awaiting our return. The crisis of days off had been resolved and normality had been restored; Abu and Salimah now took time off when we were not around.

51

The East Coast

A public holiday was about to come up so I suggested to Julia that we went for a trip to the east coast of Malaysia by plane. There was a small airstrip by the sea at Kuala Dungun where we could land and then spend a couple of nights on the beach.

She though it a lovely idea but hoped that I would prepare the flight efficiently, unlike before, and that I had suitable maps.

I had been fortunate, for when the RAF departed Malaysian shores I procured a set of maps that were used by RAF aircrews and were therefore comprehensive and up-to-date.

I phoned the club and booked a plane. Have I been checked out at Kuala Dungun, I was asked by the instructor on duty. Of course I have, I replied. I have flown frequently there. When was the last time, I was asked. Can't remember, look it up, I told him. Another busybody, always interfering. Silence. How many hours have you flown recently, he asked me. Enough, I replied; probably on many more jungle strips than you.

What about your recent landing at Carey Island, when the runway was out of bounds, my inquisitor continued. I knew this subject would eventually be raised, for I had landed at Carey Island when a drain was being dug across the width of the runway to release the water from the adjacent golf course.

Of course I had had no idea the drain was being dug and only found out as I was landing, when I noticed workers scurrying about and an excavator hurriedly retreating to the runway edge. By this time, I had committed myself to land and on hitting the ground I increased speed, lifted the nose and leapfrogged the drain.

Robin, what are you doing, shouted Pat Baskett, the manager of the estate, when I had taxied up to the far end by the club. I have come to see you; why the hell are you digging up the runway, I exclaimed angrily. Because there are certain H&C directors and Government officials who wish to play golf at the weekend and this is the easiest way of getting rid of the water. Which, you may observe, surrounds us, if you open your eyes, and has now flooded the course to a depth of a foot.

After a hundred years without a drain, you have, today, decided to dig one; on the very day I have come to visit you, I answered.

But surely, Robin, you read the notice board, notifying all pilots that Carey Island was out of bounds? Perhaps, on the other hand, you haven't yet read the notice board. Pat knew full well that I had not and gleefully mused upon the reverberations which would float around once my landing had become common knowledge. Let's go and have a drink before you take off, he invited. One only, said Pat, you are married now with responsibilities.

After two beers and a chat I decide to leave. If you start right back into the coconuts you should be airborne just before the drain and then, with an extra touch of flaps, away you go, says Pat, or splash into the drain. He chuckles, enjoying the episode, but without malice, for he is one of the most even-tempered and serene individuals one could ever meet.

I get into the plane. Don't forget to turn on both magnetos, he mocks me. For once while flying with him I only switched on one, which could have led to a disaster if he hadn't leant over and turned on the other.

I then motor to the far end of the runway and turn around by hole No. 7, a bunker close to my starboard wing. What a bloody silly place to put a bunker and hole, I say aloud to myself; what a ridiculous game hitting a stationary ball into a little submerged wee-wee pot.

I wave to Pat, who speeds off in his Land Rover to find the best vantage point, exactly in line with the new drain. Most of the workers have also become spectators, to view what they hope will be a minor catastrophe.

The excavator driver is now positioned, balanced on the boom, which allows him the best view of the action; probably praying for a crash, which he can then elaborate upon to all who may be eager to listen.

I put on 15 degrees of flap and push in the throttle for maximum power, but at the same time I hold the plane back by keeping the brakes on. Then once a head of steam is built up, I release the

244

brakes and off we trundle towards the ditch. How slow is a Cessna, I think. Then just as we approach the drain I lift the nose and up and over we go, up and away. Pat waves and so do the workers.

I land at the club; no questions are asked. I check in and start a soothing cold beer. No scowls, nor an excuse me could I have a word with you. Nothing. I relax and wait for Julia to return from her music.

Thus, I am surprised when a couple of months later this instructor should suddenly broach the subject. I wanted to have a quick look at the drain, I told him. Pat was using my excavator, you know, I lent it to him. I thought you were on Welch Estate; that's all hills, surely you don't need an excavator there, he queried. Oh yes I do, I replied, I have just constructed a reservoir. He did not know that I had borrowed Mr Tan's.

The instructor did not want to get into an argument as I had many more short-strip hours than him. He had just passed his instructor's licence a month or so back and was enjoying the power that went with it.

I want to go to Kuala Dungun on the public holiday, which is Friday returning Sunday. As I am here in North Johore and you are there at the Royal Selangor Flying Club, I would be very grateful if you would sign me in for those days, I told him. And after some hoarse panting and snuffling down the other end of the phone he booked us down for Kuala Dungun.

Julia was looking forward to renewing her acquaintances with small planes and we arrived early morning at the club. Hamdan, who had driven us, was going to stay with his relations in town; Abu and Salimah had two days off.

I filed a flight plan and took it to the control tower. They gave me the weather forecast, fine all the way, but told me to keep clear of the haze over Bentong.

The instructor was in the club, trying to look important and was just about to take up a student. Beware of the haze over Bentong. Yes, yes, I said of course I will. He was a lecturer at the university and earned a poor salary and looked upon the planting fraternity with considerable disapproval, tinged with a certain degree of envy.

We loaded our gear and lined up for take off. The instructor and his student were behind us. Can I take off from the intersection without back tracking, I asked control. Affirmative, they replied; what is your weight? Two POB (persons on board), some curry puffs, plus a couple of bottles of wine, I told control. Continue, the tower replied.

At that moment the instructor came over the intercom: all club planes must start off from the end of the runway not from the intersection. Ref. NOTAMS section 4:2-3. WILCO, I replied, but permission already granted; so off we went.

The instructor won't like that, said Julia. No, I know he won't, but the tower has it on tape so he cannot do anything about it. Except be disagreeable with you, she continued. Oh well, tomorrow is another day. We started our climb over the Bentong Pass and the thickening haze which darkened the sky around us.

It was a beautiful day for flying, and having trimmed up the plane, we enjoyed the scenery below and the jungle-clothed mountains that reared hugely close to our port wing.

Although this was the third time we had flown together in Malaysia, I reconfirmed what we had to do if there was an emergency which necessitated a forced landing. I explained how important it was to keep one's eyes open for possible landing spots and, of course, the two-tree shock absorber contingency plan as a last resort.

Julia took it all in and spent the rest of the journey bringing to my attention possible landing sites and any two trees positioned together which could be used as a fuselage braking system, should the need arise.

Needless to say, the journey was uneventful and we flew merrily along to Kuala Dungun. The strip was located 400 yards from the sea, surrounded by coconuts, with kampongs dotted about amongst the palms and *padi* fields.

The landing presented no problems and we taxied up alongside a small shack used as a pick-up point. There were lots of children around, so I searched around for an old man who would keep an eye on the plane. There seemed any number, so I selected the most robust.

We then walked to the beach and found an ideal spot which was sheltered from the sea breezes, where we could build a fire to cook our meals. The sun shone, we bathed and went for walks; it was perfect. As it was the turtle-breeding season we watched the turtles come up the beach at night-time to lay their eggs and then slowly return to the water, leaving their eggs behind. From the jungle which bordered this part of the beach, monkeys came to the sea edge, hoping to grab any morsel of food left behind.

The two days went by far too quickly. For there is nowhere more beautiful than a beach in the tropics, where an azure sky and blue sea almost fuse together, and can only be seen apart as the sea appears darker towards the horizon while the sky becomes a paler blue.

We had not washed for two days, except in the sea, and felt scruffy and sweaty. It had been a lovely break and we strolled back to the plane and the dutiful old man, who was grateful for the money I gave him.

Once we were airborne I contacted Kuantan Control and then KL. I decided to fly overhead the airstrip at Kuala Tahan, which we glimpsed through some fluffy speeding white clouds.

We will fly in there sometime, I say to Julia. Whatever for, she asks, the airstrip looks awfully short. It is a beautiful location and the mountain scenery is stunning, I reply. It is indeed, she says, but we can see it now, overhead; why go down? I am stumped, for I seldom fly with Robert nowadays and thus there is little reason to land at Kuala Tahan. I thought you might enjoy seeing a jungle airstrip, I tell her. Not really, she replies, I am happier being up here than being down there.

We fly on over the jungle, past the mountains, and then on to Bentong. I call KL and give them my position. They respond and I join the circuit, then the approach and land and taxi to the hangar.

Just made it, says the engineer. What do you mean, I ask. You have only fifteen minutes of fuel left, he retorts. Ah yes, I know, but we have a stock at Temerloh, I tell him. We sent 400 litres up there when Tan and I were taking photos of flood damage after the rains. He looks blank and departs, muttering under his breath as he walks away.

Are there, asks Julia. In actual fact, yes, but not 400 probably only 50–60, but that would be enough to get us back. She looks slightly disapproving and we both walk back up to the clubhouse. The end of a blissful weekend.

We order tea before our journey back to Welch. The instructor is

247

lingering awkwardly; so I call him over with his pretty Chinese girlfriend. Come and have some tea, I invite them. Julia chats with the girlfriend, who is also a lecturer at the university, while we talk flying.

I then asked him how he knew I landed at Carey Island those few weeks back, and why had he not brought the subject up before. He seemed to be in a talkative and good-humoured mood. Well, he said, the reason I know is because the committee asked me to inspect the runway prior to it being opened for club planes. So when I landed there, by chance, I learnt that another plane had landed before the drainage pipes had been laid and the drain was still open. And, on the log sheet you were the only one who had filed a flight plan via Carey Island. So I presumed it was you that had landed. Why didn't you report me, I asked. Because I was not an instructor then, he replied. Otherwise, if I had been, I would have.

We continued our tea in reflective silence. What authority did you have to verify whether or not the runway was safe and operational, I queried. Only the club captain can do that.

Quite correct, he affirmed, but the club captain provided me with that authority. Why you, I asked. Probably because I sought his permission, which he gave, and possibly because I am going to marry his daughter. With that they both got up, thanked us for the tea and left the club.

Interesting, said Julia. The old boy network is as strong here as anywhere else. I thought it might be different, she pondered, but alas it isn't; it's just the same everywhere.

52

Elephant Droppings

On those sombre notes we departed the club for Welch and arrived home early evening.

The journey usually takes two to three hours, depending on traffic, the roads being windy and narrow. Abu welcomed us. Julia went to the kitchen to find out what he had prepared for the evening and noticed in the refrigerator two rather large dark brown mounds of what she thought was stew, placed in two bowls wrapped in a thin plastic covering.

Stew for dinner, asked Julia, delicious, although she was surprised that Abu had prepared stew, which he had never done before. Julia lifted the dark mounds out of the fridge. Can you bake some potatoes, and let's have some leeks too.

Abu looked perplexed; he had never been asked to prepare anything before for refrigerated elephant turds, which she was now holding and admiring, and wondered why Julia thought it necessary. Abu knew full well the mounds were two of Robert's specimens, to be taken away for analysis at a later date, and until such time kept preserved in the fridge. He didn't approve of this practice, but had to put up with the inconvenience. Just as others were willing to do on other plantations up and down the country, all for the sake of elephant conservation,

However, it began to dawn on him that Mem (Madam) thought they were eatable mounds of meat. Disgusting, he thought; stews he understood were for army barracks, not for dinner at an estate manager's house. Surely there must be a mistake. Taking immediate action he came onto the veranda and agitatedly called me to the kitchen, where he recounted the conversation he had just had with Julia concerning the turds.

This had to stop. I decided to talk to Robert next time we met up.

Julia inspecting the elephant turds

The turds were returned to the fridge for safe keeping and Abu happily continued preparing the fish curry that he had started before our return.

Julia was surprised that fish was now on the menu and not the stew. I asked Abu to prepare stew, she said. I am afraid you were mistaken, what you saw in the fridge was not stew but elephant turds Robert had brought here for safe keeping prior to his return to KL.

Do you mean to say that he is using my fridge to keep his samples in? Silence. Yes, in actual fact, yes, I am afraid so, he has nowhere else to keep them, I replied. Well never again, she responded firmly, I might have eaten them by mistake. Supposing Abu or you had not been here and I had been on my own and started rummaging through the fridge looking for a snack and took a quick bite of a turd. Disgusting, she grimaced.

I certainly would not recommend elephant turds, I said, though they don't smell very much. Anyway, Abu knows. What a good job he is always here and not having a day off. She scowled with annoyance at being reminded of her now forgotten programme of equality for everybody.

Robert was informed in no uncertain fashion that leaving elephant turds in the fridge was an act of the past. No more, said Julia, never again. Robert remonstrated. Abu smirked with relief and went around the house with a smug know-all smile on his face. Things were changing, thanks be to Allah.

Robert purchased a portable fridge which could run off his VW Combi batteries and thus it all ended happily thereafter.

53

Visitors

It was easy to afford hospitality to visitors because one always had house staff to help.

As Robert had purchased a visitors' book with his name frequently entered, it was interesting to record the many different and varied persons who came to Welch and stayed.

On one evening when Julia and I were returning home, we were told by the night watchman guarding the estate entrance that a couple had arrived seeking a bed. We were expecting nobody and were therefore surprised. When we got home Abu told us two persons were staying at the assistant's house. As we had not informed him that we were to have guests, he suggested they stay with the assistant, who kindly obliged.

Usually one was informed when visitors were imminent. However, sometimes the odd person or couple would turn up unannounced, having been told through a friend, or friend of a friend, that a planter's house was always welcoming.

In the morning I met up with the assistant, Toh, in the office and asked who these people were. He did not know either; they arrived exhausted by taxi from the railway station at Segamat. They apparently had our name and nothing else. Not even money; Toh had to pay for the taxi.

I sent Hamdan round to Toh's house to pick them up and transfer them up to our bungalow. I then left the office and with Hara started my morning rounds.

By the time Hamdan had caught up with me I was far away in the field. You took a long time, I said. He replied, they were asleep so I waited. And then after awakening I took the couple up to the house. Who are they, I asked. They are *orang puteh* (white people), he answered, but he had never seen them before and he thought they had come from China.

252

They had indeed arrived from China, where they had been teaching English when the Cultural Revolution had caught up with them. They had then departed in considerable haste to avoid being interned. I asked them how they knew of us. Their only link appeared to be Simon Michel, who was now living in Hong Kong, where the couple had journeyed. How they met, I could not ascertain. Certainly they were fairly poverty-stricken and needed feeding up. And when one day I asked Simon about them he had no clue as to who they were either.

Although both enjoyed Julia's kindness and hospitality, they tended to disapprove of the way we lived and the house staff we employed. To them it was extravagant and mildly opulent, but at the same time they were certainly very eager to indulge themselves in whatever was on offer, and poor Salimah was kept very busy with their washing, ironing and cleaning, with little gratitude shown.

However, they were easy guests and their stories of life in Red China were certainly enthralling. They both could speak Cantonese, which impressed Mr Tan, who invited us all to dinner. But he was less impressed when they criticized the right-wing policies of Malaysia, and the obvious wealth that abounded throughout the country compared to China.

By the weekend both Julia and I had had enough and we put them on the train to Singapore. Having little money on me, I bought third-class tickets, which did not please them.

We never heard from them again, no thanks, no best wishes, nothing. It was always the same, though: people with left-wing tendencies indulged far more greedily in one's hospitality than those who were obviously better off and from a less radical background. Such guests were always kind, considerate and appreciative of their surroundings, and also of the staff. So opposite to those with socialist tendencies.

Sue Birch, a great friend of Julia's, arrived for a holiday. They drove to Kuantan and stayed there for a few days, and I flew down for the weekend and met them on the beach. Sue was a generous and considerate guest to entertain and was full of life and good humour.

Robert visited frequently, so did Pat Baskett, who drove a nippy Alfa-Romeo and was always good company.

Julia's cousin serving in the Gurkhas based in Hong Kong visited, and of course Jimmy Gilbert came for his half-yearly visit. Now that I had a wife he elected to stay the night in order to sample the cuisine, which a bride would probably help to engineer and prepare. It certainly was better fare than in previous years and Julia and Jimmy got on well. He was in an ebullient mood and the visit was a moderate success.

Dicky Doyle from Papua New Guinea arrived unannounced. After a heavy week of drinking with Denis Pager he jumped into his hired car and sped off to us on Welch, where he hoped he would be able to dry out.

Dicky's stories were numerous and ribald. At the same time he could talk seriously on most topics under the sun, due probably to his isolated life on Witu Island off New Britain, where he read avidly.

He and Mr Tan got on extremely well. Mr Tan at the time was looking for new partners and wanted an introduction into PNG or anywhere else. He was looking for foreign business now, not just local, which would provide him with international status. He was a wise man for he sent his children to Japan to be educated, regarding Japan as a future industrial and commercial giant. Just as the country has turned out to be.

We had other visitors; many just arrived for a drink. A Chinese or two who had started growing fruit trees on the lower slopes of Mount Ophir, visited and enjoyed our English teatime custom.

One afternoon when Julia and I were driving around the estate after work, we stopped and chatted with an old Chinese smallholder whose property bordered the estate. He spoke no English and not much Malay, but we conversed disjointedly and spent much time admiring his pigs. He was a nice old boy and he worked long hours in order to provide his children with a first-class education. As the children were away at school, Julia suggested that during the holidays they should come and visit us. He was very pleased and said that he would tell them once they returned.

We forgot all about the forthcoming visit until one day the old man arrived on his bicycle at the office and asked if his children could come over and visit us. It would be good for them to practise their English, he said.

The next day they duly arrived at the house at teatime. They were not children at all. The eldest was studying medicine at Guy's Hospital, London, another was a law student and the girl was at the Royal Academy of Music. Julia had studied at the Royal College of Music.

Their English, needless to say, was flawless and they were intelligent and amusing company. The girl, Lucy Chong, and Julia talked music and then Julia got out her clarinet to be accompanied by Lucy. The two young men and I talked politics and where they would eventually like to work. Here, Malaysia, was the answer, provided there still were opportunities for the Chinese, not just in business.

Many felt that the Government was over-promoting the Malays to the detriment of the other races, and to such an extent that they feared their education and professional standards would not be recognized. They thought that it might be difficult to find employment in the future. I agreed current policies favoured the Malays, but there had to be a catching-up process for them, otherwise they would be left too far behind, not only in business but also in the professions. Most Chinese accepted that the Government's policy was irreversible. At the same time, they felt a level playing field should be the principal stage upon which everybody ought to be judged.

My Chinese smallholder was rightly proud of his children and it was beyond imagination how he had scrimped and saved to ensure they received the best education possible.

On the northern boundary of the estate was a small estate of 400 acres, also Chinese-owned. I hardly ever met the owner except in passing, but I learnt the estate was up for sale and H&C expressed some interest.

Julia and I went visiting and found the owner in his office. His English was fluent and he possessed gentle manners, a characteristic I seldom saw exhibited by the Chinese. We talked around the subject of his estate, and I eventually found out that he wanted to sell, although at a price H&C would never be willing to pay. I knew he would come down, but when I quoted the possibilities to H&C they appeared to be uninterested. Which was a pity as it would have fitted nicely onto Welch.

However, negotiating with the Chinese is always difficult and in the end one is never quite sure who the owners really are and who holds the key to the transaction. The machinations of Chinese ownership are generally very hard to fathom and in the end one often discovers there is a little old lady in the background who can make or break an opportunity.

Fortunately, we got on well with this owner and he invited us to come to Malacca for an evening out with him. Julia licked her lips in anticipation of the meal ahead.

We arrived at his home, which was in the old Chinese quarter of Malacca. From the outside, the street of houses looked hardly sumptuous, but inside the house stretched far back and was elegant and stately. In the middle of the house was an open courtyard, which permitted the rain to fall down inside and thereby cool the adjacent rooms.

He possessed beautiful and rare furniture, pictures, porcelain and artefacts of all sorts, which he told us were smuggled out from mainland China at the time of Mao Tse-tung's communist take-over, when he fled with Chiang Kai-shek's forces to Taiwan. He had no wish to return to Taiwan and instead opted for Malaysia in order to invest in this new, developing country.

We found out that he went to England quite often and by coincidence knew not only the small village my parents lived in, but had also visited the watermill with his son, who lived close by, as it ground the barley and corn for the horses he was breeding. It was so surprising to meet somebody from another hemisphere whose offspring lived practically in the same village as my family.

After a delicious meal and copious quantities of excellent rice wine, he told us of his adventures while escaping from the communists and the trials and tribulations he experienced before arriving in Malaysia. Like all Chinese, he was not at all maudlin and his tales of fighting, fleeing and poverty were related without emotion or rancour. It was as if he was recounting a bus trip to London.

We departed from Malacca just before midnight. Hamdan was driving so we could doze on the way back.

If he was so poor when he arrived, how is that he has amassed so many riches, queried Julia. Mao's still in power, just about; he would never have been able to remove such valuable antiques whether during the past, or present, eras, she continued. Perhaps they are all from Taiwan or were previously stashed away in Hong

Kong, I replied. How very lucky to have such beautiful porcelain, Julia mused. It was very unlikely that I would ever be able to afford such exquisite ornaments and paintings on an H&C salary, I thought.

54

Kuala Tahan Revisited

Robert asked if we could drop some equipment off for him at Kuala Tahan, and I said I would if he paid. We eventually agreed upon half and half; he was very persuasive.

Have you been checked out, I am asked, when booking the plane. Repeatedly, I answer. You know that, I have flown in with Robert Olivier many times. Yes I know, but you should be checked out at least every quarter before flying into these difficult strips, the Indian instructor tells me. Whatever for, I cry. Nobody ever minded in the past, why now is this inhibiting strictness becoming all-pervasive. The resultant scowl says it all. What a bunch of arseholes, I think to myself.

In exasperation, I go to the Chinese chief instructor. Will you sign this please? Mr Leong looks harassed, but he always does, so it is not surprising. He was around in the RAF days, and is therefore a little more compliant than the other newer instructors. Leong signs, and off I go to fill in a flight plan and prepare the plane.

Julia has more sympathy for the instructors than I, realizing the burden of responsibility they carry. Well, if they cannot carry the weight of responsibility then they shouldn't be instructors, I retort uncompromisingly.

We loaded in Robert's gear and took off and climbed steadily over Bentong to a flight level of 5,000 feet.

The journey was calm all the way. As we approached Kuala Tahan, close to the runway was a group of aboriginals who, on hearing the plane, moved further towards the trees bordering the runway. I descended and landed, at which instant a young man rushed out onto the strip. Christ, I shouted. The boy suddenly dropped to the ground as the wing passed over him. Bloody fool, I said, opening the window. Julia looked pale, but said nothing.

By now the others were gathering around the fallen man, who looked sheepish and embarrassed. I got out of the plane and walked back to where everybody was alternately cooing and chiding the young man.

That was a near miss, somebody said behind me. Still, he appears not to have suffered any damage. I noticed the speaker was a Malay official. This could be trouble, I thought. However, nothing further was said and I returned to the plane to taxi to the pick-up point in order to unload Robert's baggage.

Without further mishap we took off for Ipoh, where we were going to spend the night. Our course took us over the Cameron Highlands, 6,000 feet high, where tea estates and vegetable gardens had been established.

As we flew over I suddenly heard a sharp cracking sound. I jerked into consciousness. What was that, I wondered. In order not to cause alarm I said nothing to Julia; instead I looked out at the wings to see if they were about to fall off. No, they were intact. Then suddenly again another sharp crack. Did you hear that, I asked Julia. No, I didn't hear anything, she replied. We continued and then landed at Ipoh. Julia got out and walked across to the clubhouse, while I went around the aeroplane looking for any abnormality which could have made a cracking noise. I found nothing.

We stayed the night at the Ipoh Club, and next morning, after another check, we get in and set off. You are very thorough with your checks today, nothing wrong, I hope, Julia queries. Oh no, just making sure.

We leave Ipoh and set course for KL. It is a fine morning with little turbulence. Suddenly there is this cracking noise again. What's that, I ask. What's what, asks Julia. That cracking noise, I reply. Surely you heard it. I didn't hear anything. I hope everything is all right, she queries. I just cannot understand it, there is this continual sharp cracking noise which I hear and you don't. Well if I don't hear it, then it is difficult for me to comment, she replies, with her usual feminine logic.

We continue our flight. Julia is looking out of her window at the never-ending cluster of estates below, when I hear the crack again. I look over towards Julia, who is fiddling about with something in her hand. What are you doing, I ask. Looking out of the window, she replies. No, what is in your hand. Oh, this, an old elastic band. Why, she wants to know. What are you doing with it, I demand to know. I am doing this, said Julia and flicks it against the window. The resultant sharp cracking noise returns.

Have you been doing that all the time, I question her wearily. Well, not all the time, just occasionally. Why, does it disturb you? Oh, no, I said. Good, and she pulls back the band and flicks it against the window again. The mystery is solved.

We land at the club and I check in. Leong comes over. I hear you almost hit an aboriginal. Well pretty adjacent, I admit. He ran across the field in front of me, but no harm done.

He and the aboriginal officer have complained that you could have stopped before you almost ran over him. If I could have stopped I would have, I tell him. Which direction did you approach from, he asks. From the jungle, not the hill; it's easier. He grimaces. Perhaps we can resolve this one; or if not you will be suspended.

I am suspended for six months for almost hitting an aboriginal.

Told you so, says Robert. If you must land in that direction and you have an officious park officer on site you are asking for trouble. Balls, the guy would have been 'almost hit' whichever approach I had taken, I reply.

Oh well, let's go and have a beer, he says. I will pay. What a treat, responds Julia.

55

A Wedding Ceremony

Because we were married in England, Welch staff and labour felt hard done by. After our return and amidst all the other activities of estate life, it was decided that we should also get married on Welch.

A day was pronounced compatible and auspicious, and Julia and I in our finest clothes were taken in a procession down to the estate recreation hall. The drummers beat our progress, and boys and girls waved banana leaves and flags and danced and gambolled beside us. It was a very moving and happy experience. In the hall everybody was dressed up in their best clothes and we were seated at the head of the assembly.

The local *kathi* (priest) intoned majestically about the virtues of marriage and lots of other things, and after speeches of good wishes and the blessing of the community of Welch, we went up to our estate *surau* (a small mosque). In procession we slowly and solemnly walked through the workers' line site, now alight with coconut oil lamps, and up the path to the *surau*, lined by children carrying little lamps.

There were more blessings of the community, but being Christians we did not enter the *surau*. Then, after more speeches, we were led to the feast, which had been laid out on the badminton court, overspilling onto the adjacent grass gardens of the workers' quarters.

It was a magical evening and we both thoroughly enjoyed ourselves. A wedding gift was presented, a drum on which Islamic blessings in Arabic had been written on the covering skin.

The drum still holds pride of place at our home in the UK.

A large party was organized for the entire district, and attended by most of the planters, their wives and many assistants and some of the local civil servants. Mr Tan did not come, which was a pity. Probably he was fearful of being accosted for money, donations, charity, etc. by the civil servants who were present at the party.

We had invited the local politician, Musa Hitam, whom I had met on previous occasions when he visited his local constituency. He enjoyed the custom of English tea, which he would always partake of at the appointed hour of 4.45 p.m. But unfortunately he was unable to make the journey from KL.

Abu and Raman's wife, plus Salimah, cooked the most delicious satay and *luntong* (small rice cakes eaten with satay). Raman, the gardener, and Abang, the *mandor*, served drinks. Raman was in his element and was soon conversing with some of the planters on local politics and the price of goods in the shops. Although garrulous when slightly under the spell of drink, as he called it, Raman still remained attentive and diligent. But by the end of the evening his presence became more desultory and soon he was seen being helped home by his children, who managed to prop him upright as he swaggered down the hill, calling bye-bye, my dear everybody.

Hamdan, meanwhile, was gossiping with the other drivers. Most drove Mercedes, while our car was a not very elegant Rover. There is nobody snootier than a driver whose boss owns the newest car model on the market. Poor Hamdan felt the pressure, for my car was sedate and unglittery and had been purchased at a set of traffic lights in Malacca after a game of cricket when its driver, a young Chinese, drew up alongside my battered Ford while waiting for the lights to change. I had leant over and asked if he wanted to sell his car, which looked much more presentable than my Ford, and which was also reaching the end of its active life.

How much, he asked. I said a figure. Done, he replied immediately, so I knew I had agreed to pay too much. We swapped addresses and eventually I became the proud owner of a Rover 200 that was comfortable and not bad looking, but not as elegant or swish as the modern Mercedes, Volvos and Italian makes.

Hamdan was loyal and always repeated the same story that I was looking for something suitable, not Japanese junk, as it was often referred to then. Probably not a Mercedes, something different, he would try to explain. But as I flew everywhere, he would sniff importantly at the other drivers, unlike their bosses, a car was not a priority. It certainly wasn't, but the Rover, after Mr Tan's mechanic

262

had tinkered with it, was comfortable and contained an air-conditioner that worked.

We seemed to get invited to many more functions and parties than when I was bachelor.

The Sultan of Johore arrived at Segamat, and a request to be present duly arrived by post. Julia looked very elegant, and the Sultan made a speech, in Malay, which sounded as though it was being delivered by an Englishman. He was supposed to prefer speaking in English, and when conversing with a foreigner would never use the Malay language, although he insisted that all foreigners living in his state should be able to speak Malay. If you could not, then you were in trouble.

Julia had begun to learn Malay and was progressing extremely quickly. A young Malay schoolteacher came regularly to the house to help her converse. Because Abu could not speak English, she quickly learnt the rudimentary requirements for managing a house and then progressed rapidly, finding the language easy to learn, and was soon able to communicate with little difficulty.

56

A Chance Meeting

In 1977 I met a director of Unilever at an Incorporated Society of Planters meeting. He was looking for a manager for their Solomon Islands plantations. I said I would be interested, and thought no further about it.

I enjoyed Welch but it was getting to be boring, and I felt that if I did not leave soon, we would spend the rest of our lives in Malaysia. Julia thoroughly enjoyed Welch and Malaysia, but had not yet become fully wedded to the idea of remaining in the country for ever. Therefore she thought it sensible to make the break now, if possible, or not at all.

Malaysia had not lost its charm, although muted rumblings were heard, particularly from the Malays, who were gradually realizing how far they were being left behind in all matters economic and social. A more dogmatic and strident Islam was also rearing its head and the free and easy life enjoyed by the Malays was now being scrutinized by those who mattered, the religious leaders.

We were due to go on leave when I heard that the position of Manager of Levers Plantation in the Solomon Islands was being offered to me. Would I be interested? Julia was less hesitant than I was. Having spent over sixteen years in Malaysia, I was going to find it an awful wrench to part company.

Jimmy Gilbert, who was visiting at the time, thought it was a career opportunity as Unilevers were carrying out a big plantation expansion programme, mainly in Zaire, where they owned about 200,000 hectares of land, and also in the Pacific.

At the same time some Malaysian companies had their eye on possible future take-overs of foreign-owned estates, which could mean the demise of the old companies such as H&C, Guthries, Dunlops and others. This turned out to be the case, for by the late

1980s H&C Malaysia did not exist and answered only to the name of Golden Hope Limited.

When the time came and I had accepted the Levers Solomons offer, the wrench of leaving Malaysia was lessened by H&C's ambivalent attitude to the remaining expatriate planters, who now numbered just under 30 persons. A weeding-out of those managers who had been greedy and corrupt had started and a small flow of families departed Malaysia, reducing the planting fraternity by even more.

It was sad. A general malaise had set in and poor man-management by H&C had exacerbated the situation. I was pleased to be leaving H&C but not Welch nor Malaysia, which had been my home since departing the UK in 1961. Julia was also sad, although at least she was not embedded in the life to the same extent as I was.

Hara knew something terrible was about to happen and lay in miserable discontent on the veranda. I had hoped Pat would take him over, as he had done so before when I went on leave. But Pat had too many dogs of his own and just could not take on any more, even Hara. Fortunately, the new manager of Welch was Lian, an ex-assistant, and he and his wife Dorothy were quite happy for Hara to stay with them.

We left Welch with a minimum amount of fuss: no cheering crowds, a small wave, a farewell here and there, a shaking of hands. Neither of us wanted a farewell party, although Mr Tan invited us around and found it strange that we should want to leave. Don't you like Malaysia, don't you like Welch, it is a good place, happy estate, why do you want to go? And, when Julia was not listening, do you want another wife? Good cook, he elaborated, always practical. No, I replied to all his queries, it was time to go, see another country, join another company. He did not really understand our desire to leave, but looked very sad. He had enjoyed working on Welch with me, and now what would happen. New manager, too much change, he said. I quashed his fears: Lian was excellent, he would just follow on where I had left off. Tan looked doubtful. We shook hands and we left his shop for ever.

We arrived in England during those awful years of union dominance when successive governments, Conservative or Labour, seemed

265

incapable of governing. It was hopeless; garbage lay about the streets, trains were late, prices were high. Managers left work early. There was no discipline. Nobody knew what to do and the Government was powerless against the striking workers.

I went to Unilever's office in Blackfriars then wrote formally to H&C telling them of my departure. I received a polite letter back accepting my resignation. A week later I received the princely sum of GBP11,292.03, my provident fund after sixteen years of employment. That won't buy much, Julia retorted, when I told her the amount.

We left for the Solomons in 1978. That year we learned Hara

Burying Hara on Welch

266

had died. He had been getting old, but apparently after our departure he seemed no longer to be interested in life and however well Lian cared for him, his spirit was gone. Sadly, he died of heartbreak. Abu and Abang, Hamdan and Raman buried him amongst the orchids which Murray had established when he had been manager of Welch. Some of the older workers came up to see him buried and a few threw little cupfuls of rice onto his grave. Everybody missed him, he was loved by all.